FIFTY STRATEGIES
for TEACHING
ENGLISH LANGUAGE
LEARNERS

ADRIENNE L. HERRELL

California State University, Fresno

Merrill
an imprint of Prentice Hall

Upper Saddle River, New Jersey   *Columbus, Ohio*

Library of Congress Cataloging-in-Publication Data

Herrell, Adrienne L.
  Fifty strategies for teaching English language learners / Adrienne
L. Herrell.
    p.   cm.
  Includes bibliographical references.
  ISBN 0-13-923855-7
  1. English language—Study and teaching—Foreign speakers.
I. Title.   II. Title: 50 strategies for teaching English language
learners.
  PE1128.A2H467   2000   99-39793
  428′.007—dc21   CIP

Editor: Debra A. Stollenwerk
Editorial Assistant: Penny S. Burleson
Production Editor: Mary Harlan
Design Coordinator: Karrie Converse-Jones
Text Design and Production Coordination: Clarinda Publication
Services
Cover Designer: Ceri Fitzgerald
Cover Photo: ©Photo Edit
Production Manager: Pamela D. Bennett
Illustrations: The Clarinda Company
Director of Marketing: Kevin Flanagan
Marketing Manager: Meghan Shepherd
Marketing Coordinator: Krista Groshong

This book was set in Garamond by The Clarinda Company and was
printed and bound by The Banta Company. The cover was printed by
The Banta Company.

©2000 by Prentice-Hall, Inc.
Pearson Education
Upper Saddle River, New Jersey 07458

Printed in the United States of America

10 9 8

ISBN: 0-13-923855-7

Prentice-Hall International (UK) Limited, *London*
Prentice-Hall of Australia Pty. Limited, *Sydney*
Prentice-Hall of Canada, Inc., *Toronto*
Prentice-Hall Hispanoamericana, S. A., *Mexico*
Prentice-Hall of India Private Limited, *New Delhi*
Prentice-Hall of Japan, Inc., *Tokyo*
Prentice-Hall (Singapore) Pte. Ltd., *Singapore*
Editora Prentice-Hall do Brasil, Ltda., *Rio de Janeiro*

· ·

To Dr. Rose Lee Patrón
for lowering my affective filter and
Dr. Armando Baltra for providing
patient, comprehensible input.
Thank you both!

CONTENTS

....

PREFACE

·····················

As teachers are asked to teach more diverse classrooms with students from multilingual backgrounds or multidimensional experiences, they often need to employ innovative strategies to make the content accessible to all students. This book is a compilation of strategies that have been field tested in multilingual classrooms and found to support student learning.

These strategies were developed by teachers and researchers working together to provide an education to children just learning English. Strategies were selected on the basis of their usefulness in making rigorous core curriculum meaningful to students whose knowledge of English might otherwise hinder their academic progress.

In addition to non-native English speakers, some native English-speaking children in school today have had limited exposure to the standard English language spoken in school and to the ways in which questions are asked. Adaptation of language and the use of supportive strategies are especially vital when children are being asked to learn in a language unfamiliar to them. With the strategies explained in this book, teachers can help English language learners acquire both English and content-area knowledge. A basic premise of the book is that curriculum should not be simplified for students just acquiring English; instead, teachers should employ strategies to make the curriculum understandable while teaching the English vocabulary connected with that curriculum.

Bilingual programs, designed over the years to support children in acquiring English as they continue to be taught in their home languages, have been well documented in their power to support learning. The content of this book is not intended to replace strong bilingual programs. In California and several other states, the need for bilingual teachers exceeds the number of such teachers available. Many of our English language learners are being taught by monolingual English teachers, with or without the support of bilingual teaching assistants. The intent of this book is to provide these teachers with effective strategies for teaching in English, while supporting their students' understanding of content materials and acquisition of English speaking, reading, writing, and listening skills.

▶ THE PURPOSE OF THIS BOOK

This is a practical book. The focus is on what to do in the K–12 classroom to support learning of English language learners. The research and theory base is explained in the theoretical overview section. The strategies are explained in alphabetical order with a definition and explanation of each strategy, step-by-step instructions on how to use the strategy, and several classroom applications. A matrix follows the theoretical overview section so that teachers can quickly locate strategies for specific teaching purposes. Suggestions for further readings are also given in many cases.

This book provides strong implementation examples of effective teaching techniques for English language learners based on the work of such linguistic and second-language acquisition researchers as Stephen Krashen, Jim Cummins, Tracy Terrell, and Merrill Swain. The use of their research as the basis for principles for teaching English language learners is explained in the theoretical overview. This book also relies heavily on research in a year-long study of exemplary teaching practices in classrooms in the Fresno Unified School District during the 1997–98 school year.

ACKNOWLEDGMENTS

Many of the classroom application examples are taken from hours of observation, videotaping, and hands-on involvement in the classrooms of such remarkable teachers as Sally Rowden at Hidalgo Elementary, Stephanie Collom at Balderas Elementary, Susan McCloskey at Lowell Elementary, Mary Park at Lane Elementary, Eileen Boland at Tenaya Middle School, and David Reynolds at Avenal High School.

The following professors took time to review the manuscript and give valuable suggestions for improvement: Judy Eby, San Diego State University; Christian Faltis, Arizona State University, Tempe; Margaret Ferrara, Central Connecticut State University; Joyce Lynn Garrett, Indiana University of Pennsylvania; Susan Hahn, St. Mary's College; and Mary Lynn Hamilton, University of Kansas.

A very special thanks must also be given to three people who gave tirelessly of their time and energy in reading drafts of the manuscript and making suggestions for improvements. Dr. Gail Tompkins and Dr. Armando Baltra of California State University, Fresno, both contributed not only to the quality of the manuscript but to the depth of the content. My son, Sean Bateman, not only read drafts and gave suggestions but also served as my technology consultant. His patience in this capacity is only surpassed by his persistence.

Adrienne L. Herrell

ABOUT THE AUTHOR

....

Adrienne L. Herrell is a professor of Reading/Language Arts at California State University, Fresno. She received her Ph.D. in Early Childhood Education from Florida State University after teaching for 23 years in Florida public schools. Her teaching career and research interests focus on strategies for supporting students as they acquire reading, writing, speaking, and listening skills in English. Dr. Herrell recently completed a year-long study of exemplary practices in teaching English language learners, in which she examined the teaching approaches of four highly successful teachers of students just acquiring English. Many of the strategies contained in *Fifty Strategies for Teaching English Language Learners* are a result of that study.

THEORETICAL OVERVIEW

···

The research in language acquisition has been rich and productive over the past 20 years. Linguists and educators working together (Krashen & Terrell, 1983) have discovered effective ways to support students in their acquisition of new languages and content knowledge. It is vital that classroom teachers understand the implications of the language acquisition research so that they can provide the scaffolding necessary for their students to be successful in the classroom.

LANGUAGE ACQUISITION THEORY AND THE CLASSROOM TEACHER

In order for classroom teachers to make good decisions about instructional practices for English language learners, they must understand how students acquire English and how this acquisition differs from how foreign languages have traditionally been taught in America. Many teachers have experienced classes in Spanish, French, or other languages in which they have practiced repetitive drills and translated long passages using English-French (or Spanish) dictionaries. While these approaches have been used for many years in the United States without much success, it should be noted that linguists such as Jim Cummins and Stephen Krashen have been researching new approaches to language acquisition.

Stephen Krashen (1982) in his study of language acquisition makes a distinction between language acquisition and language learning that is vital to the support of students in the classroom in their gradual acquisition of fluency in a new language. Krashen states that language acquisition is a natural thing. Young children acquire their home language easily without formal teaching. This acquisition is a gradual thing based on receiving and understanding messages, building a listening (receptive) vocabulary, and slowly attempting verbal production of the language in a highly supportive, nonstressful situation. It is exactly these same conditions that foster the acquisition of a second language. The teacher is responsible for providing the understandable language (comprehensible input), along with whatever supports are necessary in order for the students to understand the messages. Using approaches and materials that add context to the language—props, gestures, pictures—all contribute to the child's acquisition and eventually to the production of language.

Krashen and Tracy Terrell (1983) also stress the need for English language learners to be allowed to move into verbal production of the new language at a comfortable rate. Students must hear and understand messages in the target language and build a listening vocabulary before being expected to produce spoken language. This does not mean that the English language learners should be uninvolved in the classroom activities, but that the activities should be structured so that English language learners can participate at a level of comfort. Questions asked of them should be answerable at first with the use of gestures, nods, or physical responses. This language acquisition stage is called the silent or preproduction period, and it is a vital start to language acquisition. The subsequent stages and implications for teaching and learning are explained in chapter 25, Leveled Questions.

The role of the classroom environment in supporting children's language acquisition cannot be ignored. Meaningful exposure to language is not enough. Students need many opportunities for language interaction. Swain (1993) proposes that a classroom where children work together to solve problems and produce projects supports their language development in several ways. It gives them authentic reasons to communicate and gives them support in refining their language production. It also provides students with the realization that their verbal communication is not always understood by others. This realization helps to move the child from receptive, semantic processing (listening to understand) to expressive, syntactic processing (formation of words and sentences in order to communicate). If children are left to simply listen and observe without the opportunity or necessity to communicate they remain in the preproductive stage for an extended period of time. The structure of communicative classroom activities, those which necessitate communication and verbal interaction, prevents this from happening.

Another important component supportive of children's language acquisition is their discovery of what they can do with language. Halliday (1978) identified seven functions of language or purposes for using language, which serve to provide impetus for children's verbal communication. The functions that Halliday identified are:

Instrumental. The use of language to cause things to happen. For example, "Bathroom" causes the teacher to take notice and excuse the student to use the bathroom.

Regulatory. The use of language to control events or the behavior of others. For example, "He hit me!" causes the teacher to intervene in the child's behalf.

Representation. The use of language to communicate facts and/or knowledge. For example, "I have two pennies" tells the teacher that the child understands the number concept.

Interactional. The use of language to get along with others. For example, "Sit with me" is used to make a friend.

Personal. The use of language to express personality feelings or emotions. For example, "I sad" is used to convey feelings.

Heuristic. The use of language to acquire knowledge. For example, "Show me" is used to gain access to information.

Imaginative. The use of language to create an imaginative world for pleasure or play. For example, "Pretend we are on a train" is used to create a fantasy play situation.

Many researchers (Krashen, 1982; Krashen & Terrell, 1983; McLaughlin, 1990) have studied the role of emotions on the acquisition of language. Krashen calls the impact of emotions on learning the "affective filter." When a learner is placed in a stressful situation in which language production or performance is demanded, the student's ability to learn or produce spoken language is impaired. This underscores the responsibility of the teacher to provide a supportive classroom environment in which the student can participate at a comfortable level without having to worry about being embarrassed or placed in a situation where he/she will be made to feel foolish. Krashen's Affective Filter Hypotheses stresses that in order for the student to learn effectively the student's motivation and self-esteem must be supported while diminishing his/her anxiety. This provides an opportunity for the English language learner to take in information, process vocabulary, and eventually produce language because his/her stress levels are low and his/her affective filter is not interfering with thinking or learning.

Jim Cummins's research (1986) contributes to the understanding of language acquisition and effective classroom practice in several ways. First, Cummins differentiates between social language, called basic interpersonal communication skills (BICS), and academic language, called cognitive academic language proficiency (CALP). While students may acquire BICS and be able to communicate in English while on the playground or in asking and answering simple questions, this is not the same thing as having the level of language proficiency necessary to benefit fully from academic English instruction (CALP) without additional support.

Cummins also helps us to understand what must be added to instruction to make it comprehensible to students. He identifies two dimensions of language, its cognitive demand and its context embeddedness. Using a quadrant matrix Cummins demonstrates how the addition of context supports the students' understanding of more cognitively demanding language such as the language of content instruction in the classroom.

Cognitively Undemanding Language

Social conversation
  (with gestures)
Storytelling with props

Social phone call

Note left on the refrigerator

Basic Interpersonal Communication Skills

Context-embedded language

Context-reduced language

Math lesson
  (with manipulatives)
Geography lesson with maps

Social studies lecture

Multiple choice test

Cognitive Academic Language Proficiency

Cognitively Demanding Language

Figure TO.1   Cummins's Quadrant Demonstrating the Dimensions of Language

Adapted from "Primary Language Instruction and the Education of Language Minority Students" by J. Cummins, 1996, *Schooling and Language Minority Students: A Theoretical Framework*, 2nd ed. (p. 10). Los Angeles: Evaluation, Dissemination and Assessment Center, School of Education, California State University, Los Angeles. Copyright © 1996 by Charles F. Leyba. Reprinted with permission.

By examining Cummins's Quadrant the teacher can see that even social language is made more understandable by the addition of context. Directions given orally with gestures are more easily understood than the same words spoken over the telephone without the aid of gestures. This becomes even more important in the classroom, where teachers are using academic terms that may be unfamiliar to the English language learner or using them in a different way from the customary social meaning. This is demonstrated by one English language learner's illustration of a riverbed in response to a geography lesson. The student's understanding of the word *bed* was linked to his prior knowledge of the word and did not support his understanding of the term when used to describe a geographic feature.

Figure TO.2 An English Language Learner's Concept of a Riverbed

THE UNDERLYING THEORY BASE OF INSTRUCTION FOR ENGLISH LANGUAGE LEARNERS

Strategies are defined in this book as approaches that can be used across curricular areas in order to support the learning of students. Assessment strategies are included because teachers will need to adjust their teaching strategies on the basis of their knowledge of the students' growing competencies. Because assessment can be extremely language-based, requiring exact vocabulary to read and answer questions, assessment strategies must be adjusted in order to find out how well the students understand the concepts being taught. Less formal assessment also provides an opportunity for teachers to learn more about the learners' understanding of English vocabulary and use of sentence structure. The strategies described in this book are based on the theories of the linguists described in this introductory section. The goals of the strategies are to enhance learning. In order to provide this enhancement, one or more of the underlying premises of effective instruction of English language learners are emphasized in each of the strategies. These premises are:

1. Teachers should provide instruction in a way that ensures that students are given *comprehensible input* (language they can understand).
2. Teachers should provide opportunities to *increase verbal interaction* in classroom activities.
3. Teachers should provide instruction that *contextualizes language* as much as possible.
4. Teachers should use teaching strategies and grouping techniques that *reduce the anxiety* of the students as much as possible.
5. Teachers should provide activities in the classroom that offer opportunities for *active involvement* of the students.

As teaching strategies are explained in the following chapters, the reader will be reminded of these goals by means of a graphic at the beginning of each chapter, which connects the strategy to the reasons for its appropriateness to English language learners. Strategies will be labeled as supportive of comprehensible input, contextualization of language, reduction in stress, opportunities to interact verbally, and active involvement opportunities for the learner. This will enable the teacher to select those activities that best suit the needs of the learners being taught. In addition, the matrix that follows this section provides an overview of the strategies, indicating the principles supported by the strategies. The strategies are not meant to be used in isolation. By combining strategies the teacher can plan innovative lessons, which will motivate the students to learn. The examples that are included in each chapter will serve to demonstrate ways in which the strategies can be combined and used effectively.

References

Cummins, J. (1986). Empowering minority students: A framework for interaction. *Harvard Review, 56,* 18–36.

Halliday, M. (1978). *Language as a social semiotic.* Baltimore, MD: University Park Press.

Krashen, S. (1982). *Principles and practices of second language acquisition.* Oxford: Pergamon Press.

Krashen, S., & Terrell, T. (1983). *The natural approach: Language acquisition in the classroom.* Oxford: Pergamon Press.

McLaughlin, B. (1990). *Myths and misconceptions about second language learning: What every teacher needs to unlearn.* Santa Cruz, CA: National Center for Research on Cultural Diversity and Second Language Learning.

Swain, M. (1993). The output hypothesis: Just speaking and writing aren't enough. *The Canadian Modern Language Review. 50,* 158–164.

A MATRIX OF STRATEGIES AND OBJECTIVES

Principles

1 = Supports comprehensible input
2 = Encourages verbal interaction
3 = Supports contextualizing language
4 = Reduces anxiety

5 = Encourages active involvement
Assessment = Provides assessment information
● = Major objective
√ = Secondary objective

Principles	1	2	3	4	5	Assess
1 Academic Language Scaffolding	●	√	√	√	√	
2 Advance Organizers	●		●	√		
3 Anecdotal Records						●
4 Attribute Charting	●	√	√	√	√	
5 Bilingual Books and Labels	●	√	√	√	√	
6 Cloze Activities	●	√	●	√	√	√
7 Cohesion Links	●	√	●		√	√
8 Collaborative Reading	●	√	√	√	●	
9 Communication Games	√	●	√	√	●	
10 Cooperative Learning	●	√	√	●	●	
11 Culture Studies	√	●	●	√	√	
12 Dictoglos	√	●	√	√	●	
13 Free Voluntary Reading	●		√	√	√	
14 GIST	●	●	√	√	●	
15 Guided Reading	●	√	●	√	√	√
16 Imaging	●		√	√		
17 Integrated Curriculum Projects	●	√	●	√	●	
18 Interactive Read Aloud	●	√	●	√	√	
19 Interactive Writing	●	√	●	√	●	√
20 Language Experiences Activities	●	●	●	√	√	√
21 Language Focus Lessons	●	●	√	●	√	
22 Language Framework Planning	●	√	√	●	√	
23 Learning Centers	√	√	●	●	●	√

Principles	1	2	3	4	5	Assess
24 Learning Strategy Instruction	●	√	●	√	●	√
25 Leveled Questions	●	●	√	√	●	√
26 Manipulative Strategies	●		●	√	●	
27 Modeled Talk	●		●	√	√	
28 Multimedia Presentations	●	√	●	√	√	√
29 Multiple Intelligences Strategies	●	√	√	●	●	●
30 Partner Work	●	●	√	●	●	
31 Peer Tutoring	●	●	√	●	●	
32 Performance Sampling				√		●
33 Portfolio Assessment				√	√	●
34 Predictable Routines and Signals	●			●	√	
35 Preview/Review	●		●	●	√	
36 Realia Strategies	●	√	●	√	√	
37 Reciprocal Teaching	●	●		√	√	
38 Repetition and Innovation	●	√	●	√	√	
39 Reporting Back	●	●	●	√	√	√
40 Scripting	●	●	●	●	√	
41 Shared Reading	●	√	●	√	●	
42 Skills Grouping	●	√	√	√	●	√
43 Sorting Activities	●	√	√	√	●	
44 Story Reenactment	√	●	●	√	●	√
45 Syntax Surgery	●			√	√	
46 Total Physical Response	●		●	●	●	√
47 Visual Scaffolding	●		●	√		
48 Vocabulary Role Play	●	√	●	√	●	√
49 Word Walls	●		●	√	√	
50 Writing Workshop	●	●	√	√	●	√

ACADEMIC LANGUAGE SCAFFOLDING

SUPPORTS

- Comprehensible input
- ✔ Increased verbal interaction
- ✔ Contextualized language
- ✔ Reduced anxiety
- ✔ Active involvement of the learner

A cademic language scaffolding supports students' successful participation in content-area instruction. Academic language is language associated with school subjects such as mathematics, science, and social studies. It places a higher cognitive demand on the listener or speaker.

Jim Cummins (1986) identified two types of language that students acquire. The first, Basic Interpersonal Communications Skills (BICS)—or social language—is learned more quickly and easily than the second, Cognitive Academic Language Proficiency (CALP), or academic language. Academic language scaffolding supports the student in CALP, the language necessary for the student to participate successfully in classroom learning opportunities.

In order for students to participate successfully in academic lessons in the classroom, teachers use a series of scaffolding strategies that include modeling academic language; contextualizing academic language using visuals, gestures, and demonstrations; and supporting students in the use of academic language through active learning activities.

STEP BY STEP

The steps in an academic language scaffolding lesson are:

1. Identify the academic vocabulary and language functions necessary for the students to successfully participate in the lesson being taught. The vocabulary is selected from the reading assignments and explanations that are given as a part of the lesson. The language functions relate to the ways in which the student is expected to participate verbally. See Figure 1.1 for an explanation of academic language functions.
2. Provide an introductory activity that allows the scaffolding of both the academic vocabulary and language functions in a nonstressful way. If you start with a teacher explanation, support the students' understanding by using visuals for the main academic vocabulary. Then model the use of the language in the ways in which the students are expected to participate. If they are required to ask questions, model the use of the language in question form. If they are to take notes about a science experiment, provide a model of how the notes could be taken. If the academic language is complex and spelling is important, leave the

Function	Definition	Examples
Analyze (mid-level)	Identify parts of whole, look for patterns and relationships	Using written materials or teacher explanations, the student is able to label parts and describe patterns and relationships among the parts
Classify (mid-level)	Sort or group by attributes	Describe the process used to classify. Give examples and nonexamples
Compare (low-level)	Describe how objects or ideas are alike and how they are different	Explain how objects or ideas are the same and how they differ
Evaluate (high-level)	Determine the worth of objects, ideas	List criteria used, explain priorities, support judgments with facts
Infer (high-level)	Predict, hypothesize using information gathered from scholarly sources	Describe how inferences were made or hypothesize based upon information read or observed
Inform (low-level)	Describe information or experiences	Recall and describe information obtained from another source or a personal experience
Justify and Persuade (high-level)	Describe reasons for decisions and convince others	Explain decisions and justify with evidence
Seek information (low-level)	Observe, explore, read to gain knowledge	Ask questions to gather information
Solve problems (high-level)	Identify a problem, determine a process, and follow steps to a solution	Identify the problem, describe the process used to solve it, relate it to real life
Synthesize (high-level)	Select, integrate information in new ways	Incorporate new knowledge into schema. Summarize the processes used in integrating information from different sources

Figure 1.1 Academic Language Functions (Low-level, Mid-level, High-level thinking labeled)

Adapted from Chamot & O'Malley (1994)

words posted in the room and make it clear to the students that spelling is important and the words are posted for their use in spelling. If spelling is not vital, make that clear also.

3. Include an activity that allows the students to work in pairs or small groups, interacting verbally so that they practice academic language in authentic ways.

4. Move around the room during this active learning experience so that you can monitor and encourage the students' use of academic language. Provide scaffolding for the use of academic language by commenting on the work the students are doing, modeling the use of academic vocabulary, and describing the ways in which the students are solving the problems or working with the materials. When students are asked questions it enables them to demonstrate knowledge either by physically showing the teacher what was done or by explaining the process. Model the academic language as the student demonstrates the process used or restate the student's verbal explanation emphasizing the academic language.

5. Conclude the lesson with a review of the academic language. Offer the opportunity for the pairs or small groups to report back to the whole group again using the newly acquired academic language in context (see chapter 39).

APPLICATIONS AND EXAMPLES

Ms. McCloskey's first graders are learning about things that are the same and different (see function 3 in Figure 1.1). She introduces the lesson by showing pictures of the students' favorite foods they drew the day before. Displaying two drawings of pizza, Ms. McCloskey says, "Mia and Teng both drew pictures of pizza. They drew the same things. Their favorite food is the same—pizza. Maria drew a picture of a hamburger. Her favorite food is different. It is not pizza." Ms. McCloskey then displays commercial pictures of a variety of food. She chooses a picture of a hot dog and then goes through the students' drawings from the day before, modeling the sentence, "Moua drew a hamburger. A hamburger is different than a hot dog. It is not the same." When Ms. McCloskey finds a drawing of a hot dog she tapes in on the board next to the photo of the hot dog and says, "Jose drew a hot dog. His favorite food is the same as the picture. The picture of the hot dog is the same as Jose's favorite food."

For the next part of the lesson, Ms. McCloskey introduces the question, "Is it the same?" which requires the students to compare their pictures with an example. She displays a photo of an ice cream cone and goes through the students' drawings asking, "Is it the same as the picture?" If the students answer, "Yes!" she models the confirming sentence structure, "Yes, Hsi's picture is the same. Hsi drew an ice cream cone, too."

To give the students practice in using the academic language *same* and *different,* Ms. McCloskey divides the class into pairs of students and gives each pair a large sheet of paper on which she has photocopied a series of their drawings from the previous day. The pairs are instructed to work together, cut out the pictures of the favorite foods, and paste the ones that are the same together on a piece of construction paper. As the pairs complete their task they bring their paper to Ms. McCloskey and she asks them questions to encourage the use of the newly acquired words, *same* and *different.* See chapter 39, Reporting Back, for a description of this strategy.

Tong and Moua bring their paper to Ms. McCloskey. She points to the group of hamburgers they have pasted near to each other on the paper and asks, "Why did you put these pictures together?"

Tong answers, "Hamburger!"

Ms. McCloskey models, "Yes, they are all hamburgers. They are the same." She points to each hamburger and says, "This is a hamburger." She concludes with, "They are all the same."

Miss McCloskey points to the drawings of pizzas and asks, "Why did you put these together?"

Tong replies, "They all pizza. They same."

Ms. McCloskey smiles and confirms, "Yes, they are all pizza. They are the same."

She then turns to Moua and repeats the process with her.

The students were able to participate successfully in the activity because they were introduced to the academic language they needed, they were provided with visuals to support their understanding of the concepts, and because they were supported in their authentic use of language to interact and to explain. The language was related to their experiences, and they were given opportunities to practice the use of the language in a nonstressful environment. By working in pairs, they were given support and more verbal practice. The teacher provided monitoring and encouragement. She also scaffolded and celebrated their success.

• •

Scaffolding academic language can also take place at higher grade levels. In a middle school classroom, Mr. Scott is introducing an integrated unit on living organisms. He starts by asking the students what they know about living organisms and makes a list on the overhead as they give him statements such as:

They grow.
They die.
They need food and water.
Some are animals.
Some are plants.

Mr. Scott then reads a brief selection that explains how living organisms are categorized. After he has read the selection once, he lists the five categories on a chart and asks the students to copy the list onto a sheet of paper. He labels the list, "The Five Kingdoms." Mr. Scott displays a poster of a castle and asks, "Are these kingdoms like kingdoms where kings rule and live in castles like this?" After discussing the difference in the king/castle type of kingdom and the living organisms kingdoms, the students agree that the living organisms kingdoms are divided into five because of the similarities between the living organisms in each kingdom.

Mr. Scott then rereads the original selection and instructs the students to list the living organisms that fall into each kingdom when they hear them discussed in the reading. After he completes the reading about each kingdom, he stops and the students tell him what to add to the lists on the chart. Figure 1.2 shows what this chart looks like at the conclusion of the second reading.

Mr. Scott displays enlarged photographs of the cells of the various organisms and discusses the academic language associated with cells (cell, nucleus, protean, etc.) as he points them out on the photographs.

The students are then divided into pairs to work with microscopes where they are given slides of members of each of the five kingdoms. They are to work together to draw and label the cells they see on transparency film and to compare their drawings to the enlarged photographs to determine which kingdom their slides represent.

As the students view and draw their cells, Mr. Scott circulates around the classroom, answering questions and encouraging the use of academic language.

Monerans	Protists	Fungus	Plants	Animals
• bacteria • blue-green algae	• protozoans • one-celled algae	• yeasts • molds • mushrooms	• mosses • ferns • seed plants	• birds • mammals • reptiles • insects

Figure 1.2 Mr. Scott's List of the Five Kingdoms

After the microscope work, Mr. Scott displays the transparency cell drawings made by the students and they are discussed, focusing on the accuracy of the cell drawings and the labeling. The students' work is celebrated and they are ready to move onto independent reading using the academic language they have practiced.

The students in Mr. Scott's class are successful in their study of living organisms partly because of Mr. Scott's scaffolding of their academic language. He moves them through introductory steps in understanding vocabulary and the expectations of the tasks they will do. He encourages them to work together to provide verbal interactions and support for one another as they learn in an active mode. As he circulates around the room he provides scaffolding by asking appropriate questions, while modeling the use of academic language and connecting the language being used to concrete examples of the concepts being studied. He also provides encouragement and celebrates the use of language by the students.

CONCLUSION

Academic language scaffolding is appropriate across curricular areas and at every grade level. While the words *same* and *different* may not seem difficult to adults, they are used in the classroom in a slightly different way than in social speech. Learning the multiple meaning of words, especially how they are used in different ways in content-area instruction, can be very confusing to new English speakers.

References

Chamot, A., & O'Malley, J. (1994). *The CALLA handbook: Implementing the cognitive academic language learning approach*. Reading, MA: Addison Wesley.

Cummins, J. (1986). Empowering minority students: A framework for interaction. *Harvard Review, 56*, 18–36.

Suggested Readings

Gibbons, P. (1993). *Learning to learn in a second language*. Portsmouth, NH: Heinemann.

Hernandez, H. (1997). *Teaching in multilingual classrooms*. Upper Saddle River, NJ: Merrill/Prentice Hall.

Hudelson, S. (1989). Teaching English through content-area activities. In P. Rigg and V. Allen, (eds.), *When they don't all speak English,* pp. 139–151. Urbana, IL: National Council of Teachers of English.

ADVANCE ORGANIZERS

2

SUPPORTS

- Comprehensible input
- Contextualized language
- ✔ Reduced anxiety

Advance organizers (Ausubel, 1963) are brief presentations of abstract concepts given before a lesson to help the learner make connections between his existing knowledge and the new information to be presented. The form these organizers take should depend on the age, developmental level, and existing knowledge of the learner. Two forms of advance organizers can be used, depending upon the nature of the material to be presented. An expository organizer is designed to present general concepts and principles to the learner, which will help to provide a bridge between what is already known and the new material to be learned. This form of organizer is used when the new material is quite unfamiliar.

When the material to be learned is somewhat more familiar, a comparative organizer can be used. This form of organizer serves to integrate the new material with the similar material already understood by the learner and focuses on how the new and known material differ. This is particularly important when the new material may be confused with the previously known material (Newell, 1984).

Attention to the developmental levels and previous knowledge of the learners is very important when advance organizers are designed (Ausubel, 1963). The use of advance organizers with English language learners is particularly effective because their design is dependent upon building on the past experiences of the learner and providing bridges to the new material to be taught. Because the developmental levels of the learners play an important part in the design of advance organizers, appropriate formats for organizers are shown in Figure 2.1.

STEP BY STEP

The steps in designing and using advance organizers are:

1. Identify the main concepts or understandings the students must master in the lesson to be presented. Thinking about the previous knowledge and experiences of the students, develop a way to connect this previous knowledge to the new information to be presented.
2. Design a visual, hands-on learning experience or discussion topic that will encourage the use of known vocabulary and relate new vocabulary to what is already understood. As you design the advance organizer, examine Figure 2.1 for suggestions as to appropriate formats for the developmental levels of your students.
3. Present the organizer you have designed, encouraging discussion and questions. Relate the new vocabulary to known experiences and vocabulary using gestures, visuals, and restated explanations.
4. Teach the new information, relating it back to the advance organizer when appropriate.

Developmental Levels	Attributes of Learners & Suggested Formats for Advance Organizers
Preoperational preschool/ kindergarten	Need concrete experiences like field trips, hands-on activities, role plays, Venn diagrams with pictures, realia, photographs
Concrete-operational elementary grades	Depend less upon concrete props as they get older; ELL will still need some of the supports named for preoperational students for language development; activities like 20 questions, debate, oral readings, Venn Diagrams with words can now be used
Abstract-logical middle and high school	Learners' dependence on concrete props decreases, they are able to go beyond the "here and now"; ELL will still need concrete props to demonstrate new vocabulary; activities like debates, use of biographies, current events, interviews are now appropriate

Figure 2.1   Appropriate Formats for Advance Organizers

APPLICATIONS AND EXAMPLES

Ms. Flores has noticed that the only shape her kindergarten students recognize as triangles are isosceles triangles. To help them understand that all three-sided figures are triangles she designs an advance organizer to introduce a lesson on triangles. Because her students are only five and have limited English language ability, Ms. Flores knows that she must present the advance organizer in a concrete, hands-on form.

To build on the students' prior knowledge, Ms. Flores brings in five tomatoes she has selected because they all have different shapes.

She begins by showing the tomatoes and asking, "What are these?"

The students answer, "Tomatoes."

"How do you know they are tomatoes?" asks Ms. Flores. "What makes them tomatoes?"

"Red," answers Xiong.

"Round," suggests Tina.

"Yes," Ms. Flores agrees. "They are red and round. But they don't all look alike. How do you know they are tomatoes?"

"They smell like tomatoes." Nico says. "We could cut them open."

"Good suggestion," says Ms. Flores and she takes a knife and cuts two of the tomatoes in half.

"They have seeds inside," says Michael.

"Yes," agrees Ms. Flores. "We know they are tomatoes because they are red, they are round, they smell like tomatoes, and they have seeds inside."

Ms. Flores then takes out a green tomato and puts it on the table as she asks, "Is this a tomato?"

The students giggle and say, "Yes! But it's green."

"It will get red when it's ready," says Nico. "It's still a tomato, it's just not red yet."

"You are too smart for me," says Ms. Flores. "I want to show you something about triangles."

Ms. Flores takes out large cardboard examples of right, isosceles, and several obtuse triangles and places them on the chalk tray. "These are all triangles. They don't look exactly alike but they each have three sides." She runs her finger along the sides of each triangle as she counts, "One, two, three."

She then passes the cardboard triangles to the students and encourages them to run their fingers along the three sides of each example, counting the sides. She brings out enough examples for each student and they pass them around, touching the three sides and counting them. Ms. Flores then introduces a sorting game using the cardboard triangles and other cardboard shapes. The students place the shapes together, categorizing them as circles, squares, triangles, and rectangles even though the shapes within the categories are not all the same size. The students place the various types of triangles together and categorize them all as triangles.

Even though the students in Ms. Flores's kindergarten had previously recognized only isosceles triangles they were able to use the advance organizer to help them understand that just as all tomatoes did not look exactly the same, there were different kinds of triangles.

• •

Ms. Burton teaches ninth grade social studies in a highly diverse neighborhood. She is planning a unit about pluralistic society in America and wants her students to recognize the value of diversity in society instead of focusing on rigid allegiance to their own cultural group. As she reads the information to present to the students, she decides to use an advance organizer to prepare the students to incorporate the new information with their existing knowledge.

Building on the old ideal of America as a "melting pot" of cultures and the pluralistic view of America as a "salad bowl" of cultures, Ms. Burton plans an activity. She decides that an eating activity may help the students to better understand the concept of the valuing of both differences and similarities in a pluralistic society.

Ms. Burton brings in a crockpot and a salad bowl to class. She takes some cheese, salsa, and chopped vegetables and demonstrates the combining of them into the crockpot as she explains, "Years ago in America when people moved here from other countries, they were all expected to blend in together. America was called the melting pot of cultures. We're using this crockpot, or melting pot, today to demonstrate what happens when the cultures melt together."

After the ingredients melted together, Ms. Burton asked each student to take a tortilla chip and scoop some of the mixture onto their chip and taste it. After they had taken a taste, she asked them questions about the exact ingredients they had eaten.

"I think I got some peppers and salsa in my scoop," said Angel. "I definitely tasted something hot."

"Because the ingredients were all melted together, it was hard to identify exactly what you ate," agreed Ms. Burton. "This is exactly what happened to the new immigrants as they came to America. They learned to melt into American society and in many cases their languages and cultures were lost."

"My grandmother never lost her language," said Jose. "She stayed at home and took care of the children and only speaks Spanish to them."

"This is true," said Ms. Burton. "The older members of the families often stayed at home and did not melt into the American society."

"But, now let's look at what happens in a society where the differences among people are appreciated," says Ms. Burton as she takes out the salad bowl and the salad ingredients. "In a salad bowl, which is the description of what happens in American society now, all the ingredients are mixed together. Instead of melting their flavors together as they did in the melting pot, each ingredient retains its own identity and flavor. The salad is better because of the variety of ingredients—lettuce, tomatoes, cucumbers, cheese, dressing, and even onions. As you eat the salad you can enjoy the unique flavors of each of the ingredients."

As the students enjoyed small cups of salad, they talked about each of the ingredients they were tasting. "I like the tomatoes best because they taste sweet," says Jesse.

"I think tomatoes are best in a salad," says Moua. "I don't like tomatoes by themselves."

A bowl of salad is like American society today," says Ms. Burton. "America is strong because of all the different groups that have come here. The groups are trying to keep their identities and teach their children about their heritages."

Ms. Burton pauses to make this next important point, "In order for the different groups to keep their cultures and traditions and still be able to fit into American society and be accepted, we must learn to value and celebrate the contributions of each individual and group. This is called *pluralistic* society. It means that there is not just one right way to live, but that we can all participate in jobs and school and still celebrate our religions and cultures and even keep speaking our languages in business and within our family groups. For this to happen though, we must appreciate the ways people are different and the ways they are the same. Let's talk about these differences and similarities."

Ms. Burton then moves the students into a discussion of their cultures, languages, and traditions as the students help her to make a list of these things on the board. She continues to use the terms *melting pot* and *salad bowl* to support the students' understanding of the importance of maintaining the value of diversity if a pluralistic society is to be peaceful.

CONCLUSION

Ms. Burton and Ms. Flores have found ways to help students build on their background knowledge by using advance organizers to help students understand unfamiliar concepts. By presenting an advance organizer before moving into instruction, teachers activate prior knowledge in their students, explore unfamiliar vocabulary, and support students in seeing similarities between familiar knowledge and new applications or concepts. The bridges formed by advance organizers are especially supportive of English language learners because they tend to reduce the students' anxiety levels and make English instruction more comprehensible.

References

Ausubel, D. (1963). *The psychology of meaningful verbal learning.* New York: Grune and Stratton.
Newell, J. (1984). *Advance organizers: Their construction and use in instructional development.* ERIC Document ED 298908.

ANECDOTAL RECORDS

3

SUPPORTS

- Assessment appropriate for use in planning lessons based on the needs of the individual student

Anecdotal records (Rhodes & Nathenson-Mejia, 1993) are a form of assessment that allow the teacher to document the growth and accomplishments of students. They are based upon the teacher's observations as the students engage in classroom activities. This form of assessment and documentation is especially appropriate for English language learners because the teacher can ask questions of the student, record language samples and note ways in which the student demonstrates understanding (Genishi & Dyson, 1984).

The teacher is free to discuss the observations with the student and celebrate the growth that is documented. This serves to encourage and motivate the student and may even serve to lower classroom anxiety that will, in turn, increase participation and learning (Garcia, 1994). An anecdotal record always includes the student's name, the date of the observation, and a narrative of what was seen and heard by the teacher. It is not intended to be a summary of behavior but instead a record of one incident or anecdote observed by the teacher. Such things as quotes, descriptions of interactions with other students or teachers, and demonstration of knowledge through use of manipulatives or learning centers are easily documented through these narratives. If anecdotal records are taken on a regular basis and placed in sequential order, they are a good indication of the student's progress and provide a basis for instructional planning. A sample of an anecdotal record of a first grade child working at the writing center is shown in Figure 3.1.

Maria	**4/15**	**Writing center with Delores**

Maria and Delores are sitting at the writing center looking at labeled pictures of birds. On the table is a collection of books about birds. The students are to write one page for a book about birds they are compiling this week.

"What this word?" Maria asks Delores, pointing to the word *eagle.*

Delores answers, "Eagle." Maria, "That a pretty bird. I write about eagle." She writes, "Eagle is a prty brd." and draws a very detailed picture of the eagle.

The teacher asks her why she thinks the eagle is pretty. Maria says, "Eagle have shiny feathers." The teacher asks if she can write that. Maria smiles and says, "I try." She writes, "Eagle hv shne fethrs."

Figure 3.1 Anecdotal Record for an English Language Learner

Focus Area	Monday	Tuesday	Wednesday	Thursday	Friday
Writing center	Ana Blia Carol Helen	Dan Ivana Maria Susana	Jose Earl Patrick Wally	Luis Rosa Tomas Franco	Gina Karen Ned Otto
Literature circles					
Writing conference					
Guided reading					

Figure 3.2 Schedule for Conducting Observations for Anecdotal Records

STEP BY STEP

The steps in implementing anecdotal records are:

1. Decide what system you will use for keeping anecdotal records. They can be kept on index cards, in a notebook, on peel-off mailing labels (later transferred in sequence to an anecdotal record form), or in any format that helps the teacher to keep track of student progress.
2. Decide what you want to document and make a schedule for observing the students. A sample schedule allowing a teacher to observe a class of 20 students—four per day—in four areas a month is shown in Figure 3.2.
3. Set up a conference schedule and discuss your observations with the students and/or parents. This is also a good time to discuss language development and the setting of language and content-area goals.
4. Use the records to plan appropriate lessons for your students or to focus on language acquisition goals and progress. See the Language Framework Planning section in this text for an example of how this could be done.

APPLICATIONS AND EXAMPLES

Ms. Crandall is concerned that her second grade English language learners do not comprehend what they have read. She decides to conduct individual interviews with her students once a week to document their understanding of the books they are reading and to determine vocabulary to target in her language development lessons. Ms. Crandall sets up an interview schedule that allows her to interview four students a day. To document the language usage and reading comprehension of her students, she decides to keep anecdotal records of the interviews so that she has a record of their verbal interactions. A sample of one of these records is shown in Figure 3.3.

**Vang   3/26   Discussing *Alexander and Horrible, No-Good,
                                          Very Bad Day***

"I read Alexander. He have a bad day."
Why was his day so bad?
"He have gum in he hair. He call Australia. He get no dessert."
Why did he call Australia?
"He going to go there."
What did you like about the book?
"He funny."
Teacher's note: Work on possessive's and verb tenses (has and have).

Figure 3.3   Ms. Crandall's Anecdotal Record about Vang's Reading Conference

By documenting her interactions with her students in an ongoing way, Ms. Crandall has accomplished several things. She has a written record of the student's discussion of their reading; she has documented their English proficiency on a given day; and she has identified some important teaching points based upon their individual performance. Anecdotal records are a powerful strategy for individualizing instruction and documenting growth at all grade levels.

• •

Ms. Miller is using anecdotal records to document her eighth grade students' oral presentations in social studies. She models an effective oral presentation and shares the following expectations with the students:

1. Prepare and use a visual showing the main points of your presentation.
2. Prepare and use a clear opening statement and conclusion.
3. Make eye contact with the audience.
4. Speak loud enough to be heard.

Ms. Miller prepares a scoring rubric to be used to give the students feedback on their oral presentations, combining the use of the rubric with anecdotal records. She shares copies of the scoring rubric with the students ahead of time so they know how their presentations will be scored.

As the students give their presentations, Ms. Miller documents their language usage and their level of effectiveness related to the guidelines she set up for them. An example of one of her records is shown in Figure 3.4.

After the students give their presentations, Ms. Miller meets with them and discusses the rubric and anecdotal records she has written. They work together to set goals for the next presentation the students will give, identifying ways to improve the effectiveness based upon the feedback form and Ms. Miller's observations.

Student's Name _____ Jose _____

Topic _____ Electoral College _____   Date _____ 3/4 _____

Use of the Visual

< – | – – – – – – 2 – – – – – – – 3 – – – – – – 4 – – **X** – – – 5 – – – >

not used   used but not   used well,

                                          effectively   added to the

                                                                             presentation

Used the visual well. There were times when it could have been referred to, but was not.

Opening Statement

< – | – – – – – – 2 – – – – – – – 3 – – – – – – 4 – – – – – – 5 – **X** – >

not used   weak   fair   good   outstanding

Very attention-getting opening, "Many people think the electoral college should be redesigned."

Closing Statement

< – | – – – – – – 2 **X**– – – – – – – 3 – – – – – – 4 – – – – – – 5 – – >

not used   weak   fair   good   outstanding

"This is why the electoral college should be reorganized." The *why* wasn't made clear.

Eye Contact

< – | – – – – – – 2 – – –**X**– – – 3 – – – – – – 4 – – – – – 5 – – >

none   some   fair   good   outstanding

Reads notes too much.

Voice

< – | – – – – – – 2 –**X**– – – – – 3 – – – – – – 4 – – – – – – 5 – – >

too soft   weak   fair   good   outstanding

Very hard to hear.

Comments: _____ Presentation was well organized. It was clear that a lot of time was spent _____

researching the report. Visual was clear and easy to see. Voice was tentative. Gestures and posture _____

were somewhat distracting. Too much waving of hands. _____

Figure 3.4   Ms. Miller's Rubric/Anecdotal Record of Jose's Presentation

· ·

CONCLUSION

The students in Ms. Miller's class are supported and geared to be successful in several ways. Ms. Miller models an effective presentation and shares her expectations for the student presentations. She shares the scoring method she will use and helps the students to focus on points that will help them to present an effective report. Ms. Miller uses the rubric and anecdotal records she has written to discuss the students' performances and to assist them in setting goals for the future. In her use of anecdotal records, Ms. Miller has made her expectations clear and has given the students specific information about the ways in which they can improve their performance—and their grades.

In a less formal way, Ms. Crandall used anecdotal records to document changes in her students' behaviors and competencies. The use of anecdotal records is especially effective with

English language learners. The teacher is able to document the use of gestures, manipulatives, and body language that students in the early stages of English language acquisition tend to use in order to demonstrate their understanding of academic tasks.

References

Garcia, G. E. (1994). Assessing the literacy development of second-language students: A focus on authentic assessment. In K. Spangenberg-Urbaschat & R. Pritchard (Eds.), *Kids come in all languages: Reading instruction for ESL students* (pp. 180–205). Newark, DE: International Reading Association.

Genishi, C., & Dyson, A. H. (1984). *Language assessment in the early years.* Norwood, NJ: Ablex Publishing Company.

Rhodes, L., & Nathenson-Mejia, S. (1993). Anecdotal records: A powerful tool for ongoing literacy assessment. *The Reading Teacher, 15,* 503–509.

ATTRIBUTE CHARTING

4

SUPPORTS

- Comprehensible input
- ✔ Increased verbal interaction
- ✔ Contextualized language
- ✔ Reduced anxiety
- ✔ Active involvement of the learner

Attribute charting, also called semantic feature analysis (Peregoy & Boyle, 1993), is a way of visually organizing information to support students' understanding of the attributes of the concept being studied. For example, if students are engaged in the study of continents, an attribute chart of the continents could be constructed where the students look at maps and note which continents are found in the northern hemisphere; which are connected to other continents; which are surrounded by water; and which are mountainous, flat, or a variety of elevations. This strategy supports English language learners because the chart they make clearly visualizes their understanding of the main attributes of the topic—in this case continents. By making a chart of these attributes the continents can be more easily compared and contrasted. The students are involved in active research to determine which of the attributes are possessed by the individual continents and they are given opportunities to interact verbally as they construct the chart. The students' chart of the continents is shown in Figure 4.1.

STEP BY STEP

The steps in teaching the use of an attribute chart are:

1. Determine if the concept you are teaching lends itself to the charting of attributes. If it does, make a list of the attributes, traits, or characteristics that could be charted.
2. Involve the students in the discussion of the traits or attributes of the examples that illustrate the concept being taught. Provide the students with a set of clear instructions and encourage them to contribute to the completion of the attribute chart by examining the examples to see which attributes are present in each. Demonstrate how to use a marking system for the task. For example, an attribute might simply be checked on the chart or it could be marked with another symbol showing how closely it fits a given parameter. For example, under the attribute of connectedness, the continents of Europe and Asia would be marked with a plus sign because they are connected across a large area of land, while North and South America would be marked with a check mark because they are more minimally connected. Australia would be marked with a minus sign because it is not connected to any other continent.

Continent	Island	Connected	Mountains	Flat	Rivers	Desert	Forest	Ice
Africa	−	✓	−	✓	✓	+	−	−
Anarctica	−	+	✓	✓	✓	−	−	++
Asia	−	+	✓	✓	✓	−	✓	−
Australia	+	−	✓	✓	✓	+	✓	−
Europe	−	+	✓	−	✓	−	+	−
North America	−	✓	✓	✓	✓	✓	✓	−
South America	−	✓	✓	✓	✓	✓	✓	−

Figure 4.1 The Continents

3. Engage the students in the exploration of resource materials available to support their understanding of the attributes being marked. When charting animals, students might look at pictures of animals. When charting continents, students would want to examine maps and photographs. Give multiple opportunities to view realia or photographs to assure the understanding of the concept and its attributes. Model the use of the academic language being learned and help the students make connections between the academic language, their background knowledge and colloquial language (BICS).

4. Provide a follow-up activity that encourages the students to use the information on the attribute chart. This might be a writing assignment in which they must use the chart to compare and contrast two of the examples. It might also be an activity where the students illustrate and label the attributes of one of the examples from the chart.

APPLICATIONS AND EXAMPLES

Mr. Villalobos and his first graders are looking at pictures of animals and discussing where the animals live in preparation for a unit on the zoo. Since the class will be visiting the zoo, Mr. Villalobos wants the children to understand that the habitats in which the animals are housed are not exactly the same as where the animals live in the wild. Since the class has just completed a study of farm animals, the discussion of the pictures also involves the comparing and contrasting of zoo and farm animals. As the discussion continues, Mr. Villalobos decides that the children will benefit by the construction of an attribute chart. As he begins to draw the chart, he engages the children in

Animal	Farm	Zoo	Natural Habitat land	water	4 Legs	2 Legs	Wings	Hair	Babies live	eggs
Duck	✗		✗	✓		✗	✗			✗
Horse	✗		✗		✗			✗	✗	
Elephant		✗	✗	✓	✗			✗	✗	
Lion		✗	✗		✗			✗	✗	
Pig	✗		✗		✗			✗	✗	
Giraffe		✗	✗		✗			✗	✗	

Figure 4.2   A First Grade Attribute Chart of Farm and Zoo Animals

discussion of each animal, its natural habitat, and whether it is a farm or zoo animal. The chart they construct is shown in Figure 4.2.

Mr. Villalobos begins the discussion by activating the children's background knowledge of the farm animals they have recently studied and their visit to the farm. He shows the children a picture of a duck and asks, "Who remembers the name of this animal?" Tua raises his hand tentatively, "A duh?" he asks. "Yes," Mr. Villalobos replies. "It's a duck. Everyone say duck with me." The children all repeat the word *duck* together.

"Now, what do we know about ducks?" As the children reply, Mr. Villalobos writes their words, sounding them out aloud to model the sound/symbol relationships. "A duck has w-w-ing-s," Mr. Villalobos says as he stretches the sounds of the letters and writes *wings*. He repeats this process with *two legs* and *eggs*.

Next, Mr. Villalobos shows a picture of a horse and the process is repeated. The children say that the horse is a farm animal, with four legs and hair. They also add that horse babies, foals, are born alive. They know this because they saw a live birth on their farm visit.

As the children add information about the animals whose pictures they are examining, Mr. Villalobos says, "I have an idea! Let's make a chart so we can remember all about these animals. You have talked about where we see them, on the farm or at the zoo." He writes *farm* and *zoo* on the attribute chart.

"You have told me where the animals live, on land or in the water." He writes *land* and *water* on the chart.

"You have told me how many legs they have." He writes *2 legs* and *4 legs* on the chart.

"You have also told me how their babies are born, live or from eggs." He writes *live* and *eggs*. Mr. Villalobos then adds the words *duck* and *horse* under the word *animal* on the chart and explains, "This word says duck. Now I will mark what you told me about the duck. The duck is a farm animal." Mr. Villalobos makes an ✗ under the word farm. "He lives on land and in the water. I have to mark both these words. He has two legs and duck babies come from eggs."

Once Mr. Villalobos has modeled the marking of the chart for the duck, he involves the children in marking the chart for the horse's attributes. The children read and reread the attributes on the chart as they decide which traits should be marked for each animal. Once they have completed the chart they are shown what to do next.

Mr. Villalobos holds up a piece of construction paper as each child does the same. He models the folding of his paper in half and monitors as the children do the same. He models the drawing of two animals, one on each half of the paper. The children do the same, choosing the two animals they want to compare. Mr. Villalobos then models the writing of sentences about each animal, focusing on the attribute chart as the source of the words they will need. "The horse lives on a farm. He lives on land and has four legs. He has hair and his babies are born live."

Jeremy adds loudly, "We KNOW. We saw him born. The baby is called a foal."

Mr. Villalobos grins widely. "You can add that to your story, Jeremy."

The children's language and concept acquisition is supported by the use of the attribute chart. Mr. Villalobos combines the use of the chart with the use of modeling, both writing and resource use, to enable the children to successfully integrate their understanding and completion of a short writing assignment.

•••

Just as young children benefit from seeing their ideas and assignments visualized, older students also gain insight when charts are used to support their learning and planning.

For example, Ms. Vue has noticed that her seventh grade science students don't always use the strategies they have learned to support their understanding of the science concepts they are using. The science fair is approaching and all the students are supposed to be preparing projects for the fair. Ms. Vue decides that an attribute chart could be used to review the learning strategies involved in preparing a good science project.

"Today, I want to review the steps in the scientific process you are using to prepare your science project," Ms. Vue says as she projects a blank attribute chart on the overhead projector. The chart she displays is depicted in Figure 4.3.

Ms. Vue points to the steps in the scientific process on the overhead chart and reviews what each step means. She then goes back to the top row of the chart to ask, "Why do you think I wrote these particular things across the top of this chart? What do they have to do with doing a science project?"

Rodney raises his hand and Ms. Vue acknowledges him. "I think those are the strategies that are needed to actually do the steps in the project."

"Exactly," replies Ms. Vue. "Each of the steps in the scientific process involves the use of some of the learning strategies listed—and maybe some I haven't listed. Let's talk about how they are related to the steps in the scientific process."

As she points to the first step in the scientific process, Ms. Vue asks, "What does asking a question involve? Do you need to have any prior knowledge of the subject in order to ask a question?"

Stefan answers, "I think you have to know something about the subject you are going to use for your project or you won't know what kinds of questions to ask."

"Yes," replies Ms. Vue. "That is true. So, having prior knowledge is important to being able to ask a question. We could say that using prior knowledge is a trait or attribute necessary to do this step in the scientific process well. What about *resourcing?* Who remembers what that term means?"

Adriana replies, "It means using resources like encyclopedias and textbooks. You'd have to use resourcing in order to do a good job of asking a scientific question. If you didn't you may ask a question that has already been answered many times."

"That's true," said Ms. Vue. "What about note taking? Why is that listed?"

"You won't be able to remember everything you read," replied Josef. "That's why you have to take notes. But I'm not sure you need to do it just to ask a question. That's more what you do later on in the process."

Steps in the Science Process	Prior Knowledge	Resourcing	Note Taking	Planning	Communicating
Ask a question					
Make a hypothesis					
Collect data					
Record data					
Analyze data					
Answer the question					
Prepare a display to share your processes and results					

Figure 4.3   Ms. Vue's Attribute Chart

Adapted from Chamot & O'Malley, 1994.

As Ms. Vue works through the steps in the scientific process and relates them to the learning strategies needed in order to do a thorough job of the science project, the students can see by the chart exactly what they will need to do in order to complete each step. The last item on the chart, communicating, elicits some spirited discussion.

"You'll be doing all this work for nothing if you can't communicate to others. You need to be able to make your steps and results clear," said Alberto.

"And how do you do that?" asks Ms. Vue.

"By drawing pictures and listing your methods and results in order. Oh, and you have to make sure that you define your terms well so everyone knows what you are taking about," Alberto answered.

"So being able to communicate also takes some planning. Some of these attributes are connected," replies Ms. Vue. "That's why I wanted you to get to see them in chart form. Maybe a chart would help you to communicate your steps, methods, data gathering, and results."

CONCLUSION

Again, by using an attribute chart to demonstrate the attributes of a good science project, Ms. Vue has helped her students to visualize what is required of them. In the process she has taught them an organizational strategy that might be helpful to them as they communicate their scientific processes and results. The students have been given an opportunity to see the fifth and sixth language arts, *viewing* and *visually representing,* in action. This lessens their dependence on *reading, writing, speaking,* and *listening.*

References

Chamot, A., & O'Malley, M. (1994). *The CALLA handbook: Implementing the cognitive academic language learning approach.* Reading, MA: Addison Wesley Publishing.

Peregoy, S., & Boyle, O. (1993). *Reading, writing, and learning in ESL: A resource book for K-8 teachers.* White Plains, NY: Longman.

BILINGUAL BOOKS AND LABELS

5

SUPPORTS

- Comprehensible input
- ✔ Increased verbal interaction
- ✔ Contextualized language
- ✔ Reduced anxiety
- ✔ Active involvement of the learner

Books and labels written in two or more languages including English are appropriate for use in bilingual or multilingual classes for several reasons. First, they validate the students' home languages and allow them to use their knowledge of the home language to support their understanding of the text. The books and labels written in the home languages of the students bring some of the students' native culture into the classroom. They also provide opportunities for all the students in the class to be exposed to multiple ways of expressing thoughts and value systems. In classrooms where students have learned to read and write in their first languages, labels and books in those languages provide access to information. Some of the books contain the entire text, written in two languages, and support the transfer of reading ability from the home language into English.

In classrooms where the students do not read and write in their native languages, the books and labels provide some exposure to the written systems of the native languages and to the customs and traditions of multiple cultures. Some may encourage parents to read and discuss the books with their children. There are now many books available in which the cultures are depicted by stories, in English, with some samples of common expressions in the first language added for a taste of the language. For example, in the poem *"I Am Cucaracha"* (Johnston, 1996) the Spanish words *señora, señor,* and *por favor* are integrated into the English version and serve to add a Spanish lilt to the rhyme and rhythm. Many of these books, while not truly bilingual books, are written by authors familiar with the cultures about which they are writing and are very helpful in supporting multicultural studies in the classroom (Tomlinson & Lynch-Brown, 1996). See Figure 5.1 for a listing of some of these books.

STEP BY STEP

The steps for implementing the use of bilingual books and labels are:

1. Determine the home languages represented in your classroom and the stages of English development achieved by each student.
2. Provide opportunities for the students to verbalize the words for common items in the classroom using their home language. Involve the students in the writing and placing of labels

Books With Text in Two or More Languages

Spanish/English

Bofill, F. (1998). *Jack and the beanstalk—Juan y los frijoles magicos*. San Francisco: Chronicle Books.

Johnston, T. (1996). *My Mexico—Mexico mio*. New York: G. P. Putnam's Sons.

Lachtman, O. (1998). *Big enough—Bastante grande*. Houston, TX: Piñata Books.

Reisner, L. (1993). *Margaret and Margarita—Margarita y Margaret*. New York: Greenwillow Books.

Reisner, L. (1998). *Tortillas and Lullabies—Tortillas y cancioncitas*. New York: Greenwillow Books.

Hmong/English

Campbell, R. (1992). *I won't bite*. Union City, CA: Pan Asian Publications.

Thao, C. (1993). *Only a toad*. Green Bay, WI: Project Chong.

Vietnamese/English

Truyen, T. (1987). *The little weaver of Thai-yen Village—Co be tho-det lang thai-yen*. San Francisco, CA: Children's Book Press.

Books Available in More Than One Language

Hmong/Spanish/English

Coburn, J. R., & Lee, T. C. (1996). *Jouanah, a Hmong Cinderella*. Arcadia, CA: Shen's Books.

Books Written in English With Multicultural Themes

Cheltenham Elementary School Kindergartners (1991). *We are all alike . . . We are all different*. New York: Scholastic.

Dooley, N. (1991). *Everybody cooks rice*. Minneapolis, MN: Carolrhoda Books.

Dooley, N. (1996). *Everybody bakes bread*. Minneapolis, MN: Carolrhoda Books.

Hyun, P. (Ed.). (1995). *Korean children's songs and poems*. Elizabeth, NJ: Hollym.

Lessac, F. (1984). *My little island*. London: Macmillan.

Levine, E. (1989). *I hate English!* New York: Scholastic.

Morris, A. (1989). *Bread, bread, bread*. New York: Lothrop, Lee & Shepard Books.

Morris, A. (1989). *Hat, hats, hats*. New York: Lothrop, Lee & Shepard Books.

Morris, A. (1995). *Shoes, shoes, shoes*. New York: Mulberry Books.

Musgrove, M. (1977). *Ashanti to Zulu—African traditions*. New York: Dial Books.

Roland, D. (1986). *Grandfather's stories from Mexico*. El Cajon, CA: Open My World Publishing.

Steptoe, J. (1987). *Mufaro's beautiful daughters*. New York: Scholastic.

Trezise, P. (1988). *The cave painters*. Australia: Angus & Robertson.

Figure 5.1   Bilingual Books

within the classroom. For example, the words *door, la puerta, window, la ventana, chalk, la tiza* would be displayed in a Spanish/English first grade classroom. In classrooms with older students the labels can be complete sentences such as *Pongan sus tareas de casa aquí*.

3. Provide bilingual books, with the text written in both English and the home languages of the students, for use in read-aloud or independent reading according to the abilities of the students to read in their home language. If the students do not read in their home language, enlist the help of a bilingual parent or instructional assistant to read the text aloud in the home language(s) of the students before reading the English version. Take time to stop dur-

ing the English reading to compare the words and sentences in the different languages. Draw attention to any similar words. Discuss the books and the similarities and differences in the customs and situations depicted in the books. Encourage the students to discuss how their experiences and family customs are similar to or different from the situations described in the books. Support the students in seeing that there is a range of customs and beliefs within any culture and that people from many cultures share similar customs and beliefs. See the "Culture Studies," "Learning Centers," and "Shared Reading" chapters for additional ways to use bilingual books and labels.

4. Provide translations of important texts whenever possible. Students can often assist with these translations. These can be read aloud by bilingual parents or instructional assistants or put on tape for the students to use in the listening center.

5. Periodically engage all students in the learning of key vocabulary in multiple languages. They can all learn the names of colors, counting, and asking basic questions in multiple languages. In addition, engage the students in discussions of the customs depicted in the multicultural literature that is being shared in the classroom

APPLICATIONS AND EXAMPLES

Ms. Torres teaches a fifth grade class in a border town in California. A number of her students move across the border to Mexico for a few months each year. Some of the students attend school regularly while they are in Mexico, but some of them do not. Ms. Torres is determined that the students will learn to read and write in English while they are in her class. She has decided to make the most of the students' reading and writing abilities in Spanish to move them toward more fluent literacy in English. Ms. Torres and her students label everything in her classroom in both English and Spanish. They provide bulletin board captions in both languages and Ms. Torres encourages the children to write in the language with which they are most comfortable. If the students write in Spanish then she asks them to write a sentence or two in English giving the main gist of the page. By doing so, everyone in the class can read and enjoy the stories that have been written. She also encourages collaboration so that her students can publish bilingual books, with both English and Spanish texts.

Ms. Torres regularly reads picture books in English after her instructional assistant has read the same book in Spanish. After the book has been read in both languages, the students help her to add words to the word wall—matching the English and Spanish words and cross-listing them alphabetically. This encourages the Spanish speaking students to build their English vocabularies—and the English speaking students to build their Spanish vocabularies. With longer texts like chapter books, Ms. Torres reads one chapter in English and the next in Spanish. She then asks a student to summarize each chapter in the language which was not used. She finds that both her English and Spanish speakers are learning to listen carefully and are understanding both languages well.

One day, Juan, one of her Spanish speakers who regularly spends a few weeks in Mexico each year, comes to her with a special request. "My grandmother is very sick. I am afraid she is going to die. My mother would like for me to write the story of her life so that we will all remember her. Will you help me to translate it from Spanish to English so that my parents can read it and also my brothers and sisters?"

Ms. Torres is excited about the project and shares the idea with the whole class. "I think we all have relatives who have interesting stories. Why don't we each choose someone to interview. We can write biographies for our class library and learn more about our family history at the same time."

The students are interested in the idea of conducting interviews, although they are not sure about the writing part of the project until Ms. Torres suggests that they can publish their biographies using the word processing program on the computer.

The next step in the project is to formulate interview questions the students can ask. The students work in small groups brainstorming the questions that will help them to learn more about the life stories of their relatives. The groups share their lists of questions and then the students go home to conduct their interviews.

Each day the students return with more of their questions answered and they begin to write the biographies. They work in pairs most of the time to help each other with vocabulary and sentence structure. Some of the more fluent Spanish writers finish their Spanish versions very quickly and then struggle over the English translations. Some of the English speaking students are able to help with the translations because of the bilingual word wall and the number of Spanish/English dictionaries in the classroom. The English speaking students use the same approach to writing in Spanish that Ms. Torres requires of the beginning English speakers. They write a sentence or two in Spanish to convey the gist of the story to the Spanish readers. The Spanish speaking students serve as assistants to the English speakers when they need help with this.

Toward the end of the school year all the biographies are complete, illustrated, and bound, and the class decides to have a celebration to share the books with their families. They sit in groups and read their favorite parts of the biographies to the visitors. Ms. Torres is touched by the attendance and the enthusiasm for the project. One of the grandmothers shares, "I never thought I would have a book written about me. And my relatives in Mexico can read it. So can my grandchildren who speak only English."

• •

Students of all ages benefit from the use of bilingual literature, labeling, and sharing. Mr. Fong's tenth grade class is preparing a Thanksgiving assembly for the nearby elementary school. They want to help the younger students to understand the concept of the various groups of pilgrims who have come to America from all over the world. To begin their research they read books about emigrant groups that have come to America to escape war and oppression. The students decide to focus on several different pilgrim stories to illustrate how America is still receiving pilgrims today. They begin with a brief reenactment of *Molly's Pilgrim* (Cohen, 1983) and then create a time-line of all the major immigrations to America. As they unroll the time line across the stage, each tenth grader reenacts a scene from the life of one of the pilgrims they have researched. They begin with Juan de Oñate, and the group of Mexican pilgrims who escaped to Texas 23 years before the Mayflower arrived, and continue the reenactments all the way to the Bosnian pilgrims who are still arriving today. To make their presentations authentic, each student has researched the language of each of the pilgrim groups and learned to say, "Thank God! We have arrived in America and now we are free!" in the language appropriate to the group they represent.

Mr. Fong is so impressed with their research and dedication to the project that he makes a videotape of their production to motivate the next year's social science group. When he interviews the students about the project he is surprised by some of their comments.

"I never knew there was more than one group of pilgrims."

"The hardest part of the research was learning to speak in Armenian—and it was only two sentences."

"I found out that my grandmother was a pilgrim. I never knew that."

"I never knew how hard the pilgrims had to work in order to survive."

• •

CONCLUSION

The use of bilingual books and labels in the classroom encourages students to value other cultures and languages. English language learners are validated by the use of their home languages in the classroom and the study of their literature and culture. Native English speakers are given an opportunity to experience the challenge of remembering vocabulary in a second language. The comparison and celebration of a variety of approaches and beliefs helps to build a cohesive community in the classroom.

References

Cohen, B. (1983). *Molly's Pilgrim*. New York: Bantam Books,

Johnston, T. (1996). *My Mexico—Mexico mio*. New York: G. P. Putnam's Sons.

Tomlinson, C., & Lynch-Brown, C. (1996). *Essentials of children's literature* (2nd ed.). Needham Heights, MA: Allyn and Bacon.

CLOZE ACTIVITIES

6

C loze activities are activities based upon written text in which some words are left out and blanks are inserted. Cloze paragraphs are often used to assess reading comprehension because the word choices students make provide the teacher with an opportunity to evaluate their understanding of the meaning of the text. Cloze activities, when used with English language learners, provide an opportunity to teach English vocabulary and reading decoding skills in a meaningful context. When done in pairs or small groups these activities also provide an opportunity for students to discuss their choices and justify their selection of words.

Teacher-designed cloze activities are especially valuable because they can be adapted to the specific needs and language levels of students. Based upon observation of students' oral reading or running records, the teacher is able to identify students who are not using cross-checking of phonological and meaning cues. Creating paragraphs with words left out requires the student to use multiple sources of information like context to predict words which make sense in the sentence. Cloze sentences can also demonstrate to students the fact that they don't have to be able to read every word of the paragraph to understand the meaning. The context of the sentence, in combination with phonic and syntax cues, is very helpful in supporting the reader in the identification of unknown words. Figure 6.1 shows the variety of ways one paragraph can be used to provide practice adapted to individual student needs.

STEP BY STEP

The steps in using cloze activities are:

1. Observe your students as they read and note their use of phonological, meaning, and syntax cues as well as the self-monitoring they do. Also note the categories of the words that seem to be giving them difficulty. A running record is an easy way to do this. Figure 6.2 presents an example of such a running record.
2. Examine your students' running records to determine which students are experiencing similar difficulties, then group these students together.
3. Prepare a cloze paragraph by choosing a selection from a reading assignment at the students' instructional reading level and deleting words using one of the following methods:

Type of Cloze	Definition	Example
Traditional	Leave out words selected randomly.	I went for a walk to the _____. I wanted to _____ a _____. I watched carefully but I was to be _____.
Syntactic	Structure words are deleted.	I went _____ a _____ the sea. ____ wanted ____ see ____ dolphin. I watched carefully ____ I was _____ be disappointed.
Semantic	Content words are deleted.	I went for a walk to the _____. I wanted to _____ a _____. I _____ carefully but I was to ____ disappointed.
Graphophonic	Some letters are deleted.	I w_____ for a w_____ to the s_____. I wanted to see a d_____. I watched c_____ but I was to be d_____.

Figure 6.1   Cloze Activities to Support Reading and Language Acquisition

Adapted from Gibbons, 1993.

- Copy the paragraph onto poster board or chart paper and cover selected words with wide correction tape. Be sure to use the type of tape that is easily removed.
- Copy the paragraph onto transparency film, leaving blanks in the text.
- Copy the sentences from the selection onto sentence strips. Cut the words apart and leave some out as they are placed into a pocket chart.

4. Work with the groups of students asking them to read the selection silently. Have students write down the words they think would best complete the selection. Ask each student to read the selection orally and insert the words they believe are needed to make the selection make sense. After the students read the selection with their chosen words inserted, have them explain how they decided which words to insert. Have them point to or read the parts of the selection that gave them clues. If they selected different words have them discuss which words seem to fit best and why.

APPLICATIONS AND EXAMPLES

Ms. Mendez has noticed that some of her second grade students tend to look at the first letter of a word and then guess. They don't seem to be monitoring to make sure the words they are

Passage	Errors	Self-Correct	Errors MSV	Self-Correct MSV
✓ ✓ ✓ ran ✓to✓ ✓ Jack and Jill went up-the hill	2		Ⓜ Ⓢ V	
✓ find ✓ ✓ ✓ ✓ To fetch a pail of water.	1		Ⓜ Ⓢ V	
✓ ✓ ✓ ✓ ✓ ✓ head Jack fell down and broke his crown,	1		Ⓜ S V	
✓ ✓ ✓ ⌠ falling too ⌡ SC And Jill came tumbling after. ⌡ R		2	Ⓜ Ⓢ V Ⓜ Ⓢ V	ⓂⓈⓋ ⓂⓈⓋ

Figure 6.2 Sample of a Running Record

MSV refers to the cueing system the child was using. M = Meaning, S = Structure, V = Visual (phonological).

reading make sense. She designs a cloze activity that will force them to think about the meaning of the words in the passage. It looks like this:

Jack and Jill _____ up the _____ . They wanted to _____ some _____ . On the way, Jack _____ and Jill helped him by _____ .

After the students read the passage, guessing words that make sense, Ms. Mendez shows them the same passage but this time each blank has the first letter of the word displayed. The passage now looks like this:

Jack and Jill r_____ up the r_____ . They wanted to f_____ some bl_____ . On the way, Jack f_____ and Jill helped him by st _____ .

The students read the passage again, using the phonic cues to help them to decide which words fit into the blanks. They discuss how their choices are different. The teacher displays the passage a third time, without any blanks, and the children read it again.

Jack and Jill ran up the rock. They wanted to find some blossoms. On the way, Jack fell and Jill helped him by stopping.

Ms. Mendez and her students discuss how they have to think about what makes sense in the sentence and even when they know the first letter of the word it is still possible to choose the wrong word. Ms. Mendez cautions them to be sure to look at the whole word. After this lesson, Ms. Mendez will remind her student frequently about the importance of thinking about the words they read and the sense they make.

• •

Cloze activities can be used at any level. They force the reader to think about the meaning of the passage and to choose words to insert in the blanks that fit the meaning, structure, and genre of the piece.

Mr. Tompson notices that his eleventh grade English language learners have difficulty making sense of poetic language in narratives. To assist them in making sense of what he calls tough text, he prepares the following cloze passage:

E _____ for the moment at least from the t_____ of fantasy, Jose in a short time set up a s_____ of order and work which allowed for one bit of 1_____: The freeing of the birds, which since the time of their founding, had made m_____ with their fl_____, and installing in their place m_____ clocks in every house. (Marquez, 1970.)

The students read the passage and discuss what they think it means. Mr. Tompson leads them to the conclusion that, although they can't read every word, they can understand the main idea of the passage. They work as a group to sound out and discuss the words *emancipated, torment, system, license, flutes, merry,* and *musical.* The teacher's goal is met. The students feel that they can understand this tough text even without knowing every word. They also learn some new vocabulary as a result of the lesson.

• •

CONCLUSION

As shown by these two examples, cloze activities are helpful in supporting English language learners to focus on meaning in reading. Although new vocabulary may be difficult for the readers, cloze activities help the students to learn ways in which the context of the reading passage—in combination with their knowledge of phonics, syntax, and prior knowledge about the topic—can support their understanding of the text they read.

References

Gibbons, P. (1993). *Learning to learn in a second language.* Portsmouth, NH: Heinemann.
Marquez, G. (1970). *One hundred years of solitude* (p. 45). New York: Avon.

Suggested Reading

Tompkins, G. E. (1997). *Literacy for the 21st century.* Upper Saddle River, NJ: Merrill/Prentice Hall.

COHESION LINKS

7

C ohesion links are the important parts of written and spoken paragraphs that connect sentences so that they form a cohesive whole. These links often appear in the form of pronouns that refer back to a person, place, or thing in a previous sentence or references that require the reader to recall a previously stated fact or condition. Cohesion links that are frequently used in spoken and written English are often confusing to English language learners. This is because the use of pronouns or use of ellipses where words are understood—but not spoken or written—are not always easy to connect to words used in previous sentences. Cohesion links lessons make these links more visible and understandable to English language learners and are valuable in supporting their understanding of both spoken and written material. The forms of English writing and speaking that English language learners find most confusing are shown in Figure 7.1.

STEP BY STEP

The steps in teaching a cohesion links lesson are:

1. Prepare an overhead transparency of a paragraph at the students' reading level that contains pronouns, conjunctions, substitutions, or ellipses. Start with a fairly simple paragraph and then gradually add complexity in future lessons. Write the paragraph so that you can uncover one sentence at a time.
2. Cover all but the first sentence of the paragraph and have the students read that sentence aloud with you. Discuss any words that substitute for others or refer the reader to another word in the sentence. Uncover the second sentence and repeat the process, supporting the students in making connections between words in the first sentence and references in the first sentence. Use an overhead marker to draw an arrow back to the proper noun that has been replaced by a pronoun or other word that has been replaced to make the connections visible to the students.
3. Work your way through the entire paragraph in this way. Make connections between pronouns and nouns, sequence words, conjunctions, and multiple ways of referring to the same thing.
4. Follow up this lesson by dividing the students into pairs and giving the pairs each a paragraph written on transparency film. Encourage the pairs to work together to draw arrows from pronouns to the words in other sentences to which the pronouns refer. Have them label the conjunctions and circle words that describe the same things.

Cohesive Tie	Example	Problem
Reference	A tall figure was standing outside the door. The figure turned quickly toward her as Sally stepped onto the porch. As she regained her composure she watched as he turned without a word and walked away toward the bus stop in the rain.	These underlined reference words often refer back to something already mentioned in the text. English language learners often do not recognize the relationship between the sentences and words used to refer back to a previous sentence.
Conjunctions	He worked all day although he was tired. Finally he laid down his hammer. He wasn't finished but his work was getting sloppy. So, he was afraid of ruining his work unless he got some rest.	Conjunctions are key words in helping the reader to determine the connections between ideas and the sequencing of events. English language learners do not always understand the connections that conjunctions demonstrate and so they often misunderstand the text being read or heard.
Substitution	He was given a new pair of shoes for Christmas. His old ones were too small.	When one word is substituted for another, English language learners often do not recognize that both words are referring to the same thing.
Ellipsis	He sat down, ✓ stood up, and then ✓ sat down again. He said, "Some people like to dance and others don't ✓."	The checks in the example show places where words are left out but the reader or listener assumes meaning as if the words were present. English language learners may not recognize what is missing or may not be able to supply the meaning because of the omitted words.
Lexical cohesion	The giant was now in a land of tall *trees* and flowing *rivers*. He was still running hard although he was slowing down considerably. He went galloping over an enormous *forest* and on into a huge *range of mountains*,	If an English language learner does not see the connections between the underlined words or the words in italics, this selection will not make as much sense as it should.

Figure 7.1 Cohesive Ties in Written and Spoken English and the Difficulties They Cause English Language Learners

Adapted from Gibbons, 1991, and Halliday & Hasan, 1966.

5. Have the students display their paragraphs on the overhead projector and discuss their conclusions after the pairs have completed their work. Have the entire group discuss the connections in the paragraphs that help build meaning as the paragraph is read.

6. Review the connections found in future reading assignments on a regular basis by asking questions such as, "To what word in the first sentence does the word *he* in this sentence refer?"

APPLICATIONS AND EXAMPLES

Ms. Collom's kindergarten class is writing a language experience story about their trip to the pumpkin patch. The first sentence they dictate is: *We went to the pumpkin patch*. She stops and asks, "Who went to the pumpkin patch?" The students respond, "We did!" Ms. Collom asks, "Who is *we?*"

Philip answers, "Ms. Collom's class—all of us!"

"You are right, Philip. We use the word *we* because it is shorter and easier to say than, *Ms. Collom's class went to the pumpkin patch*. When we say *we*, we mean Ms. Collom's class."

The class then dictates, *We saw a scarecrow. He was funny*. Ms. Collom asks the students, "Who was funny?"

The students laugh, "The scarecrow!"

"Yes," Ms. Collom says. "We don't have to say, We saw a scarecrow. The scarecrow was funny. We can say *he* was funny because we already said we were talking about the scarecrow."

Ms. Collom knows that pronouns are sometimes difficult for English language learners to understand. She is providing support that will aid their listening and reading comprehension in the future.

Ms. Barnes is teaching a lesson on revising with her eighth grade writing class. She displays a paragraph on the computer screen, projected on a large monitor so that all the students could see it. The paragraph says:

I was walking down the garden path when I met a small, round man. The small round man was dressed all in green with pointed shoes and a round bowler hat. The small round man's face was round and his cheeks were red. I felt as if I had seen the small round man somewhere before.

Ms. Barnes reads the paragraph aloud to the students and asks them if there is anything that bothers them about the paragraph. When the students reply that the phrase, "the small round man," is repeated too many times, Ms. Barnes asks for suggestions as to how that could be fixed. The students help her to replace "the small round man" with pronouns so that reading the paragraph sounds better. After the students help her to replace the noun phrase with pronouns, Ms. Barnes questions the students about the pronouns and to whom they refer. The students have no problems understanding the paragraph although many of the English language learners do not know anything about leprechauns.

The students work together to make the paragraph more interesting. One of the challenges Ms. Barnes issues is, "Can you think of some more interesting words to use so that this paragraph isn't so boring?"

Gradually, using suggestions from various students and discussing the meanings of the words added, the class revises the paragraph so that it finally reads:

I was walking slowly down a winding garden path lined with a wild variety of blossoms in every possible color when I met a squat, rotund man with a shiny red face. He was dressed all in green, emerald jacket and trousers, brilliant green velvet shoes with glittering gold buckles and a round green satin bowler hat. His face was so round that he looked like a characature of every leprechaun I had ever seen in a book. Even though I knew that leprechauns are usually found in the imaginations of Irishman and fools who have consumed too much malt, I couldn't wait to get home to describe him to my family. He was the happiest vision one could possibly see on the seventeenth day of March!

As Ms. Barnes and her class revise the paragraph they discuss the uses of pronouns, the meanings of the words they use, and the images they portray. They connect the sentence, "He was dressed all in green" with the phrase that follows, "emerald jacket and trousers" and arrive at the conclusion that the phrase illustrates the reference to "dressed all in green" since emerald is a shade of green.

The students discuss the importance of varying the words so that the readers can envision the sight of the leprechaun and his vivid clothing surrounded by the spring flowers along the garden path. They also have learned that using pronouns helps make the narrative sound more natural, but it is important to know to whom the pronouns refer or the narrative doesn't make sense. The students also add a number of new words to their personal writing dictionaries that day.

CONCLUSION

Cohesion link lessons support students in making sense of English language, both spoken and written. Teachers help students to understand the formats by explaining the meaning of pronouns, ellipses, conjunctions, substitutions, and other abstract references in text and spoken language; by giving examples; and by providing students with guided practice in analyzing English text. They also encourage students to take time to analyze the reasons for their own misunderstanding. Demonstrating the connections by writing the sentences and drawing arrows to the words that are needed to make sense of the sentences makes the cohesion links more comprehensible to the reader or listener.

References

Gibbons, P. (1991). *Learning to learn in a second language*. Portsmouth, NH: Heinemann.

Halliday, M., & Hasan, R. (1966). *Cohesion in English*. New York: Longman.

Suggested Readings

Irwin, J. (1991). *Teaching reading comprehension processes* (2nd ed.). Boston: Allyn and Bacon.

Tompkins, G. (1996). *Literacy for the 21st century*. Upper Saddle River, NJ: Merrill.

COLLABORATIVE READING 8

Collaborative reading (Gibbons, 1993) is a strategy that is helpful to English language learners when they are reading for information. This strategy also allows a teacher to support readers of various abilities to work collaboratively as they study a specific topic. Students use a variety of library and/or textbooks with information on the topic being studied. These books are selected to provide a wide range of reading levels to meet the needs within the class. The group has the advantage of reviewing information from four or five different sources, depending on the number of students in each group. Members of the group then discuss the information gathered so that everyone becomes an expert on the topic. Collaborative reading provides a method for all students—regardless of reading ability—to participate in a group research activity. Because the teacher selects books appropriate for the reading levels within the group of students, each student can make a significant contribution to the collaborative task. English language learners are supported because, if necessary, they have texts with simpler language and illustrations. Each member of the group can contribute in unique ways. English language learners may contribute by drawing a visual to represent the main points of the collaborative research. This allows them to provide a translation of the information by reporting orally to the group if there are other students who share the same home language, or providing information related to the difference in use of the concept being studied in the students' home cultures.

STEP BY STEP

The steps in a collaborative reading lesson are:

1. Gather books on the topics to be studied, making sure to include books at various reading levels so that all students will be successful in finding information.
2. Carefully considering the strengths and needs of the students, organize your students into groups of four or five to explore topics. Make sure that each group contains a student with strong reading and writing skills. Either have each group explore a different topic or a different aspect of one topic. Instruct the groups to brainstorm questions they want to answer about their topic. These questions can be included on a **KWL** chart, a chart where the students note the things they **K**NOW about the topic, the things they **W**ANT to know about the topic and, after the collaborative reading, the things they **L**EARNED about the topic.

They may just simply brainstorm their questions on a list. Depending upon the topics, it sometimes works to have the whole class brainstorm questions and then have each group answer the same group of questions on their topic. Provide each member of the group with a book on the group's topic. Be careful to match the books with the students' reading levels. Each member of the group researches the group's questions using a different book on the topic.

3. Instruct the members of the groups to find the answers to the group's questions in their books and take notes about the information they will share with their group. You may have to teach a mini-lesson on how to read and take notes, jotting down important facts.

4. After group members have completed their note-taking, have them discuss their findings, create a data chart—a form of information matrix—or other visual, and plan how they will share their research with the whole class. A data chart form is shown in Figure 8.1.

Group Members _____

Topic _____

	Questions				
	How does it look?	**What does it eat?**	**Where does it live?**	**What are its natural enemies?**	**Other important information?**
Sources and Readers					
Book: Reader:					
Book: Reader:					
Book: Reader:					
Book: Reader:					
Book: Reader:					

Figure 8.1   Data Chart Form

Adapted from McKenzie, 1979.

5. Have the groups work on their group presentation and then share their research and visuals with the whole class.
6. Document the group's success in working together, following instructions, gathering information, and presenting their information to the group. You can do this documentation through anecdotal records, checklists, or rubrics. See the chapter on Anecdotal Records for suggestions.

APPLICATIONS AND EXAMPLES

Ms. Frederick's third graders are studying insects. Because the students' reading abilities vary greatly and the science textbooks are too difficult for many of the students, Ms. Frederick decides to gather a number of library books for them to use in researching insects. The media specialist at her school is extremely helpful in locating books at varying reading levels and Ms. Frederick locates four or five books or chapters in books for each of the insects the students have identified as interesting. Ms. Frederick arranges the books by topic: bees, ants, beetles, grasshoppers, and roaches. She labels the books with correction tape so that she will be able to give students books at their reading levels. The easiest books are marked 5, next easiest 4, and so on, with the most difficult labeled with the number 1.

The students sign up for groups depending upon their interests, but Ms. Frederick makes sure that there are some able readers in each group. Before she lets them start their research, Ms. Frederick does a lesson on note-taking. Using an informational book on spiders, she reads aloud and models note-taking on the overhead projector. She stops after a few examples and involves the students in deciding what notes she should add. Before she has finished, the students understand how to select important information for their notes and they also have learned why spiders were not included on their list of insects to be researched. The next part of the mini-lesson involves finding research questions. Ms. Frederick leads the class to ask basic questions, which she writes on the transparency of the data chart. This enables the students to discover how to look for information, answer the research questions, and note the information in the proper box on the chart. She models the use of several books on spiders to demonstrate that the students will not find the answers to all the questions in the same book. She also points out some conflicting information in several of the books.

Ms. Frederick then moves the students into their interest groups and they begin to read their books and take notes. Toward the end of the period, she instructs the students to add their information to the group data chart. The students are then given a few minutes to discuss their findings within the group.

During science period the next day, the students get back into their groups and discuss how they will present their findings to the class. One group decides to make a fact book about bees and read it aloud to the class. One group decides to make a poster about grasshoppers with a large labeled picture of a grasshopper and small posters surrounding the large one with facts about grasshoppers. The ant group wants to make a model of an ant with paper mache. They will write facts about the ant on large green paper shaped like blades of grass and place the ant in the grass. The beetle group decides to put their data chart on poster board and give an oral presentation using the data chart. Each group is busy preparing their visual and their presentation.

Ms. Frederick's class was able to learn many things through their collaborative reading projects. Every student contributed information to the group reports. All the students learned much more about the topics than they could have learned reading independently. They felt like researchers and were successful in presenting information orally.

Ms. Stacy is a fifth grade teacher with a multicultural class ranging in reading abilities from first grade level to eighth grade level. She decides to do a collaborative reading project on the human body. Ms. Stacy follows much the same procedure as Ms. Frederick did but with one interesting twist. The day of the presentations Ms. Stacy moves all the desks in her classroom to one side. She sets the chairs up in a large semicircle, three chairs deep. At the door of the classroom that morning, Ms. Stacy has each child sign in and get a name tag, a folder with a yellow pad and pencil, and a paper robe that she purchased at a medical supply house. Her students are all presenters at a mock medical conference. She has invited the local television station to come and tape the conference, and she has set up a lectern, microphone and sound system—transforming the students into medical professionals at a conference. They present their reports and visuals solemnly, smiling for the camera only when they're finished with their reports. After their reports, the groups must field questions. They handle the questions well. They have obviously done their research thoroughly. Each group seems to know which member of the group is likely to know the answer to the question. One student, when stumped for an answer, replies, "I'll have to get back to you on that one."

CONCLUSION

Collaborative reading can be used to provide students with knowledge from a variety of sources. It supports the formation and strengthening of a classroom community by providing students with an activity in which their unique gifts (such as speaking more than one language, drawing, or using computer or other technology to create visuals) supply a valuable component to the group presentation. In the process of creating, practicing, and presenting the group report the students are given several opportunities to acquire new vocabulary, to write and reread English and home language summaries of the material read and written, and to communicate in English for a meaningful purpose.

References

Gibbons, P. (1993). *Learning to learn in a second language.* Portsmouth, NH: Heinemann.

McKenzie, G. (1979). Data charts: A crutch for helping pupils organize reports. *Language Arts, 56,* 784–788.

Tompkins, G. (1997). *Literacy for the 21st century.* Upper Saddle River, NJ: Merrill/Prentice Hall.

COMMUNICATION GAMES

9

SUPPORTS

✔ Comprehensible input
● Increased verbal interaction
✔ Contextualized language
✔ Reduced anxiety
● Active involvement of the learner

Communication games (Gibbons, 1993) are activities set up in the classroom for the purpose of creating opportunities and purposes for verbal communication practice. Many times the purpose of the communication in these games is to convey information or cause something to occur as a result of the activity. Some of the games provide practice in the use of a particular language function such as giving directions or asking questions. Other games require students to work together and communicate in order to solve a problem. Suggested communication games are shown in Figure 9.1.

STEP BY STEP

The steps in teaching communication games are:

1. Identify a language function in which your students need practice. Following directions, asking questions, and conveying academic information are among some of the most commonly used in communication games. Choose a category of communication game from Figure 9.1.
2. Model the way the game is played by involving one or more students in demonstrating the game to be played. Review the rules carefully and post them in the room so the students can refer to them during the activity.
3. Organize the students in pairs or small groups, making sure you have a fairly fluent English speaker in each pair or group. Give the pairs or groups their tasks and get them started.
4. Move around the room providing support and encouragement.
5. After the activity, ask the students to share their experiences, any problems they had, and the solutions they devised. Make a list of the vocabulary they found helpful and discuss how it was used.

Activity	Description	Example
Barrier games	Two students sit back-to-back or behind a screen (barrier). One student is given a complete set of instructions that must be conveyed verbally to the second student, who completes the task.	One student has a set of small colored blocks that must be arranged in a certain configuration. The other student, working from a diagram, gives oral directions to the student with the blocks so that the blocks end up in the proper configuration.
Information sharing	Each student has part of the information necessary to complete a task or solve a problem. They must share their information to accomplish the task.	Students are given materials to fold an origami flower. Each student has one section of the directions. Using the sequence words as a guide, the students take turns reading the directions silently and then conveying them orally so the members of the group can complete the folding task.
Inquiry & elimination	A small group of students works together. One student has a set of information that must be obtained by the others through questioning and elimination of irrelevant items. The group then decides the solution based upon their inquiry.	The class has been studying insects. The child designated as the expert in the group is given the name of an insect and a set of facts about that insect. By asking questions, the students must gather enough information about the insect so that they can determine which insect is described. When they have guessed the correct insect, they have also reviewed their knowledge of that insect.
Rank ordering	Students work together in a small group to suggest solutions to a problem and then reach consensus as to the rank order of the usefulness of each of the solutions.	The groups are asked to make a shopping list of important supplies to purchase for a camping trip. They are to brainstorm items, and then rank-order the importance of the items so that they could survive if they could take only the top five items. Food and water don't have to be listed; the groups are assured of having them.

Figure 9.1 Suggested Communication Games

Adapted from Gibbons, 1993.

APPLICATIONS AND EXAMPLES

Ms. Darling's kindergartners are learning colors and shapes. She wants them to have experience in using the new vocabulary they are learning so she designs a barrier game using attribute blocks—blocks in various geometric shapes and colors. (Construction paper shapes in a variety of colors will also work.) She explains to the students that they will be playing a game. She asks Tony to help her teach the game. Tony comes up to the front of the room and uses the shapes designed for the overhead projector to follow Ms. Darling's oral directions. Ms. Darling shows the class the drawing she is holding and tells them, "This is the design that I want Tony to make. I will give him directions. He can't see the design. I have to tell him how to make it."

"The design is in a straight line. I will tell you the shapes to put in the line. Start at the left and move across the glass from left to right, like you do when you read. First, find the large red circle and put it at the top of the projector," Ms. Darling tells Tony.

Tony places the large red circle at the top of the glass, on the left side. Ms. Darling is standing with her back to him so she waits until he tells her that he is ready for the next direction.

"You will be sitting behind a screen so you won't be able to see what your partner is doing. You have to talk to each other in order to build the design," Ms. Darling reminds the students.

"Next, find the small green circle and put it next to the large read circle," Ms. Darling says. Tony follows her directions.

Once the demonstration is complete, Ms. Darling arranges the students in pairs and puts up small science project boards between the pairs as barriers. She starts each pair with a simple design. They come to her for a new design when they finish one and they take turns giving instructions. Ms. Darling moves around the room giving encouragement and language scaffolding as needed.

After the activity the class discusses the words that they used. Lara says, "It was hard. You had to remember a lot of things to say. The shape and the color and the size—a lot!"

Ms. Darling acknowledges Lara's comment. "Yes, it was hard. You had to use a lot of math language. You did a good job!"

Mr. Standford's tenth grade English class is completing a study of *The Canterbury Tales* (Chaucer, 1365/1934). Because the language in the tales is so difficult, Mr. Standford reads the Geraldine McCaughrean (1984) version of the stories aloud, comparing the simplified, illustrated version with the language in the older, more traditional version. Occasionally, Mr. Standford even reads the Old English words to give the students a feel for the original. To provide a review of the work before the unit exam, Mr. Standford decides to give the students practice in discussing the tales and reviewing the information they have about each of them. He begins the lesson with an explanation, "Today we will be reviewing *The Canterbury Tales* so that you will all do well on the exam on Monday. You will be working in small groups to identify the main characters in the tales, their characteristics, and their stories. Let me show you how this will work."

Mr. Standford asks three students to come up to the front of the class and ask him questions about the tales. He sets the stage for them. "You can ask me questions, which I must answer truthfully. You cannot ask me to name the character or tell you things directly about the character, but you can ask questions that can be answered by 'yes' or 'no.'" The person who is being questioned will have the character's name and the information about the character and tale so that the answers given will be accurate."

One student asks Mr. Standford if the character is a man. He answers, "No."

The next student asks if the character had animals. Mr. Standford answers, "No."

The third student asks if she was married several times. Mr. Standford answers, "Yes."

The first student then asks, "Is it the Wife of Bath?" Mr. Standford answers, "Yes."

The group then discusses how they eliminated characters as the questions were answered. They agreed that eliminating the men really narrowed the possibilities. They then reviewed the information about the Wife of Bath and her tale on the review sheet.

Mr. Standford divides the class up into groups of four students and gives one student in each group a review sheet so that they are ready to field questions. He makes sure that there are strong students in each group. Each group has a copy of both the simplified, illustrated version and the more traditional version of the tales so they can check the accuracy of their answers.

Mr. Standford moves around the room as the questioning takes place. As each group reviews the characters, they take turns fielding questions. Mr. Standford saves the more easily recognizable characters for the English language learners and supports the students in returning to the texts whenever anyone needs help in answering questions. The students find they knew a lot about the characters and the tales.

• •

CONCLUSION

Communication games can be used in many grade levels and across all curricular areas as shown by the vignettes. By providing students with authentic reasons to communicate in English, they are given opportunities to practice their English communication skills in a low-stress environment. Students are more likely to be successful because the situations are explained in advance, the vocabulary is practiced, and the context is built into the exercises. By lowering the stress, making the activities game-like, and providing examples of vocabulary and sentence structure, the teacher reduces the affective filter for all students involved in the activity.

References

Chaucer, G. (1934). *The Canterbury tales.* (J. Nicolson, Trans.). New York: Crown. (Original work published 1934)

Gibbons, P. (1993). *Learning to learn in a second language.* Portsmouth, NH: Heinemann.

McCaughrean, G. (1984). *The Canterbury tales.* Chicago: Rand McNally.

COOPERATIVE LEARNING

10

SUPPORTS

- ● Comprehensible input
- ✔ Increased verbal interaction
- ✔ Contextualized language
- ● Reduced anxiety
- ● Active involvement of the learner

Cooperative learning (Johnson & Johnson, 1984) is a term used for a collection of strategies in which students work together to accomplish a group task. The group task is structured so that each member of the group is expected to perform an assigned task. Because of the unique tasks assigned to the members of the cooperative group, cooperative learning is much more effective than ordinary group work usually done in classroom situations. These approaches are especially effective for English language learners because the students have more opportunities for verbal interactions in small groups (Kagan, 1989). They are encouraged by the members of the group and can participate at the level at which they are able. English language learners working in cooperative groups must be given assignments according to their levels of English proficiency, which requires the teacher to be aware of their stages of language acquisition. (See the chapter on Leveled Questions) and their levels of ability in English reading and writing.

Cooperative learning activities must be preceded by some team-building (see suggestions in Figure 10.2) in order for the team to understand the value of working together and getting to know the strengths of each of the members of the team. In addition, teachers must make their expectations clear if cooperative learning activities are to be successful. Some of the principles of cooperative learning are explained in Figure 10.1.

STEP BY STEP

Steps in using cooperative learning strategies in the classroom are:

1. Divide the class into cooperative groups. Provide a team-building activity as "warm-up" for helping students to see the advantages of cooperation and getting to know each other. Each time a new team is formed there should be a team-building activity to help members become familiar with each other's capabilities. Suggestions for team-building activities are given in Figure 10.2.
2. Give the team members cards which identify their assigned roles and clear descriptions of their duties. Usually one member is designated as the leader, one as note-taker, one as reporter, one as time-keeper. It is also helpful to give each member a name tag which designates the role to be played so that all members of the group are aware of the roles of all the members. Tasks especially appropriate for English language learners include artist, vi-

Principle	Example	Benefit to English Language Learners
Cooperative tasks are designed so that individuals must work together in order for the task to be accomplished.	Jigsaw activities involve each member of the team being given a piece of the information so that they must work together or no one will have all the necessary data.	English language learners must be encouraged to participate in the tasks or the whole team will fail to accomplish their assignment.
Positive interactions are developed and encouraged.	The group's evaluation is based on individual and group marks. Group members are rewarded for peer tutoring and supporting weaker students.	Because peer tutoring and group support of individuals are encouraged and rewarded, all students are supported to succeed.
Students have opportunities to work in different teams.	A variety of plans are used for grouping, such as interest groups, random groups, heterogeneous groups, etc.	English language learners have an opportunity to get to know other students in meaningful ways and to demonstrate their competence in a variety of ways.
Social, language, and content skills are all learned in the process of interacting with the group.	Social and academic language interactions in cooperative groups help the students to learn pro-social behaviors as well as content knowledge.	English language learners benefit from the verbal interactions, learning social norms and content-related language.

Figure 10.1   Principles of Cooperative Learning

Adapted from Meyers, 1993.

sual creator (drawing or computer-generated), mime, or translator—providing a physical reenactment or second-language translation of key points for other second-language learners in the classroom.

3. Give each team a task to complete and remind each member of the team of the roles they are expected to serve in order to assist the others in completing the task. The leader keeps everyone working and focused, the note-taker keeps records of the team activity, the reporter shares the information or results with the class at the completion of the activity, and the time-keeper makes sure they are on task and moving toward completion of the task within the time limit.

4. Provide an opportunity for the groups to report back to the class at the end of the assigned time. Each group should share their solutions.

5. Give each group an opportunity to debrief, discussing the process and the roles each team member played in the success of the group. Have each group fill out a group report form that focuses on both product and process. A sample group report form is shown in Figure 10.3.

Activity	Rules
Arts project	Team members work together to create an artistic display of the team members' names.
Assembly line	Using a arts or crafts project, team members assemble a product in assembly line fashion. One team member starts the project and passes it to the next member, who adds to it. Each member contributes to the final product.
Brainstorm	Teams work against the clock to try to find three commonalties among the team members. Following the rules for brainstorming, which are: accept all ideas, build on other people's ideas; teams try to find a category in which they can all agree; three favorite things that are common among the team, three things they all hate to do, or three movies they all liked, for example. One team member suggests a category, the others quickly give their favorites in that category until they are able to find an area of agreement.
Group task	Group works together to complete a puzzle, word search, or brain teaser.
Line up	Team members work quickly to line themselves up according to a given stipulation such as height, age, birthday, number of brothers and sisters, etc.
Team identity	Team works together to reach consensus on a team name, logo, and motto.

Figure 10.2   Common Team-Building Activities for Cooperative Learning Teams

Adapted from Meyers, 1993.

APPLICATIONS AND EXAMPLES

Ms. Truit's fourth graders are working in cooperative groups to use their math and problem-solving skills to plan a party for the end of the year. Each group of four has been given a budget of $25 to spend and they are to decide on the refreshments, decorations, and games to be played. At the end of the planning period, each group will present its plan for the party complete with a drawing of the decorations, a detailed refreshment list including costs figured from a grocery store price list and a presentation detailing the process the group used to solve the problems and make decisions. The group with the best plan will actually get to do the shopping, make the decorations, and be in charge of leading the games. The winning group will have a full school day without other assignments in order to complete their party preparations.

The groups work diligently to complete their calculations and draw their decorations. The group leaders are encouraging everyone to work together. The note-takers are in charge of preparing the detailed plans, while the reporters are working along with the others to practice what they will say in their oral presentations. The time-keepers are keeping a close eye on the clock. Motivation and cooperation is high. Everyone wants to have a chance to actually give their party.

Group Name _____		
Task _____	**Date** _____	

Group Member	**Contributions**	**New skill practiced? (yes, no, or comment)**
_____	_____	_____
_____	_____	_____
_____	_____	_____
_____	_____	_____

Comments

_____

_____

_____

_____

_____

Group Member's Signature

Note: Each group member must fill out a form. The group must agree on the new skill to be practiced. Suggestions: taking turns, sharing materials, staying on task, asking questions, summarizing ideas, encouraging others, restating suggestions, etc.)

Figure 10.3   A Cooperative Group Report Form

Adapted from Meyers, 1993.

Ms. Hill's math students at Mountain High are using their calculators to solve problems related to the state budget. One of the gubernatorial candidates is promising a 12% reduction in state income tax if he is elected. He is also promising an increase of 6% in state spending for education. Ms. Hill has formed cooperative groups for the purpose of figuring out the answers to some weighty questions.

Each group leader is given a list of line items on the state budget. The group comptroller has been given a detailed list of state income from income taxes, the state education budget, and anticipated revenues for the coming year. Each group secretary has been given a list of bills currently being considered by the state legislature and their anticipated cost. The group calculator has been given the task of making calculations as requested by other members of the group.

The groups have been given the following tasks:

1. Figure the effect of a 12% reduction in state income taxes.
2. Figure the effect of a 6% increase in state education funding.
3. Figure the cost of new legislation if all of the bills currently being considered are passed, or if only 50% of them are passed.
4. Figure by what percentage the state revenues must increase in order for it to be possible for the gubernatorial candidate to be able to carry out his promises (listed in tasks #1 and #2).
5. Create a visual on transparency film showing your calculations and what combination of factors would make the candidate's promises possible. In this task you may decide which bills could be passed, what the increase in revenues would have to be, on any combination of factors.

6. Watch the clock to make sure the group will be able to complete the task within the time limit. You should be finished and ready to present in 45 minutes.

7. Group leaders will present the results at the end of the class period. They may enlist the help of any (or all) of the group members in making the presentation.

The groups are working hard to make professional presentation visuals, double-check their calculations, and make sure they haven't overlooked any bills that might make a big difference in their calculations. They are learning a lot about calculator math and state government, including vocabulary unfamiliar to a number of them. The teacher is circulating to monitor the group efforts, define unfamiliar words, or refer the students to resources within the room—including the computer on-line services.

· ·

CONCLUSION

Cooperative learning provides an opportunity for communication, planning, research, and oral and visual presentations in the classroom. Quality group cooperation does not occur overnight, however. Taking the time to build teams, monitoring the group interactions, and debriefing are all vital pieces of the cooperative learning process. The groups are not just learning content but valuable interpersonal interaction skills, as well. Videotaping the group interactions and having the group watch the video and examine their own behaviors, strengths, and weaknesses is a supportive activity when creating the learning community (Herrell & Fowler, 1997).

References

Herrell, A, & Fowler, J. (1997). *Camcorder in the classroom: Using a video camera to enrich curriculum*. Upper Saddle River, NJ: Merrill/Prentice Hall.

Johnson, D. W., & Johnson, R. T. (1984). *Circles of learning: Cooperation in the classroom*. Alexandria, VA: Association for Supervision and Curriculum Development.

Kagan, S. (1989). *Cooperative learning: Resources for teachers*. San Juan Capistrano, CA: Resources for Teachers.

Meyers, M. (1993). *Teaching to diversity*. Toronto, Canada: Irwin Publishing.

Suggested Reading

Chamot, A., & O'Malley, J. (1994). *The CALLA handbook*. Reading, MA: Addison Wesley.

Additional Resources

Lesson Planning

Ellis, S. S., & Whalen, S. F. (1990). *Cooperative learning: Getting started*. New York: Scholastic.

Johnson, D. W., & Johnson, R. T. (1985). *Structuring cooperative learning: Lesson plans for teachers*. Edina, MN: Interaction Book Company.

Video

Cooperative Learning. (1996). Alexandria, VA: Association for Supervision and Curriculum Development.

CULTURE STUDIES

11

Culture studies (Freeman & Freeman, 1994) are studies in which the students research and share information about their own cultural history. These studies will vary greatly depending upon the ages of the students in the class but generally fit well with the history or social science goals in most school districts. Many different language arts skills can be supported by culture studies. Students are required to use reading, writing, speaking, listening, viewing, and visual representation of ideas to interview their parents, grandparents, and other members of their culture. The key to making this strategy work is the way the word *culture* is defined. Any culture study should begin with a discussion of culture and what makes up a culture. This can be done effectively by examining the culture of the classroom and what makes it unique. The use of time, the attitude toward learning, the expectations for participation, the rules about how to get along with each other, and the structure that is in place regarding the use of materials all contribute to the culture of the classroom.

Once the students understand the broad definition of *culture* that is to be investigated, they can begin to organize the study of their own culture. Some teachers have found it profitable to encourage students to work in pairs or small groups so that they can begin to compare and contrast cultural norms as an ongoing part of the study. For possible approaches to culture studies see Figure 11.1.

STEP BY STEP

The steps in implementing culture studies are:

1. Decide on a project that is appropriate for the ages of your students and will support the objectives for your grade level. Examine the objectives in both social sciences and language arts to determine ways to integrate both curricular areas. See Figure 11.1 for suggestions.
2. Identify the purpose of the projects to be done and whether the research and activities should be done individually, in pairs, or small groups. If a main goal is to get the students to interact and share the information they are gathering, then pairs or small groups should be used. Make a visual with the students that clearly identifies the steps they are to take in their research and the products they will be expected to create. For an example of this visual, see Figure 11.2.

Group	Projects	Activities
Kindergarten	Family portraits Working together	• Draw a picture of your family. • Tell about what your family likes to do together. • Draw a picture of some work that your family does together. • Tell about how the work is divided and who does each part. • Tell about the things each family member can do to help the work get done. • Is there anyone in your family who teaches other people in the family how to do things? What things?
Primary grades	People are different, people are the same The way we do things changes from generation to generation	• Group investigation of basic ways in which cultural groups are the same and different. Choosing one aspect at a time, have the students interview people of their own cultural groups about how the particular aspect is regarded. (For example, the use of time, the importance of education, the regard for animals, the significance of different colors, the role of food in celebrations, the division of work, etc.) • Individual students interview and research family photo albums for examples of how things have changed from generation to generation. Questions asked of family members should also examine how these changes have affected the use of time and the value system of the family.
Upper elementary grades	Our state and nation	Each student researches the impact of their own cultural group on the history of the state and nation. The child's own family history should be examined first to determine the reason for immigration, if any, or the family work history and how the occupations of generations fit in with the history of the state and nation. The changes in value systems, occupations, and places where the family moved should be compared to the general trends in the state, nation, and world history when applicable.
Middle school	Values and history	Students examine their family's values in relation to how time is spent, the priorities for the expenditure of money, the differences in expectations for male and female children, any inequalities in the past or present in the division of work or responsibilities within the family. The celebrations and rituals which have continued over time and the use of language and interactions in solving problems or disputes should also be examined.
High school	Nation building	Students examine the movements in history which affect the building of nations and how their culture has followed or differed from the general trend. The contributions of women, minorities, the effect of world events are all considered in light of the building of nations across the world. The changes that have taken place in the students' own families and cultures as a result or in response to these events should also be considered. The construction of time lines and personal family histories in relation to world events is appropriate.

Figure 11.1   Culture Studies Appropriate for Different Grade Levels

Please note that suggestions are given in relation to the broad themes recommended in the California History/Social Science Framework, 1988.

1. Introduce yourself to your group, telling your name and the cultural group with which you identify yourself. If you do not identify yourself with an ethnic group, try to identify your broad cultural affiliation such as Mexican-American, German-American, European-American, or White Anglo-Saxon protestant. You may even have to identify the cultural group from your mother's side and your father's side.

2. As a group use your social studies book to research the history of the world from 1900 until today and create a time line of major events. Hint: Several of these time lines are included in your textbook. Each member of your group should make a copy of the general time line and place his/her own birth on the time line.

3. The group should brainstorm questions they will ask as they interview members of their family about the events on the time line that they remember. The purpose is to learn as much as you can about how the world events since 1900 affected your family. Did any members of your family fight in any of the wars? Did the family move to another city or country because of world or economic events? (See #5 for other ideas.)

4. Each member of the group should arrange to interview members of his/her own family or other members of their cultural group and report back each day to share the interviews that have been conducted and the information that has been revealed. Events shared by the interviewees should be charted on the time line and written in narrative form.

5. At the conclusion of the week groups should meet together to plan a presentation format for sharing the information they have gathered with the whole class. Be creative and include visual or reenactments! Each member of the group should have a speaking part in the presentation. Information that should be highlighted in the presentation:
   • In what ways were the family events affected or family histories altered by world and economic events?
   • In what ways were the different cultural groups impacted by these events?
   • Which cultural groups seemed to be least affected by the world and economic events?
   • How did the world and economic events affect the basic values and priorities of the different cultural groups?

Figure 11.2   The Steps You Will Take to Create Your Family Time Line

3. Encourage the students to identify the main elements of a good project and create a rubric or checklist based upon their suggestions so that they know what is expected of them and how their report will be evaluated. See Figure 11.3 for a sample of a cultural study checklist.

4. Plan a celebration involving school administrators and families so the students can share their research and results.

APPLICATIONS AND EXAMPLES

Mr. Watanabe's fourth graders have been studying California history all year. They have explored the history of the state from the pre-Columbian settlements and people through modern day immigrations and rapid population growth. They have created a time line of the history of the state with major events prominently noted. As Mr. Watanabe introduces the final segment of the study of California history he shows some pictures of his family. "This is a picture of my family. This is my grandfather and my grandmother. This is my father and this is my mother. And this is me," He points to the small child in the picture. "I am going to tell you about how my family's history fits on the time line of California history we have created."

"My grandfather was a fisherman in the San Francisco area in the 1930s. When the Japanese bombed Pearl Harbor in 1941, the American people became very suspicious of all Japanese

Before you present your culture study, check to make sure you have all the following:

_____ I made a visual to help me show what I learned.

_____ My visual is large enough to see easily.

_____ I have checked the spelling and grammar.

_____ I have note cards prepared, which will help me remember the main points I want to make.

_____ I have included information in my report from interviews of people in my generation, my parents' generation, and my grandparents' generation.

_____ I have included information in my report about the main historical events that affected my family history.

_____ I have included information in my report about the changes in values and priorities from generation to generation.

_____ I have included interesting family stories in my report so that "the flavor" of my cultural heritage is evident.

_____ My visual and note cards will be submitted to my teacher at the conclusion of my report.

Figure 11.3 Checklist for Culture Study Reports

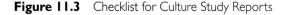

people and the American government moved all the Japanese families from the west coast into camps to that they could not conspire with the Japanese government to attack the west coast of America. The picture I showed you was taken at the Manzanar War Relocation Camp here in California where my family lived for four years. I went to school there. My whole family lived behind barbed wire like criminals simply because we were of Japanese heritage. You would think that my mother and father would be very bitter about this part of history and how they were treated. My parents, however, see it as something that was natural. They say that people get frightened in time of war and do unreasonable things. Part of my Japanese culture is the value of serenity. I think that an important part of my culture is thinking serene thoughts so that the aggravations of life do not upset the higher thoughts of the mind. My father wrote some beautiful music while he was in the relocation camp. He used the time he was given to create something of beauty."

Mr. Watanabe placed a card along the class time line under January, 1942 that said, "Mr. Watanabe's family goes to Manzanar War Relocation Camp." He then talks about what he wants each member of the class to do as a part of their final study of California history.

"As your final study of California history I want you to interview the members of your family, your clan elders, your priests, or older people you know who belong to your culture. I want you to find out how long your family or people have been in California, what caused them to come, and what part they played in any of the California events that we have been studying. If your parents do not know the answers to your questions, ask your grandparents or other elderly people in your families. What other ways can you think of to get information about this study?"

"We could look in old photograph albums," answers Juanita.

"My grandmother has a family Bible that has the whole history of our family in it!" exclaims Jerrod.

"That will be very helpful," says Mr. Watanabe with a smile.

By the end of the week the time line is bulging with three-by-five cards noting events in the families of the students. Some of the students are amazed at how long some of the Mexican and Native American families have lived in California.

"I thought the Mexican families were all new immigrants," said Melissa. "My family only moved to California in 1980. Maria's family has been here for generations. Compared to her family, we are the new immigrants."

• •

Ms. Jeffreys teaches twelfth grade English in a high school where most of the students are from white protestant families. Her husband teaches the same grade level and subject in a highly multicultural school and they often discuss how different the students at the two schools are in their views of the world. One night, over dinner, Mr. and Ms. Jeffreys decide that they want to do a project that will help the students from the two schools to get to know each other and their differing viewpoints. They decide that each of their students should write a cultural autobiography to be shared over the Internet with a student in the other's class. The Jeffreys decide to call the project, "Cultural Conversations." They begin the study by identifying a piece of literature that they can explore with their classes. Each student is asked to reflect on the incidents discussed in the book and how it relates to the customs, values, and interactions in their own families and cultural groups. The Jeffreys choose the book *Plain and Simple: A Woman's Journey to the Amish,* by Sue Bender (1989), because the book tells about one woman's visit to another culture and how the things she learns about another culture cause her to reflect on her own.

The Jeffreys assign conversation partners from their fourth period classes. They intend to start small and see how well the project is accepted. They agree to read and discuss the first chapter of the book on Monday, having their students reflect on the chapter, talk to their families on Monday night, and post their first e-mail conversations on Tuesday.

The first chapter of the book talks about how the author falls in love with Amish quilts—their simple designs and bold colors—and begins to think about the Amish people. She compares her lifestyle and values to those of the Amish people and wants to create an area of calm peace in her life. As the Jeffreys read the first chapter they stop periodically and discuss their own lives, values, and cultures and how their family heritages contribute to their beliefs. They ask the students to think about the values Ms. Bender lists in the first chapter and how they equate their own personal and family's values to those the author discusses. The students are then given a list of things to discuss with their families that evening and told that they will be discussing their self-reflections and information gained from their families via e-mail with a student at the "other high school" the next day. The students all chuckle, knowing exactly how they are connected to the "other high school."

The next day in the computer lab, the students are all busily writing to their new conversation partners. The Jeffreys ask the students to save the correspondence each day so that the information they share and gather from their conversation partners can be used in the future. There is a lot of concern about spell-checking and proper English sentence structure because of the cross-town rivalry between the high schools, but the teachers and fellow students are all happy to give assistance.

On Wednesday, the discussion begins with what has been learned through the conversations. Many of the students are amazed to discover the differences in the use of time and the priorities expressed by their conversation partner. "My partner has lessons every day after school. He's taking trumpet lessons, French lessons, and being tutored in calculus. He has no time for fun. He goes from school to lessons, to homework, to bed." says Mikel.

"What does that tell you about his values?" asks Mr. Jeffreys.

"I think it tells more about his family's values because he doesn't seem to want to take all those lessons," replies Mikel.

"That may be so—but he's doing it," says Mr. Jeffreys.

"Oh, I see your point," Mikel replies. "His values involve going along with his parents' expectations of him, improving himself in areas of music and languages. He did say he was expecting to go to college on a music scholarship."

After their discussion of the first day's conversations the Jeffreys read and discuss the second chapter of *Plain and Simple,* where Ms. Bender struggles with her interest in the Amish, her values, which seem to directly conflict with those of the Amish, and her desire to know more about the Amish culture. The chapter explores the value of the finished product in comparison to the value of the process of creating, the need to establish balance in life, and the impact of religion on the rules of the culture. The Jeffreys give the students their next assignment which is to reflect on the chapter and their own family values related to these issues.

The study continues in this pattern over the next two weeks. After the book has been read and the conversation partners have discussed a number of issues related to culture, they are assigned a report to be written collaboratively and presented at a joint meeting of the two classes. The partners are to bring some artifacts from their cultures that represent the values they have discovered as they reflect on the book and exchange ideas. The partners are to share the things they discover about their own cultures and how their belief systems are formed, including the influence of their families, their religion, their interests, their school, their friends. The Jeffreys plan a seminar where the two classes will get together for a Saturday morning to work on their presentations, eat lunch together, and then present their findings to their school administrators and families in the afternoon. Each student is invited to contribute a paper to a journal they will compile collaboratively, entitled, "Our Stories, Cultural Conversations." The Jeffreys are pleased to see that almost everyone contributes a story to the journal. The stories contributed show a respect for the students' own cultures and the new information they have gained about their partner's culture.

CONCLUSION

Culture studies provide a way for teachers to build the classroom community while engaging their students in an in-depth social studies project that requires research. Language arts skills such as interviewing, note taking, using the steps in the writing process, and oral and visual presentations must be taught. The classroom community is greatly enhanced when the teacher shares his/her own culture study and discusses the multiple ways in which the study was conducted. Appreciation of the values, customs, and unique contributions of the different cultures is heightened through the process of investigating multiple cultures through firsthand accounts of personal experiences.

References

Bender, S. (1989). *Plain and simple: A woman's journey to the Amish*. New York: Harper Collins.

California State Department of Education. (1988). History/social sequences framework. Sacramento, CA: California State Department of Education.

Freeman, D., & Freeman, Y. (1994). *Between worlds: Access to second language acquisition*. Portsmouth, NH: Heinemann.

DICTOGLOS

> ### SUPPORTS
> - ✔ Comprehensible input
> - ● Increased verbal interaction
> - ✔ Contextualized language
> - ✔ Reduced anxiety
> - ● Active involvement of the learner

Dictoglos is a strategy developed by Ruth Wajnryb (1990) for use with high school students, but it can be adapted for use with all ages. It is especially effective with English language learners because the strategy focuses on fluent academic language and supports learners in listening and recalling good English language models (Gibbons, 1993).

Dictoglos involves students in listening to repeated, fluent readings of English text. At first they just listen but on subsequent readings they take down as much of the text as possible. They then get together in pairs and again in fours to combine their notations and re-create as much of the text as possible. The activity provides an authentic reason for communication and practice in re-creating, rewriting, and rereading English text.

▶ STEP BY STEP

The steps in teaching a Dictoglos lesson are:

1. Select a content-related text and read it aloud at a normal speaking pace. At first, the students are instructed to "Just listen carefully."
2. Reread the text twice more. The students are now instructed to "Jot down key words and phrases."
3. Have the students work in pairs to re-create as much of the text as possible using the notes taken by each of the partners to write the text as closely as possible to the original text as read by the teacher.
4. Have two pairs meet together and pool their re-creations of the text to reconstruct it more completely.
5. Have the group of four work together to write down as much of the text as possible. Their aim is to re-create it as closely as possible to the original.
6. Ask one member of each group to read the group's re-creation of the text and ask the other groups to see how closely it matches their versions. Display the groups' re-created texts, and compare and discuss them, noting the sections in the text that were difficult to re-create.

APPLICATIONS AND EXAMPLES

Because Laura Ingalls Wilder is one of her students' favorite authors, Ms. Leonard reads aloud from Carol Greene's biography of Wilder (1990) to her third grade class. Reading the excerpt from the book where Greene describes how Wilder got ideas for her books, Ms. Leonard instructs the students, to listen carefully so they will be able to remember Ms. Greene's words.

The second and third times she reads the text aloud, Ms. Leonard asks the students to jot down key words and phrases so they can recall the author's exact words. Ms. Leonard then pairs the students, instructing them to put their notes together so that they can rewrite the text in Greene's voice. Once the pairs have a text written that combines the words each of the pair was able to recall, the students meet again in fours to try to make their text even more complete. Once the groups of four are satisfied with the text they have re-created, they are instructed to use the text and illustrations to make a big book.

Each group of four is given time to present their big book to the class. The groups then discuss the sections of the text that were easiest to recall and compare and contrast the text of the big books. The groups agree that they used more colorful language in the writing of their big books because they were trying to use Carole Greene's exact words instead of their own.

Dictoglos is an exciting strategy because it gives students a chance to explore literary and academic language in depth. It exposes students to spoken and written English at a level above the everyday spoken English they hear and gives them practice in listening and writing more formal English. This strategy can be used in many curricular areas.

Grade Level	Adaptations	Curricular Areas
Kindergarten	Recite poems and fingerplays, and write their notes interactively	Language arts
Primary	Paragraphs describing content knowledge— re-create and illustrate	Science, social studies
Upper elementary	Literary excerpts, famous speeches, and historical documents such as the Constitution	Language arts, social studies
Middle school	Descriptions of procedures Historical literature linking writing to periods of history Literary language—link to art, music	Science literature, history language arts, fine arts
Senior high school	Current Events—famous speakers, speeches Famous literature, poetry, historical literature	Political science, language arts

Figure 12.1 Adaptations of Dictoglos for Different Ages and Curricular Areas

Mr. Estes teaches tenth grade humanities. In celebration of Martin Luther King Junior's birthday, Mr. Estes decides to use Dictoglos to support his students in listening to and appreciating Dr. King's *I Have a Dream* speech. The students listen first, and then take notes during the second and third readings so that they can re-create the speech. They meet in pairs to combine their notes and then meet in groups of four to refine the rewriting of the speech. Lively discussion erupts as they struggle to remember the eloquent words. Discussion of the meaning of the literary language is heard throughout the room. At the conclusion of the lesson, one student from each group delivers the group's version of the speech with dramatic flourish. Although the words are not all exactly right, each group has demonstrated its understanding of the message.

CONCLUSION

Dictoglos is a strategy that can be adapted for use in many different ways. Figure 12.1 shows the ways in which it can be used for different ages of students and different curricular areas.

Dictoglos is not only valuable as a strategy for exposing students to fluent, literary English—it is an exciting way to help them to study language and its changes over time. By listening to pieces of literature written in different time periods, students become aware of the ways in which English vocabulary and usage have changed over the years and of the influence of different linguistic groups on the language of the time. The context of the language can also be emphasized so that students begin to appreciate the ways in which the choices of words and phrasing are influenced by the purpose of the writing or speaking and the audience for which it is intended.

References

Gibbons, P. (1993). *Learning to learn in a second language.* Portsmouth, NH: Heinemann.
Greene, C. (1990). *Laura Ingalls Wilder, author of the little house books.* Chicago: Children's Press.
Wajnryb, R. (1990). *Grammar dictation.* Oxford, England: Oxford University Press.

FREE VOLUNTARY READING

13

SUPPORTS

- ● Comprehensible input
- ✔ Contextualized language
- ✔ Reduced anxiety
- ✔ Active involvement of the learner

F ree voluntary reading (Krashen, 1993) is a powerful tool for involving students in the reading of English text. Free voluntary reading, or FVR, is a system for encouraging silent, self-selected reading of enjoyable books written at the students' independent levels. It has been found to support reading comprehension, writing, grammar, spelling, and vocabulary development even though the texts read are written at an easy reading level. Series of books in which the reader becomes familiar with the structure, main characters, and setting in the first book of the series and then reads sequels are especially appropriate for building vocabulary and comprehension in readers with limited English vocabularies.

Although free voluntary reading has been criticized (Hernandez, 1997) as difficult to implement because of the large numbers of books required, it has been shown to be effective for English language learners because of the power in exposing them to a large volume of English reading and the anxiety-reducing power of easy reading. A suggested list of free voluntary reading materials is shown in Figure 13.1.

STEP BY STEP

The steps in implementing free voluntary reading are:

1. Identify the independent reading levels of the students in your class and gather a number of books at their levels. Organize the books in a way that identifies the reading levels and provides easy student access to the books. To identify other sources of easy reading materials for your students enlist the help of the school media specialist.
2. Introduce the free voluntary reading program to the students, explaining that reading widely helps them to learn new English vocabulary and improves their writing, spelling, and grammar—even when the reading they are doing is not difficult. Set up a system so they can check out books freely, taking them home to read or reading them during DEAR (Drop Everything and Read) time or free time in the classroom. Provide a celebration system so that the class is keeping track of the numbers of books being read by the class members.

Grade Level	Materials
Primary	*Aliens for Breakfast and Aliens for Lunch,* Stepping Stone Series, Random House. *Clue, Jr.* Series by P. Hinter, Scholastic. *Commander Toad* Series by Jane Yolen, Coward-McCann Inc. *Horrible Harry* Series by Suzy Kleing, Puffin. *Magic Tree House* Series by Mary Pope Osborne, Random House. *Sweet Valley Kids* Series by F. Pascal, Bantam Books. *The Zack Files* Series by D. Greenburg, Grosset & Dunlap. *Ziggy and the Black Dinosaurs* Series by S. Draper, Just Us Books.
Upper elementary	*Bailey School Kids* by Debbie Dadey & Marcia Thornton Jones, Scholastic, Little Apple. *Dragonling* Series, Minstral Books. *Dragon Slayers' Academy* Series by K. H. McMullan, Grosset & Dunlap. *Full House* Series published by Minstral Books. *Goliath* Series by Terrance Dicks, Barrons'. *Nate the Great* Series by Marjorie Weinman Sharmat, Dell Publishing. *The Adventures of Wishbone* Series by A. Steele, Lyrick Pub. *The Boxcar Children* Series by G. C. Warner, Albert Whitman & Co. *The Three Investigators* Series by R. Arthur, Random House. *The Young Merlin Trilogy* by Jane Yolan, Scholastic.
Middle school	*Animorphs* Series by K. A. Applegate, Scholastic. *Babysitter's Club* Series by Ann Martin, Scholastic. *Broadway Ballplayer's* Series by M. Holohen, Broadway Ballplayer's Publishing Co. *Eerie Indiana* Series by J. Peel, Avon. *Goose Bumps* Series by R. L. Stein, Scholastic. *Sweet Valley Jr. High* Series by F. Pascal, Bantam Books.
Senior high school	*California Diaries* Series by A. Martin, Scholastic. *danger.com* Series by J. Cray, Aladdin. *Star Wars* Series by J. Whitman, Bantam. *X Files* Series published by Harper Collins. *Sweet Valley High* Series by F. Pascal, Bantam Books.

Figure 13.1   Suggested Materials for Free Voluntary Reading

Arrange for celebrations as the class reads 100, 500, and 1,000 books. Focus on the number of books being read rather than the difficulty of the books chosen. The object is to get students reading more.

3. Schedule informal literature discussions so the students can share their favorite books and talk about favorite authors. Use these discussions to provide positive feedback to the students who are reading a lot of books. Encourage wide reading by introducing new authors of easy reading books and give book talks about new books as they are added to the classroom collection. Keep these introductions informal, for example, "This is a new book by

Mary Grace. If you enjoyed her other books, you'll probably like this one. It's about an ice skating competition."

4. Keep the momentum going by adding new celebrations during the year such as creating video commercials for favorite books, keeping track of the number of students who read a certain title in order to determine the class' favorite books, scheduling guest appearances by favorite authors, holding read-a-thons where students read for a given number of hours per night until they reach self-set goals (10 hours, 50 hours), and then presenting awards such as a 10-hour reader button or a 50-hour reader button.

APPLICATIONS AND EXAMPLES

Ms. Gerrard's third-grade class shows little interest in leisure reading until she introduces free voluntary reading. Ms. Gerrard brings in a series of new paperback books to the class, reads the first book in the series aloud, and sets up a system for keeping track of the number of students who

Category	Place a sticker in a box for each book read.	TOTAL
Adventure		
Biography		
Comic books		
Folktale		
Horror		
Information		
Mystery		
Poetry		
Science fiction		
		Class Grand Total ____

Figure 13.2 The Books We've Read

read each book. Students in the class are given a new composition book in which to record the titles of the books they are reading—in school and at home. There is a tally sheet in the class library where students record tallies next to the books they are reading to keep track of the number of times each book is read by a student. One of the students is appointed class record keeper, and he keeps track of the reading being done each week in two ways. First he posts a list of the week's most popular books, and then he totals the number of books read by the entire class each week.

Ms. Gerrard provides time each day for free reading. At the end of the free reading period she encourages students to share comments about the books they are reading, such as an especially funny part or a reading recommendation. As the cumulative count of books read by class members mounts, Ms. Gerrard gives periodic celebrations. For the 100-book milestone, the class has a cookie party with chocolate chip cookies made and eaten in class. For the 500-book milestone, the students are given free time to sit under the playground trees and read for 30 minutes after lunch. Ms. Gerrard can see that her students are reading more.

• •

Mr. Tibbs's eighth graders are enjoying the introductory day of their free voluntary reading program. Mr. Tibbs begins the program by bringing in a number of comic books to the class. At first, the students don't believe that they are being allowed to read comic books in school. Mr. Tibbs makes it clear that it doesn't matter what they read, reading improves reading. He shares his goal—for each student to be reading every day. On the second day of the program Mr. Tibbs brings in a collection of easy books that can be checked out for free reading at home and he also makes the comics available for checkout. The students are encouraged to keep a list of the books and comics they are reading. Mr. Tibbs posts a chart where the students place a sticker for each book they read beside the category of the book. The chart he uses is shown in Figure 13.2.

Because Mr. Tibbs realizes that the support of the parents is vital to the success of this new reading program, he prepares a notice for the parents so that they understand the purpose of the free voluntary reading program. He encourages their participation and their assistance in providing time to read, providing a quiet place to read, and encouraging the student to meet his/her reading goals. His parent notice is shown in Figure 13.3.

The eighth graders are a little wary of the intent of this new reading program but they like the reading materials that are available to them. Slowly they relax and enjoy their free reading.

Dear Parents,

Your students may be bringing home some new reading material this week. We will be encouraging the students to read books—even comic books—to increase their reading enjoyment, fluency, and vocabulary. This program is called Free Voluntary Reading (FVR) and has been shown to benefit students in the following ways:

- It promotes reading comprehension.
- It supports vocabulary development.
- It supports writing, spelling and grammar knowledge.
   We know that NOTHING HELPS READING LIKE MORE READING. You can help by:
- Providing time for your student to read each day.
- Providing a quiet place for reading.
- Talking to your student about the books being read.
- Modeling the enjoyment of reading yourself.
   Thank you for your support!

Mr. Tibbs

Figure 13.3   Mr. Tibbs's Notice to Parents

Don Quixote	The Adventures of Tom Sawyer
The Odyssey	Romeo and Juliet
The Adventures of Robin Hood	Oliver Twist
The Strange Case of Dr. Jekyll and Mr. Hyde	Joan of Arc
A Journey to the Center of the Earth	Frankenstein
The Red Badge of Courage	Ivanhoe

Figure 13.4   Titles Available in the Wishbone Classics Series Published by Harper Collins

Each book in this series has sections that tell about the author, the book, the main characters, and the setting. The books also contain text notes to aid comprehension and a complete glossary.

Mr. Tibbs gives them a free reading period every now and then as a reward for good work or to celebrate reading milestones, such as 200 books read by the class. The free reading done by the class is showing a steady growth each week.

CONCLUSION

Free voluntary reading is an important strategy in helping students develop a love for reading and a shared literary experience. There are a number of children's and young adult writers producing series of books that build on a common theme or familiar characters. These books are especially appropriate for free voluntary reading by English language learners because the sequels are set in familiar contexts once one book in the series has been read. The authors of these series have created texts that are interesting to readers at certain age levels and yet easy to read and understand. In addition, a number of the classics have been rewritten in simplified language so that teachers can provide understandable versions of these books as class literature studies are conducted. See Figure 13.4 for a list of the classic titles available in this series.

Although access to a large number of books is necessary for this strategy to be successful, a number of the book series are available in paperback form at very reasonable prices.

References

Hernandez, H. (1997). *Teaching in multicultural classrooms.* Upper Saddle River, NJ: Merrill/Prentice Hall.

Krashen, S. (1993). *The power of reading.* Englewood, CO: Libraries Unlimited.

GIST

14

SUPPORTS

- Comprehensible input
- Increased verbal interaction
- ✔ Contextualized language
- ✔ Reduced anxiety
- Active involvement of the learner

GIST or *Generating Interaction between Schemata and Text* (Cunningham, 1982) is a strategy used for supporting comprehension of informational text. GIST is especially helpful when students are required to read long texts containing a significant amount of new information. Students work in cooperative groups and read sections of the text silently. After each short section is read silently, the members of the group work collaboratively to generate one sentence that summarizes the "gist" of the passage. In some very dense text this generation of a summary sentence is done paragraph by paragraph. Once a sentence is generated, members of the group write it on their own papers so that each group member ends up with a concise summary of the text. The teacher circulates among the groups to facilitate and provide support. This is a particularly effective strategy for use with English language learners because the group members have a chance to discuss and clarify meaning as they decide on the best summary sentence for the section or paragraph.

STEP BY STEP

The steps in implementing GIST are:

1. Identify text to be read by the students that may cause some difficulty. Decide whether the text must be read and summarized paragraph by paragraph or section by section and determine logical stopping or summarizing points.
2. Divide the class into cooperative groups and identify a leader for each group. Make sure that each group contains a strong English speaker and reader. If possible, group English language learners with other students of the same language background who can provide first language support if needed. If your main purpose is to facilitate the understanding of the text, the discussion of the meaning and the negotiation of the best summary sentence can be done in the students' first languages and later translated to English. If your purpose is facilitating English communication, then the discussion should take place in English with first language translations made only for the purpose of clarification.
3. Demonstrate the strategy by discussing background knowledge and informing the students that they will be working together as groups to create a summary of the material to be read. Post the summary points, the points in the reading at which each group is to stop, then discuss and summarize. See Figure 14.1 for an example of a summary point chart. Instruct the

Stop and summarize at these points:
1. Page 3, at the subheading
2. Page 7, at the bottom of the page
3. Page 9, after the chart
4. Page 13, at the subheading
5. Page 18, at the end of the selection

Figure 14.1 Example of a Summary Point Chart

students to read the passage silently to the first summary point and then stop and write a one-sentence summary of what they read.

4. After the students have completed their summary sentence, ask one of the students to share his/hers with the class. Discuss the sentence as a group and add details that the class feels will enhance the sentence. Instruct the students to write the summary sentence on their papers. The teacher serves as facilitator and quality controller, making sure that the summary sentences capture the "gist" of the paragraphs. It is important that the quality control be done in a supportive manner through questioning and supporting of the students' understanding of the text.

5. Explain to the class that they will be reading the entire selection in this manner. They will all read the selection to each summary point, as indicated by the chart that is posted. As they wait for the rest of their group to finish reading they should be thinking of the main points in the section and formulating a summary sentence in their minds, or writing it on a scrap piece of paper. The group should then discuss the section read and negotiate the best summary sentence they can write. Once the group has decided on their summary sentence, each member of the group writes the sentence on his/her own paper and the process begins again.

6. Once the selection has been completed, have the groups read and compare their summary sentences. This provides an effective review of the passage read and gives an opportunity to correct any misconceptions. Again, the teacher serves as facilitator and questions the students to lead them to capture the meaning and nuance of the text.

APPLICATIONS AND EXAMPLES

The fifth graders in Ms. Menashian's class have been studying the American Revolution. They have read the *Jean Fritz* biographies of the great men and women who lived at the time of the revolution and the contributions they made. Ms. Menashian wants to conclude the unit of study with the reading of Longfellow's poem *The Midnight Ride of Paul Revere*. However, she also wants her students to understand the significance of the poem so she assigns the reading of the chapter "A Centennial Celebration," in the Augusta Stevenson biography *Paul Revere* (1986).

Ms. Menashian divides the fifth graders into cooperative groups to read and summarize the chapter. Because her class has a number of English language learners, Ms. Menashian makes sure that each group has a strong reader and several students in each group who speak the same home language. She posts a chart of summary points and the students begin reading and summarizing the selection. As she moves among the groups she hears some interesting discussion.

"I don't understand this chapter. It says it was 1875," says Andre. "That's a hundred years after Paul Revere's ride."

"I think that's why it's called a centennial celebration. That's a celebration after a hundred years," says Juanita. "I think this chapter is going to talk about how they were still celebrating his ride after a hundred years."

"Oh, I get it," says Andre. "What should we write for our summary sentence?"

"How about this?" asks Tyra. "A hundred years after the famous midnight ride of Paul Revere, the people of Boston were still talking about how brave he was."

"That's good," says Margaret, "but it also said that they were proud of him because of his silverwork too."

"But they were more proud of his patriotism," added Juanita.

"What is patriotism?" asks Mario.

"It's being loyal to your country," answers Juanita. "He risked his life to warn the soldiers that the British soldiers were coming," Juanita says in English and then she repeats the explanation in Spanish.

"OK," says Mario. "So the people of Boston are proud of Paul Revere because he was a great silversmith but more because he was a great patriot."

"That's a good summary sentence," says Andre. "Let's use that one. Say it again, Mario."

As Mario repeats the sentence everyone writes it on their papers, including Mario. The group then reads the next section of the chapter.

When they have completed reading and discussing the chapter, their summary looks like this:

The people of Boston are proud of Paul Revere because he was a great silversmith but more because he was a great patriot.

On April 18, 1775 eight hundred British soldiers were going to Concord to seize the patriot ammunition and guns.

Patriot troops had to be warned that the British soldiers were coming so they could move the powder and guns.

John Hancock and Samuel Adams also needed to be told to leave Lexington before they were arrested and hanged for speaking against the king.

The patriots chose Paul Revere to make the ride to warn the troops that the British were coming.

It was a very dangerous ride because British soldiers and warships were guarding the whole area.

Lanterns in the Old North Church belfry would tell Paul Revere how the British soldiers had gone. There would be two lanterns if they had gone by water, one lantern if they had gone by land.

Paul Revere went to the sexton of the Old North Church and told him to put two lanterns in the church belfry and then Paul Revere rowed across the river.

Patriots across the river had a horse waiting for Paul Revere when they saw the lanterns.

Paul Revere stopped at all the houses between Boston and Lexington and warned everyone that the British were coming.

The Patriots all grabbed their guns and kept the British from getting to the guns. They also gave John Hancock and Samuel Adams time to escape.

Ms. Menashian was very pleased with the summaries the students wrote about the ride of Paul Revere and about the discussion of the importance of the ride that took place as the groups shared their summaries. As she concluded the study of the Revolution with the reading of the poem, *The Midnight Ride of Paul Revere* (Stevenson, 1986), she was sure that the students really understood the words and the significance of the event to American history.

• •

Some of the reading in Ms. Hughes's eleventh grade literature class is extremely difficult for her students to understand. Although she is sure that her students will enjoy the reading of Mark Twain's most famous works, she is concerned that they will not understand the political significance of his work and its place in history. Because of the difficulty of some of the vocabulary in the biographic readings about Mark Twain, Ms. Hughes decides to encourage her students to work in cooperative groups. Being in groups allows them to discuss the vocabulary, to consider the politics involved at that particular time in history, and to comprehend the nuances in meaning that they might otherwise miss.

Ms. Hughes groups her students for the reading of Bernard de Voto's (1984) introductory chapter in *The Portable Mark Twain.* She posts a chart that tells the groups to stop and summarize after each paragraph they read and she walks the class through the steps in the GIST procedure. She explains the double meanings of the term "gist" and the procedure name, which connects schemata and text.

"Who knows what it means to "Get the gist of things"? asks Ms. Hughes.

"It means that you get the general idea," answers Leon.

"That's right, Leon," responds Ms. Hughes. "And today we're going to learn a new strategy for studying that is also called GIST, G-I-S-T, which stands for *G*enerating *I*nteraction between *S*chemata and *T*ext," says Mrs. Hughes as she writes the words on the chalkboard and underlines the letters in that create the acronym GIST.

"Using this strategy is supposed to *generate* or cause something to happen. What is supposed to happen is *interaction,* or some action between some things. The interaction is supposed to happen between your *schemata,* or your past experiences that have been filed in your brain, and *text,* which is what you will be reading. This interaction, or the comparing and contrasting of your background of knowledge and the text you are reading, will help you to understand what you are reading. You and the rest of your group will work together to figure out what the reading means. Because this introductory chapter is what I call 'tough text,' difficult to read and understand, I want you to stop after each paragraph and discuss the meaning. Your group will write one sentence to summarize each paragraph. When you are finished reading the introductory chapter and writing the summary sentences you should have a good understanding of Mark Twain and his place in American history. We will talk about the chapter after you have completed the reading."

As the groups work their way through the chapter, Ms. Hughes circulates among the groups and occasionally gets drawn into the discussion. Because there are a number of difficult words in the reading, she also gathers words from the groups to add to the word wall. First language translations for the new vocabulary are added to the word wall as necessary.

At the end of the period, Ms. Hughes asks the groups to share their summaries and they choose the best sentence for each paragraph to create a class summary of the chapter. It reads:

The first truly American literature grew out of the early republic and includes such writers as Emerson, Poe, Thoreau, and Melville.

There were strands of literature and culture that clashed as influences from the South, New England, Louisiana, and the expansion West began to drift together.

A heartland culture, or midcontinental culture, began to emerge and it seemed to be pulling away from the traditional influences of Europe.

Abraham Lincoln was an important advocate of this emerging American heartland culture.

Lincoln's approach to America as an entirely new entity seems to come across loudly as a change from the tidewater republic of the new nation to the continental empire that will be the future.

Walt Whitman expressed his feeling for this emerging nation and its budding literature as "this continental inland west not yet speaking for the people or making images for their spirit."

Actually Whitman was wrong because ten years prior to this statement, in 1869, a book of humorous travel sketches written by Samuel Langhorne Clemens had been written and signed with the author's pen name, Mark Twain.

Innocents Abroad, Mark Twain's travel sketches book, was an instant success partly because of its obvious disdain for European society.

Because of the nature of this first book Mark Twain struggled for two generations to overcome literary critics' opinion of him as a clown.

Mark Twain was referred to as "the Lincoln of our literature" because of the many similarities between Lincoln and Twain in their upbringing and humor.

After the groups have read and summarized the introduction to the Mark Twain volume, Ms. Hughes asks the students to think about what they had learned and give an overall summary of the history of the time in which Twain wrote.

"I think the feeling I got was that the new nation had finally gotten past copying things from Europe and was starting to produce humorists and historians who valued America as a new country with a different kind of personality," says Monica.

"Exactly," agrees Ms. Hughes. "Although the writers of the early republic are outstanding and made contributions to literature, they are more like the European writers. Mark Twain is a new kind of voice, a more rustic, more American voice."

"But, the literary critics didn't take him seriously," adds Alberto.

"But that happens a lot, doesn't it?" asks Martina.

"I think that happens whenever writers or artists move too far away from the traditional approaches," agrees Ms. Hughes.

After the discussion of the introduction, Ms. Hughes assigns the students the first reading in the Mark Twain anthology and they discuss some vocabulary and background that they will need in order to understand the reading, *The Notorious Jumping Frog of Calaveras County*.

CONCLUSION

Students of all ages benefit from the use of collaborative strategies such as GIST. By placing students in heterogeneous groups, with a strong English reader and writer in each group, teachers can encourage discussion of the reading and give students a chance to clarify meaning and vocabulary. The group task of writing a summary sentence for each paragraph that is read provides an authentic assignment that requires the students to discuss the meaning of the paragraph and agree on a sentence that conveys the important information. Once the paragraphs are read and discussed and summary sentences are written and read, each student in the group has a concise summary of the reading assignment.

When several groups read and summarize the same text and then share their summaries, further discussion of the main ideas and supporting details frequently follows. This gives student another chance to hear the information discussed and new vocabulary clarified.

References

Cunningham, J. (1982). Generating interactions between schemata and text. In J. A. Niles & L. A. Harris (Eds.), *New inquiries in reading research and instruction* (pp. 42–47). Washington, D.C.: National Reading Conference.

de Voto, B. (Ed.) (1984). *The portable Mark Twain*. New York: Penguin Books.

Fritz, J. (1973). *And then what happened, Paul Revere?* New York: G. P. Putnam.

Fritz, J. (1974). *Why don't you get a horse, Sam Adams?* NY: G. P. Putnam.

Fritz, J. (1975). *Where was Patrick Henry on the 29th of May?* New York: G. P. Putnam.

Fritz, J. (1975). *Who's that stepping on Plymouth Rock?* New York: G. P. Putnam.

Fritz, J. (1977). *Can't you make them behave, King George?* New York: G. P. Putnam.

Fritz, J. (1987). *Shh! We're Writing the Constitution.* NY: G. P. Putnam.

Stevenson, A. (1986). *Paul Revere: Boston patriot.* New York: Aladdin (Macmillan).

GUIDED READING

Guided reading (Fountas & Pinnell, 1996) is an approach to teaching reading done in a small group setting, while providing individual coaching. The students are taught in groups of four to six all reading at approximately the same level. Teachers use running records to determine the students' reading levels, their use of cueing systems (attention to phonics, meaning, word order, sentence structure, and the relation of the text to the students' prior experiences). Running records also determine the students' use of self-correcting and their attention to self-monitoring of whether or not their reading is making sense.

A guided reading lesson begins with a book walk, in which the students and teacher look through the book and predict what will happen. It then progresses through multiple readings of the book with students reading to themselves at their own pace. During this time, the teacher moves from child to child in the group, listening to them read and giving them coaching on decoding, self-monitoring, and comprehension strategies. This coaching is done by asking the student questions like, "Does that word start with a d?" or "does that make sense?" The students continue to read until each child has been coached. Teachers then conduct mini-lessons based upon the needs of the students identified during the coaching sessions. They use this opportunity to discuss the story and determine whether or not the students need support in understanding what they have read. Vocabulary is discussed, clarifying and relating it to the story, the illustrations, and the students' background experiences. The group may then engage in writing, phonics, or other skills activities. The guided reading approach is very appropriate for English language learners because of the focus on vocabulary development, individual instruction, and opportunities for verbal interactions. Because the English language learners participate in a group discussion of the story and the vocabulary encountered, they benefit from the language interactions of the small group setting. Because their needs may be different from the native English speakers, the individual coaching provides the teacher with an opportunity to support their understanding, correct pronunciation, and clarify word meaning and misconceptions caused by reading in their second language.

STEP BY STEP

The steps in teaching a guided reading lesson are:

1. Place students in groups of four to six, based upon information learned from running records. Choose a book at the appropriate reading level for the students in the group and based upon their interests whenever possible. Although guided reading can be used with

Student's Behavior	**Sample Questions or Prompts to Use**
Guessing words	Does that make sense?
Skipping words	Point to each word as you read it. Did it match?
Inserting extra words	Point to each word as you say it. Were there enough words?
Substituting words that start with the same letter	Does that make sense? Look at the whole word.
Appealing for help from the teacher	Give it a try. How does it begin?
Incorrect reading of a word	Try that again. You made a mistake. Can you find it?

Figure 15.1 Questions and Prompts to Promote Self-Monitoring and Comprehension in Guided Reading

    any text, it is most effective when used with authentic texts that are of interest to the students.

2. Gather the group at a table and take a book walk through the book to be read. A book walk involves looking at the illustrations on each page, predicting what will happen on that page, discussing and modeling the meaning of vocabulary that will be needed in order to read the page, and building background knowledge. Sometimes it will be necessary to use visuals, gestures, or realia to support the students' understanding of the vocabulary. It is also very helpful to relate vocabulary words to words in the child's home language whenever possible.

3. Give the students copies of the book and encourage them to read aloud at their own pace. Move from student to student, listening to their oral reading and giving them instruction in decoding, reading fluently or self-monitoring, as needed. Ask questions to help them learn to self-monitor. Encourage the students to reread the story if they finish before you have listened to and coached each child. See Figure 15.1 for suggestions of questions and prompts to use.

4. Pair the students up to read to each other and listen to their oral reading one more time, coaching and celebrating their successes.

5. Introduce a mini-lesson based on the needs you see as you coach individuals. Focus on self-monitoring and problem-solving strategies. Conclude the lesson with a discussion of the story, writing the students' words down in the form of a dictated story or interactive writing lesson. Encourage all the students to participate in an oral rereading of the story written.

APPLICATIONS AND EXAMPLES

Although guided reading as described in this chapter is usually done in primary grade classrooms, it is very appropriate for English language learners of all ages because of the comprehension instruction and language development it supports.

In first and second grade, teachers are using this approach with all students. It is particularly valuable for English language learners because of the repeated reading it encourages and the vocabulary that is introduced, modeled and connected to illustrations. For example, Ms. Garcia was using the little soft-back book, *Where's Tim?* (1996), with a group of Southeast Asian students. The book tells of a child looking for his pet cat. He looks in many places, including the kitchen cupboard, and finally finds the cat under the bedspread. Ms. Garcia does a book walk, showing the pictures and having the students predict where the boy might look next. When Ms. Garcia reaches the page where the boy is looking in the kitchen cupboard, she shows them the cupboard behind her, under the classroom sink. She says, "This is a cupboard. It's like a closet, but it's usually found in a kitchen or bathroom. It's not as tall as a closet." She gestures toward the coat closet as she says the word, "closet." She repeats "cupboard," pointing to the cupboard. She repeats "closet," pointing to the coat closet.

Problem	Suggested Strategies
Insufficient background	Use realia, visuals, or videos to build background. Read aloud picture books that relate to the same topic.
Unfamiliar vocabulary	Use realia, illustrations, or skits to act out meanings. Provide translation to home language for unknown words.
Word-by-word reading	Provide a fluent model by using echo reading. In echo reading the teacher reads the sentence fluently and the student rereads it using expression and intonation echoing the teacher's model. Provide a model of reading with correct phrasing and ask the child to repeat the reading, phrase by phrase.
Reading past miscues without self-correcting	Stop the reader and focus on the miscue if it changes the meaning of the sentence. Support the reader in the use of phonics, meaning, syntax, and context so that the use of multiple cues is modeled and stressed.
Inability to answer questions after reading	Support the reader in looking back at the text to find the answers. Focus on the meaning as the text is reread. If the question is inferential, support the reader in finding clues that may help him/her to make guesses related to the question. Discuss the possibilities and agree on a likely response. Try to find ways to connect the questions and answers to the reader's background knowledge.

Figure 15.2 Guided Reading Strategies

When the boy discovers the lump under the bedspread, Ms. Garcia demonstrates a lump by covering a stuffed cat with a towel. She says, "The boy saw a lump. The cat made a lump under the bedspread." She has the students pull their hands up under their sleeves to show her how their hands make lumps under their sleeves. They then read the story. See Figure 15.2 for additional strategies for guided reading.

CONCLUSION

In upper grades, guided reading can often help students to understand content reading such as science and social studies where the vocabulary is often unfamiliar to the students. Using this approach, walking through the reading material, examining illustrations, charting and graphing, and discussing them is often very helpful in building comprehension. Reading in pairs and encouraging summary and discussion is also appropriate with older students.

References

Cowley, J. (1996). *Where's Tim?* Auckland, NZ: Wright Group.

Fountas, I., & Pinnell, G. (1996). *Guided reading: Good first teaching for all children.* Portsmouth, NH: Heinemann.

Irwin, J. (1991). *Teaching reading comprehension processes* (2nd ed.). Needham Heights: Allyn and Bacon.

IMAGING

....

16

SUPPORTS

- ● Comprehensible input
- ✔ Contextualized language
- ✔ Reduced anxiety

....

Imaging (Chamot & O'Malley, 1994) is a strategy that encourages students to create an image in their minds to support the understanding of concepts or problems to be solved. The teacher is involved in supporting students to create mind-pictures that enable them to imagine the scene being described in the text being read or the problem to be solved. Once images are created in the students' minds, the teacher encourages the students to describe what they can see. This gives the teacher an opportunity to interact with the students to support their understanding. Research in reading comprehension (Irwin, 1991) has shown imaging as an attribute of effective readers, which is often not employed by poor readers. For this reason, it is an important strategy to teach. It is especially important to teach the strategy and discuss the images, or mind-pictures, with English language learners because they may form faulty images due to misconceptions related to language misunderstanding. Possible curricular uses of imaging are shown in Figure 16.1.

....

APPLICATIONS AND EXAMPLES

Mr. Fernandez's third graders are trying to figure out some difficult word problems in math. The first problem gives the following information:

> Jan and Bob are cousins, Jan is six years old and Bob is four years older. Jan has a brother whose name is David. David is a year older than Jan but younger than Bob. Bob has a sister named Carol who is two years younger than Jan. Which of the cousins is the oldest? Who is the youngest? How old is each of the cousins?

Mr. Fernandez reads the problem aloud to the class and says, "This is a new kind of problem. There is a lot of information given but it's hard to keep track of it all. I find that it helps to create a picture to see if I have all the information I need to solve the problem. When I read the first sentence, I picture Jan as a little six-year-old girl. I picture Bob as a tall ten-year-old boy. I know Bob is ten because the problem says he is four years older than Jan. In my mind I see Jan and Bob. They look like this." Mr. Fernandez draws a stick figure of Jan and Bob.

"Now, the next part says that Jan has a brother named David who is a year older than she is. That makes him seven. In my mind I now see Jan, David, and Bob." Mr. Fernandez draws David and points to each of the stick figures as he says this. "So far I know that Jan is six, David is seven, and Bob is ten. I can picture them in my mind. Now it says that Bob's sister Carol is two years younger than Jan. That makes her four years old. I can picture her in my mind." Mr. Fernandez adds Carol to the picture. See Figure 16.2 for Mr. Fernandez's picture.

Curricular Area	Imaging Use
Vocabulary	Picture a _____ in your mind. Does it look like this? (Show an illustration or photograph.) What does yours look like?
Comprehension	Close your eyes and picture the scene in your mind. What do you see? (Question for details.)
Mathematics	Use with word problems. After the word problem is read, have the students close their eyes and picture the people, animals, and things involved in the problem. (Ask questions related to the relative size, number, and quantity in the problem.)
Summarizing	After a section of a text is read, have the students close their eyes and create a mind-picture of the text. Question about the overall scene they see and the important details pictured.
Art	Before having the students begin to create images in art media, have them close their eyes and picture what they want to create. Question them about the features of line, proportion, color, and movement that they see.
Music	As the students listen to music have them close their eyes and picture what the music is suggesting. Ask them to describe their mind-pictures.
Writing	Before the students write a passage, have them close their eyes and picture the image they want to create with words. Encourage them to verbalize the image they want to create before they write the words.

Figure 16.1   Curricular Uses of Imaging

"Now I have all the information I need to answer the questions," Mr. Fernandez smiles. "Now you try it. I'll read the next problem."

Ms. Garcia has three children, Jose, Maria, and Lidia. Each of them is exactly two years older than the next younger one. Jose is the eldest, and Lidia is the youngest. If Maria is eight years old, how old are Jose and Lidia?

As Mr. Fernandez moves around the room, he notices that several of the children have their eyes closed and are talking to themselves. They begin to write down numbers and names as they see the pictures in their minds. Gabriella is drawing pictures on her paper. Mr. Fernandez stops to talk to Gabriella.

"I see you have Maria drawn on your paper." says Mr. Fernandez. "How old is she?"

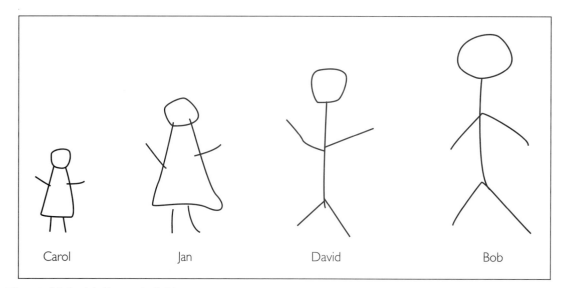

Figure 16.2 Mr. Fernandez's Picture

"Eight," says Gabriella as she writes the number under the picture of Maria. "But that's the only one I know."

"OK," says Mr. Fernandez. "What else do you know?"

"Jose is the eldest," says Gabriella. "Does that mean the same as oldest?"

"Yes," says Mr. Fernandez as Gabriella draws Jose.

"Oh, now I see," says Gabriella as she draws Lidia and adds Jose's and Lidia's ages to the picture with a big smile.

• •

The ninth graders in Ms. Patino's geography class are reading a passage in their text about the Louisiana bayou. As Ms. Patino shows the class a map of the Gulf Coast area, she talks about a trip that she made through the bayou on an airboat.

One of her students asks, "What is an airboat, Ms. Patino? I've never heard of one."

"It's a boat with a big fan mounted on the back," explains Ms. Patino as she draws a picture of an airboat on the chalkboard. "The bayou is an area of water that is not very deep. There are a lot of plants, trees, logs, and wildlife that live in the bayou. Regular boats can't move through the area because of the shallow water and all the roots that would interfere with the propeller. So, airboats are used. They skim across the top of the water propelled by the air that is blown through this huge fan. Of course, there is a big protective screen in front of the fan so no one in the boat gets hurt by the blades."

"Let's take a mind-trip through the bayou. Close your eyes and try to create mind-pictures as I describe my trip," suggests Ms. Patino.

"It's a warm sunny day as I start my trip. I am wearing shorts, a sleeveless shirt, sneakers, and a big sun hat—but it is still very hot. It's also very humid. My clothes are sticking to my back as I walk across the landing platform to the airboat. The airboat is silver with a huge fan in the back. It seats about six people and has a very tall pole sticking up from the back of it with a red flag flying from the pole. I wonder what the flag is for."

"Are you picturing the day? Can you see the steam rising from the water and the airboat with the tall pole?" asks Ms. Patino.

The students are all sitting with their eyes closed but they all nod solemnly. Their faces are showing signs of concentration.

"As I get into the boat it rocks slowly from side to side and I wonder if I really feel safe riding on this rocky vessel. As the boat fills up with people I begin to feel safer. I'm not the only one taking the risk. When the airboat pilot fires up the fan I am amazed at the noise it creates and I'm grateful for the earpieces that have been distributed so that we will be able to hear the guide's explanations of the bayou."

"I look around and see a wide expanse of water surrounded by strange trees with roots that seem to grow down from their branches. The airboat guide tells us that the trees are called Banyan trees and that they grow in very wet terrain. As we continue through the main expanse of water we soon find out the reason for the tall pole and flag as we enter an area of tall brown grass that looks like tall hay. We are soon surrounded by the grass and feel as if we are traveling through a field of wheat that separates for us as the boat cuts through it. No one could see us coming if it weren't for the flag we fly. We are moving very quickly now and I hope the pilot and guide are watching for other airboats."

"We soon emerge into an area in which we are surrounded by Banyan and Cypress trees and small logs floating in the water. The guide soon points out that what looks like logs are actually small alligators sunning themselves. The guide also reminds us to keep our arms inside the boat. I am beginning to wish I had stayed behind on the dock."

"The movement of the boat produces a nice breeze and it isn't as hot as it was back on land. We are moving more slowly now. The pilot has turned off the engine and he and the guide are using long poles to move us slowly through the swamp so we can see the wildlife. I am amazed at the number of beautiful birds standing on tall legs in the water, the number of snakes wc see swimming through the water, and the number of furry rodents and beavers we see busily building nests and chewing on trees. The guide calls our attention to a huge snake draped over a branch of a Banyan tree, his tail almost dipping into the water. I slide a little farther down into my seat. The area is teeming with movement as we creep slowly through the tea-colored water. The water has a strong odor, not unpleasant but distinctive. The guide tells us the odor and the color of the water is called tannin and comes from the bark of the Cypress trees. He also tells us that some of the natives use the bark of the Cypress trees to make tea that they claim is very healthy."

"We enter another section of high grass and the pilot restarts the engine. We are soon flying back through the grass to the wide lake-like area where we began our trip. I feel very tired as I exit the airboat. My face is burning from the wind and sun, and I feel like I've been on a journey to another world."

"Wow, Ms. Patino," says Martino as he opens his eyes. "I could really see the pictures in my mind."

"That's very good, Martino," replies Ms. Patino. Being able to create pictures in your mind helps you to understand what you read, too. Now that I've told you about my trip on the bayou, see if you can create pictures of it as you read about it in your geography book."

After the students have completed their reading, Ms. Patino goes back to the map to help them see the relationship between the scene she described, the passage they read, and the map. She wants to help them to make connections between the markings on the map and the visions they have in their heads.

• •

CONCLUSION

Imaging can be used in a wide variety of classroom situations. It is helpful to students because often their inability to image or "picture in their minds" indicates that they don't really understand. Teachers cannot assume that students know how to image since research indicates that poor readers do not image (Irwin, 1991). It may be necessary for students to actually draw pictures on paper before they can paint pictures in their minds, but teaching imaging as a tool for understanding as well as a self-monitoring strategy can help students to become more responsible for their own learning.

References

Chamot, A., & O'Malley, J. (1994). *The CALLA handbook: Implementing the cognitive academic language learning approach*. Reading, MA: Addison Wesley.

Irwin, J. (1991). *Teaching reading comprehension processes* (2nd ed.). Needham Heights, MA: Allyn and Bacon.

INTEGRATED CURRICULUM PROJECTS

17

The integrated curriculum project (Meyers, 1993) is an approach to planning curriculum in which knowledge and skills in several curricular areas are combined to accomplish an authentic task. The studies are integrated, usually around an active-learning project, so that the students are learning vocabulary and having experiences that demonstrate the need to use knowledge in multiple disciplines in order to complete real-life work. Integrated curriculum projects differ from thematic units in several ways. There is no attempt to bring all subject areas into the project. An authentic project is accomplished using only the curricular areas necessary to actually complete the objective. This approach is very appropriate for English language learners because of the use of vocabulary in multiple contexts and the focus on authentic projects, which embed the language in real tasks. In addition, the work that is done in an integrated curriculum project is almost always done with cooperative groups of students working together to create a project. This approach gives the English language learners many opportunities to interact verbally within a supportive, small-group setting, while engaging in activities that require communication.

STEP BY STEP

The steps implementing integrated curriculum projects are:

1. Be alert to curriculum possibilities related to science and social studies curricula, national or local news events, service project needs of the school, community, or in your own classroom. If no ideas emerge from that approach, interview your students to determine their interests. Ask questions like, "If you could study anything at all, what would you like to learn about?" For further suggestions see Figure 17.1. Involve the students in the planning. This will enhance their intrinsic motivation. Present the project or possible projects and engage the students in brainstorming ideas about what might be accomplished. It is very important for the students to be enthusiastic about the project and see the opportunities to really accomplish things.

Grade Level	Projects
Kindergarten	• Making our playground cleaner (prettier, safer) • Eating healthy food • Our families
Primary	• Making our neighborhood cleaner (prettier, safer, more friendly) • Making our school safer • Who are our neighbors? (Neighborhood study) • Where does our food come from?
Upper elementary	• Our friends, our world (Origins of the students and families) • Making our town (city, county) cleaner (safer, friendlier) • How our officials are elected • Lobbying for a cause • Manufacturing a product
Middle school	• Advocating for safe leisure activities • Adopting a group (peer tutoring, supporting old folks, etc.) • Beautifying a public area • Publishing a magazine or newspaper • Integrating photography, art, spokesmanship into school
Senior high school	• Uniting the community • Designing and implementing a homework center • Walking in their shoes (Cross-cultural or studies of the physically challenged) • Advocating for changes in the school system
All levels	• Studies based on a good piece of literature

Figure 17.1   Suggestions for Integrated Curriculum Projects

2. While you plan the curricular connections, required vocabulary and key lessons, keep in mind the concepts which the students will need in order to accomplish grade level objectives. Focus on the multiple uses of vocabulary and skills they will need in order to successfully complete the project. List other groups, organizations, teachers, and administrators who can be enlisted to support the project.

3. Conduct a class problem-solving session in which you and the students identify the most important products or accomplishments they want to achieve, the problems they will need to overcome, and the people who will need to be involved.

4. Form cooperative groups, making sure that the English language learners are paired with strong language models, and divide the labor so that each group is responsible for designated tasks. Provide each group with a list of their responsibilities and roles and encourage

them to work together to set a time line for accomplishments, as well as a checklist of tasks to be carried out.

5. Plan ways to involve the cooperative groups in studying, planning, implementing, and celebrating each step of the way.

APPLICATIONS AND EXAMPLES

When Ms. Frangelica's first graders hear that they are getting a new student from the same Caribbean island where their teacher grew up, they are very excited.

"Do you know her, Ms. Frangelica?" asks Sandi.

"No, I don't know her but she is coming from a school not too far away from where I went to school," replies Ms. Frangelica with a smile.

"What is it like at that school?" asks Jerome.

"Why don't we wait until she gets here and we'll ask her to tell us about it," suggests Ms. Frangelica.

"We want you to tell us about what it was like when you went to school there," says Sandi.

Ms. Frangelica smiles and says, "Why don't we wait until Sarieta gets here on Monday and we'll study all about the island. I'll even bring a book about the island and some of the music from there so we can all learn about it."

"Oh, good! A project!" reply the children, who like project studies.

As Ms. Frangelica begins to plan the study of her new student's native island she realizes that she can put together an integrated curriculum project based upon her students' interest in the new student, and her native island. She plans to build the study on Frank Lessac's book, *My Little Island* (1984), which has always been a favorite of hers. The book is rich in vocabulary related to new foods, geography, and activities that will be fascinating to the first graders but familiar to the new student. Ms. Frangelica also plans a project where her students will become pen pals to the students in Serieta's old class. Miss Frangelica lists the curricular areas she can integrate:

Music: Caribbean music, dance, rhythm

Nutrition: new foods, food groups, diet

Geography: island, Caribbean

Social studies: the impact of climate and natural resources on housing, food supplies, activities, occupations; customs and celebrations and their origins; contrasting the use of time, resources to the way things are done in the U.S.

Language arts: writing to pen pals, reading books about life and customs of the Caribbean

Vocabulary: a wall of Caribbean words, pictures and realia to illustrate them, native words and expressions

Parent involvement: bring other Caribbean parents in for interviews, demonstrations of music, dance, cooking

Because Ms. Frangelica knows how poor the schools are on her island, she plans a service learning project where the children will become involved in sending something of educational value to Serieta's old school. She will involve the children in making this decision once Serieta has arrived and can tell them more about the needs of the school. As she thinks about the integrated curriculum project that is growing in her mind, she realizes that the children will learn a great deal. She immediately gets to work to choose the music that she will play as the students arrive on Monday morning and she gets out her old sun hat to wear to help set the mood. She gathers some artifacts from the island to label and place around in the classroom. As she looks around her apartment she finds a conch shell, photos of brightly painted houses on stilts, an artificial frangipani flower, a coconut, and a stuffed iguana. Her project is underway.

Ms. Boland teaches seventh grade English is an inner city middle school. Her students are from several different cultural groups, some Hispanic, some Southeast Asian. They don't see much beauty as they walk to school each morning, but they usually come in smiling. One morning, Tia enters with an angry stomp. "I *hate* graffiti!" she states strongly. "My grandmother just painted her front fence yesterday, and it's already marked again."

Several of the other students join in the discussion but no one seems to have a solution to the problem. The discussion gets Ms. Boland thinking about the neighborhood in which her students live, however. Several of the school service groups have painted murals on the outside walls of the school. The murals do help. No graffiti is painted over them. But the walls without murals are still covered regularly, no matter how quickly they are painted. Ms. Boland is not convinced that graffiti is the main problem. She is more worried about the general feeling of despair and discouragement that she often recognizes as she confers with parents.

That evening, as she attends her photography class at the local community college, Ms. Boland has an idea. After class, she approaches her photography instructor with it. "I want to do a photography project with my seventh graders. Do you have students who would be available to help them learn how to take pictures?" she asks.

"Yes, I think we could do that," replies Mr. Stephens, the instructor. "Better than that, though, we have a service club on campus which I sponsor. We just happen to be looking for a project."

"Great!" replies Ms. Boland. "Here's my idea. I want my students to begin to see some beauty and hope in their neighborhood. I thought if they could look through the lens of a camera they could begin to see the beauty in their world and think about ways that they can contribute to their neighborhood. I plan to use the photography project to motivate their writing and their thinking about the control they have over their futures. Seventh graders are at such an important point in their education, I think maybe giving them some new interests might be helpful in inspiring them as readers, writers, and thinkers."

"Wow!" replies Mr. Stephens. "You're biting off a lot. I think I see where you are going, however. But, first things first. Do you have any cameras? Who will buy the film? Do they know how to take pictures?"

"No, I don't know, and no!" grins Ms. Boland. "That's why I need help."

"Well, the service club meets Thursday night at the student union. Can you and a couple of your students come and present the idea?" asks Mr. Stephens.

"We can do that," replies Ms. Boland, "What time?"

The next day Ms. Boland presents her idea to her first period class. She simply tells them that she thinks they will enjoy learning to take pictures as a prewriting strategy and asks if anyone is interested in the idea. Many hands go up. Tia's hand is one that is not raised.

"Tia, you don't want to learn to take pictures?" asks Ms. Boland.

"It's not that," replies Tia. "My grandmother still thinks that you steal people's souls when you take their pictures. She won't like this. And, also, I don't have a camera."

"What if we could get cameras to use and you can take pictures of scenery or buildings rather than people?" asks Ms. Boland.

"I think that will be all right," replies Tia slowly. "I'll have to ask."

"I'll be glad to talk to your grandmother if that will help," replies Ms. Boland.

The next few days are busy in Ms. Boland's class. She organizes cooperative groups to plan the photography projects. The groups plan their needs: cameras, film, release forms for people they will photograph, permission forms for walking field trips around the neighborhood. One group plans a presentation to the principal for his support. Another prepares for the presentation to the community college service club. On Thursday evening Ms. Boland and her group attend the meeting of the community college service club and get support for disposable cameras for the class. They also get help from some of the photography students who agree to come and give lessons in basic photography. The next week is spent in planning their photography projects, looking for possible pictures to meet the criteria set by Ms. Boland. The pictures are to illustrate one of the following themes:

- My culture
- My neighborhood

- Beauty in unexpected places
- Intergenerational interactions

Ms. Boland teaches the use of photography as a prewriting strategy by asking the students to think of a picture they could take and then drafting a short essay that might accompany the picture. In the meantime, students from the community college come to the first period class and teach basic principles of photography. The second week the students take a walking field trip and take pictures. Working as partners, the students each take six pictures. While one student is using the camera, the partner is writing a brief description of the picture that is taken, while jotting down any notes the photographer dictates. Once the photos are developed using funds donated by the community college service club, the students begin to work on their essays.

Ms. Boland is so impressed by the photos and the essays that she shares them with a professional photographer friend of hers a few weeks later. "I would love to have a way to enlarge the photos, mount them, and display them," says Ms. Boland. "The students are very motivated by this project. They are learning a lot about photography and writing. But, more than that, they are developing a renewed interest in their neighborhood and the people who live there. I've created a monster. We simply do not have the money to continue this approach on an ongoing basis."

"Why don't you get the students involved in some problem solving?" replies her friend. "I'll work on some ideas through the local photo gallery group, but it would be wonderful if the students themselves could help solve their own problem."

"I agree," nods Ms. Boland.

The next morning Ms. Boland presents the problem to her class. She reconvenes the cooperative groups for a brainstorming session and the groups quickly formulate a list of ideas. By the end of the period the groups each have a project they are willing to pursue in the effort to raise funds to continue their photography project. One group is going to approach the local newspaper to do an article about the project with the hope of identifying possible donors. One group is going to approach the principal for help. One group is going to talk to the cafeteria manager to see if they can sell ice cream or snacks at the end of each lunch period to raise funds. One group is going to call the photography and education departments at the local university to see if there are any funds available to support university/college partnerships. Each group has a plan of action.

Six months later Ms. Boland can hardly believe how many of their plans have produced results. As she stands and watches the parents circulating around the room looking at the beautifully mounted photos and essays she notices the local television station filming the event for the evening news. The article and full-color spread that appeared in the local newspaper is displayed prominently on one wall. The university professors, community college instructor, and students who were all a part of the project are beaming their approval. The students are all getting many opportunities for oral language practice explaining how they got their ideas and how exciting the project has become. Ms. Boland is thinking about all the knowledge of grants and budgets and advocacy that the students have gained through this endeavor and she is already planning her next integrated curriculum project.

CONCLUSION

Integrated curriculum projects are powerful because they go a step beyond the traditional thematic unit in order to complete an authentic task. Whether the task is providing books for students in a poor community, using photography to improve writing skills and community pride, or using math and science skills to design a reading loft for the classroom, students begin to see the practical applications of school subjects through integrated curriculum projects. They also gain multiple opportunities to practice their spoken and written English as they gather information, make presentations to possible supporters of the project, and participate in the planning and implementation of the project.

References

Lessac, F. (1984). *My little island.* London: Harper Trophy (Macmillan).

Meyers, M. (1993). *Teaching to diversity: Teaching and learning in the multi-ethnic classroom.* Toronto, Canada: Irwin Publishing.

INTERACTIVE READ ALOUD

18

> ## SUPPORTS
>
> - ● Comprehensible input
> - ✔ Increased verbal interaction
> - ● Contextualized language
> - ✔ Reduced anxiety
> - ✔ Active involvement of the learner

Interactive read aloud (Barrentine, 1996) is the reading of books out loud with the use of expression, different voices for different characters, gestures, and the active participation of the listener through predicting, discussion, and checking for understanding. It also involves the exploration of the structure of text and think-aloud strategies that demonstrate how the reader gains meaning from text. This form of read aloud is a powerful teaching tool for use with English language learners because it produces a strong English language model and it reduces anxiety in the students since they can listen and comprehend due to the use of voices, illustrations, and gestures (Smallwood, 1992). Students see their teachers as role models and in interactive read aloud the teachers demonstrate what good readers do (Tompkins, 1998).

Although read aloud has traditionally been used extensively with young children, its effectiveness with older students has been documented many times (Trelease, 1995). This research has led some administrators of high schools with low test scores in reading and comprehension to mandate the use of read aloud school-wide on a daily basis—with very positive results (Trelease, 1995).

Interactive read aloud is motivational. When students observe a teacher reading fluently and with enthusiasm they often choose to read the same book, or another book by the same author for leisure reading (Wood, 1994). The discussion of characters, setting, and description that is involved in interactive read aloud provides shared understanding and vocabulary that serves to support English language learners to stretch their linguistic abilities (Swain, 1993). It's been documented that students who frequently hear books read aloud have a more extensive vocabulary than those who do not (Trelease, 1995).

STEP BY STEP

The steps in implementing interactive read aloud are:

1. Choose a book that is above the instructional reading level of the students that will give you an opportunity to provide a rich read-aloud experience through the use of different voices, excitement, and drama. Set aside a time each day when you will read aloud interactively with your students.

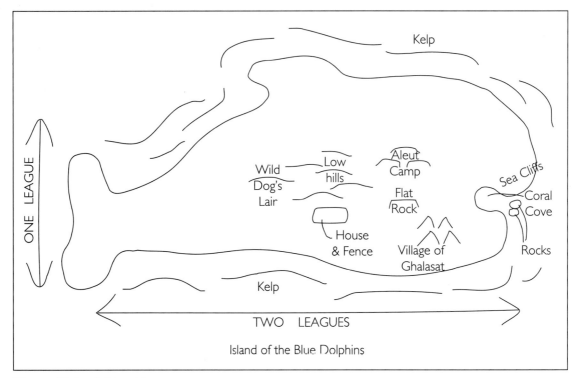

Figure 18.1 A Story Map

2. Before beginning the read-aloud sessions, read the book you have chosen thoroughly. Use post-it notes to mark places for discussion, predicting, and connections to other books the students have read or personal experiences they can relate to the story.

3. Select a 10–15 minute section of the text to read each time, stopping at logical places between readings. Read with enthusiasm, using gestures and voices, and review the events of each day's reading at the end of the session. Discuss predictions for the next day's reading and involve the students in relating the events of the day to their own experiences or similar literary experiences. Use graphic devices like story mapping or daily illustrations of the events to keep the students interested. See Figure 18.1 for an example of a story map.

APPLICATIONS AND EXAMPLES

In Mr. Castro's school district each grade level has been assigned five core books that are to be studied. Scott O'Dell's *Island of the Blue Dolphins* is one of the core books designated for fourth grade. Mr. Castro knows that many of his students will not be able to read and understand the book if they are required to read it independently. He decides to explore the book with his students using interactive read aloud.

Mr. Castro reads the book to prepare for his lessons and identifies places where the students will need to have support in understanding the vocabulary and situations. He prepares the teaching points, vocabulary, and modeling that he wants to do as he reads and plans a half an hour a day for the read-aloud and follow-up discussion. Since the book has 29 chapters, Mr. Castro plans to read two chapters a day so he can complete the book in a three-week period. He marks the points in the book where he will stop for discussion, think-alouds, and vocabulary checks. He uses post-it notes placed in the book to remind him of his plans to interact with the students and provide modeling of important comprehension processes. See Figure 18.2 for a sample of Mr. Castro's Interactive Read Aloud Plan for *Island of the Blue Dolphins.*

Chapter One

Preparing to Read

1. Look at the map and locate the Pacific Ocean and the Aleutian Islands.
2. Encourage discussion of times when the students have seen the ocean, sailboats, and tropical flora and fauna.
3. Look at the cover picture and predict what the story might be about.

During Reading

pg. 9 — Relate "Aleut Ship" to the Aleutian Islands on the map. Discuss the meaning of "it looked like a small shell afloat on the sea" and "it grew larger and was a gull with folded wings."

pg. 10 — Discuss the fact that neither of the children had ever seen a ship before. Think-aloud the possibilities and arrive at the inference that the island didn't have many visitors.

pg. 11 — Discuss the meaning of the first paragraph.
        Prediction Point —bottom of page 11.

pg. 12 — Discuss the meaning of *concealed, crouched,* and *ravine.*

pg. 13 — Discuss the meaning of the quote, "I come in peace and wish to parley."
        Discuss the explanation of the secret name and the belief that it has power.

pg. 14 — Show a picture of an otter. Discuss why the Aleuts were hunting them.

pg. 15 — Estimate the distance of 20 leagues and then look it up.

After Reading

1. Ask the students to tell what happened in this chapter and write their words on large chart paper.
2. Ask for predictions about what will happen in chapter two.
3. Review the means of *concealed, crouched, ravine,* and *mesa.*

Figure 18.2   Mr. Castro's Interactive Read Aloud Plan for *Island of the Blue Dolphins*

After Mr. Castro reads each chapter he asks the students to tell him what happened in the chapter. The students dictate a sentence or two for each chapter and Mr. Castro writes the sentences on a large chart tablet. Later in the day the students may copy the sentences and illustrate them in their *Island of the Blue Dolphins* journal or write a different summary and illustrate it. Their journal also has a section reserved for the writing of new vocabulary learned each day. The students are given a challenge to find ways to use the new vocabulary in their writing and speaking each day so that they will "own the new words."

Mr. Castro has multiple copies of the book being studied because some of the students like to follow along while he reads aloud. There are also several copies in the listening center so the students can listen to a tape of the story if they want to hear the chapters read again. The students often use the listening center to review past chapters or to catch up with the story after an absence. Although there is no reason why they can't listen ahead to coming chapters, they keep a strict code of silence about future chapters because "they don't want to spoil the story for the rest of the class."

• •

Ms. Bosic is preparing her ninth-grade students to attend a performance of Hal Holbrook as Mark Twain. The students have read several short selections written by Mark Twain and want to hear *The Adventures of Huckleberry Finn*. Ms. Bosic knows that the students will benefit more from the theater excursion if they understand the stories they will hear and decides to expose the students to Huck Finn through interactive read aloud.

After rereading the first few chapters of the book, Ms. Bosic decides that she will try to read the story in dialect and with a few props. She finds an old flannel shirt and decrepit straw hat and uses post-it notes to mark stopping points in the story. Because Mrs. Bosic is interested in teaching the use of comprehension processes to her students, she plans to model the processes as a part of her read aloud. See Figure 18.3 for an explanation of the comprehension processes.

Ms. Bosic introduces the reading of Huck Finn by showing the video of *The Adventures of Tom Sawyer.* She asks the students what they think might happen next with Huckleberry.

"I think he's going to run away," says Ramon. "He's never going to be able to live with the Widow Douglas."

"You may be right, Ramon," smiles Ms. Bosic. "We get to see in the next book, *The Adventures of Huckleberry Finn.*

Ms. Bosic opens the book and says, "Mark Twain begins this book with a warning and an explanation. Do you know what a warning is?"

"Do you mean a warning like, 'Be careful?'" asks Kelly.

"Yes, Kelly. It's something you say or read that tells you to be careful or that something is dangerous. Mark Twain starts this book with these words:"

Notice

Persons attempting to find a motive in this narrative will be prosecuted; persons attempting to find a moral in it will be banished; persons attempting to find a plot in it will be shot.

By order of the author,
per G. G., Chief of Ordinance.
(de Voto, 1984)

"What do you think Mark Twain is warning us about?" asks Ms. Bosic.

The students seemed very puzzled by the quote so Ms. Bosic decides to explore the word meanings. "Let's take the warnings one at a time. He says 'persons attempting to find a motive will be prosecuted.' What is a motive?"

"I've heard that word on television," says Carlos. "A person with a motive has a reason for murdering someone."

"That's right," says Ms. Bosic. "So Mark Twain says people who try to find a motive in this book will be prosecuted. What does that mean?"

"That's like the shoplifting signs in the stores," says Katy. "They say that anyone caught shoplifting will be prosecuted."

"And the lawyer who is trying to get the criminal put in jail is the prosecutor," adds Karim.

"That's right," says Ms. Bosic. "Mark Twain is saying if you try to find a reason for this story you'll be put in jail. Why would he say that?"

"I think it's a joke," says Michael. "He's saying not to take this story too seriously."

"I think you may be right," says Mrs. Bosic. "Because he also says if you try to find a moral you'll be banished and if you try to find a plot you'll be shot."

"What is a moral?" asks Ms. Bosic.

"We studied that when we were reading *The Tortoise and the Hare,*" says Ramon. "The moral of that story was, 'Slow and steady wins the race.'"

"Good for you!" says Ms. Bosic. "The moral is the lesson you learn from the story."

"What does Mark Twain mean when he says you will be banished?" she asks next.

"That's when you are sent away and told never to come back," says Carlos.

"You are all too smart for me," laughs Ms. Bosic. "You are doing a great job of making connections. You remember things from other stories or television that help you to understand the story. That's exactly what good readers do."

"Next Twain says if you attempt to find a plot, you'll be shot. Do you think he really intends to shoot people?" asks Ms. Bosic. "Or is he just joking again?"

"How can he write a book without a plot?" asks Karim. "This must really be a silly book."

"I think you've got the idea," agrees Ms. Bosic as she puts on her straw hat. "He also explains that the language he has written is the extremist form of backwoods Southwestern dialect. I'm going to try to read the story with that dialect."

Process	Definition	Teaching Strategies
Microprocesses	Sentence level connections Making sense of elements within a sentence	Read aloud, rereading for fluency, phrasing practice
Integrative processes	Connections between adjacent sentences within a selection	Finding cohesion links, referents, visualizing the connections between ideas
Elaborative processes	Making connections between personal experiences or other texts related to the text being read	Think-aloud referring to personal experiences or other texts that were similar to the one being read
Macroprocesses	Getting the main idea, the overarching meaning of a whole selection	Summarizing the text, stating the main idea, finding the topic sentences
Metacognitive	Monitoring your own understanding of what is being read	Stopping and taking stock and having strategies to use to support understanding; Rereading, paraphrasing, looking up words, self-correcting and monitoring

Figure 18.3 Teaching Comprehension Processes

Adapted from: Irwin, J. (1991). *Teaching the comprehension processes,* and Tompkins, G. E. (1997). *Literacy for the 21st Century.*

The students are all smiling now. They love to hear Ms. Bosic read aloud. She always uses great voices and expression. They know they'll enjoy hearing the story of Huck Finn.

Because Ms. Bosic reads the story with the dialect of the people, she manages to set a tone that helps the students to relax and enjoy the story. She stops periodically to model comprehension processes like thinking aloud when something may be confusing or talking about something in the book that reminds her of the Tom Sawyer video. She stops every now and then and pretends to be confused by a pronoun, asking the students who is meant by the word "he" in that sentence or rereading a sentence to help the students make connections. She doesn't demonstrate these strategies constantly because she doesn't want to interrupt the flow of the story, but she gives the students a lot of ideas about how she is making meaning of the text by her short explanations and demonstrations.

At the end of each day's reading Ms. Bosic reviews some of the more difficult vocabulary and encourages the students to discuss the main events in the part of the story read that day. She asks questions that require the students to infer and she encourages them to predict about what might happen next. She is modeling fluent reading, obviously enjoying the story and using the storytelling mode with the addition of the simple costume and dialect.

▶CONCLUSION

Interactive read aloud, while traditionally associated with primary classrooms, has been found to be highly effective in supporting comprehension and vocabulary development in older students. Even high school students benefit from hearing fluent, expressive reading of English text. By hearing literature read with the use of different voices, inflection, gestures, and body language, English language learners are supported in refining their reading and speaking skills.

References

Barrentine, S. (1996). Engaging with reading through interactive read-alouds. *The Reading Teacher. 50,* 36–43.

de Voto, B. (Ed.). (1984). *The portable Mark Twain.* New York: Penguin Books.

Irwin, J. (1991). *Teaching reading comprehension processes* (2nd ed.). Needham Heights, MA: Allyn and Bacon.

Krashen, S. (1993). *The power of reading.* Englewood, CO: Libraries Unlimited.

O'Dell, S. (1960). *Island of the blue dolphins.* New York: Bantam Doubleday.

Smallwood, B. (1992). Children's literature for adult ESL literacy. (On-line). Available Internet: http://www.cal.org/ncte/digests

Swain, M. (1993). The output hypothesis: Just speaking and writing aren't enough. *The Canadian Modern Language Review, 50,* 158–164.

Tompkins, G. (1997). *Literacy for the 21st century.* Upper Saddle River, NJ: Merrill/Prentice Hall.

Tompkins, G. E. (1998). *Language arts: Content and teaching strategies.* Upper Saddle River, NJ: Merrill/Prentice Hall.

Trelease, J. (1995). Sustained silent reading. *California English, 1,* 8–9.

Wood, K. (1994). Hearing voices, telling tales: Finding the power of reading aloud. *Language Arts, 71,* 346–349.

INTERACTIVE WRITING

19

SUPPORTS

- Comprehensible input
- ✔ Increased verbal interaction
- Contextualized language
- ✔ Reduced anxiety
- Active involvement of the learner

Interactive writing (Pinnell & McCarrier, 1994) is a form of shared writing or language experience lesson in which the teacher and students compose a story or text and share the pen in writing the words down on chart or writing paper. The students are supported in using conventional spelling, capitalization, and punctuation. They are encouraged to write the parts of the text they are able to write. The teacher supplies the non-phonetic parts of words as she also supports the students' decision making as they practice writing with conventional spelling and mechanics.

Interactive writing provides scaffolding for young children moving from invented spelling into conventional spelling or to older students who are in need of skill- and confidence-building. It is especially appropriate for English language learners because providing an experience about which to write is the first step in interactive writing. While discussing the experience the students provide the language to be written. The teacher helps them in creating complete English sentences, sounding out the words to be written, and teaching the use of capitalization and punctuation. See Figure 19.1 for texts and skills that can be taught through interactive writing.

STEP BY STEP

The steps in conducting an interactive writing lesson are:

1. Provide an experience to write about. Interactive writing can be done after a field trip, to share daily news, or after reading a book. The shared experience gives the group something to write about. If the interactive writing is done with an individual it still works best to have a recent experience to write about.
2. Display a piece of chart paper on which the text will be written, or a piece of writing paper if the text is to be written with an individual student. Gather markers and correction tape. Inch-wide correction tape is best when the story is written on chart paper.
3. Negotiate a sentence to be written. In the beginning it is best to start with a fairly simple sentence. Have the students help you to count the words in the sentence. This helps you to remember it and helps the students to see the individual words as they are written.
4. Say the first word in the sentence slowly, drawing out the sounds. Ask the students what letter they hear at the beginning of the word. Invite one student to come and write the be-

Texts	Skills
Labels	Letter formation
Lists	Initial consonants
Daily news	Final consonants
Parent newsletters	Short vowels
Formula poems	Capital letters
Friendly letters	Punctuation
Business letters	Drafting
Reports	Revising
Book reports	Editing
Big books	Alliteration
Alphabet books	Varying word choice
Fact books	Writing dialogue
Autobiographies	Citing sources
New versions of old books	Conventional spelling

Figure 19.1 Texts and Skills Appropriate for Interactive Writing Lessons

ginning letter, but before it is written ask, "Will you write a lower-case letter or a capital letter?" If the student answers, "Capital," ask "Why?" The idea is to provide all possible support for success as well as to verbalize the decisions to be made so that all students understand. Then, allow the student to write the letter. Note that with older—or more skilled—students you adjust this step, providing only the support that is necessary for the students to participate successfully.

5. After each word is written, go back and reread the sentence so far, pointing to each word as it is read. Continue to compose and support the children in writing the story following the same procedures. Focus on decisions that must be made as the writing is done, such as when to leave spaces, when to use capital letters, commas, periods, etc. Use the correction tape whenever necessary, but always offer support to the student who made the error and encouragement when he/she corrects it.

6. After the text is written, celebrate with the students by having the group read it aloud. Choose a student or two to illustrate it and then display it proudly in the classroom. When completed, an interactive writing lesson should produce a story that is correctly spelled, spaced, punctuated, and capitalized. Every student in the group should be able to read it, pointing to each word as it is read.

APPLICATIONS AND EXAMPLES

Mr. Benning gathers his first-grade students on the carpet at the end of each day. He asks them to tell him about the activities they have enjoyed in school that day. As they talk about their experiences, Mr. Benning conducts an interactive writing lesson. Each student is encouraged to participate as they are able. Some students can supply beginning letters in words, others can write whole words and even some phrases. Mr. Benning supports the students in sounding out words, leaving spaces, and placing punctuation marks and capital letters. After the text is complete, the students reread it together and talk about information they want to share with their parents. This daily ritual brings closure to their school day and reminds them of stories they want to share with their

Today we went to the zoo.
We saw Lots of animals.
Jose liked the monkeys the best.
Paulie liked the elephant.
We sang Songs and ate lunch at the zoo.
It was fun.

Figure 19.2 Mr. Benning's Daily News (written interactively)

parents. It also provides a daily model for the uses of writing, conventional spelling, and mechanics. Figure 19.2 shows an example of Mr. Benning's first-grade daily news texts written by students from nine different language backgrounds.

• •

Ms. Jacobs teaches eighth-grade English. Her students are reading literature related to the underground railroad and she decides that an interactive writing lesson would help the students to summarize their knowledge of the railroad while simultaneously providing an opportunity for her to teach writing mechanics in an authentic way.

Ms. Jacobs provides each student with an individual white board and dry-erase marker. She begins the interactive writing lesson with a question about the book *The story of Harriet Tubman, conductor of the underground railroad* (McMullan, 1991), which she has been reading aloud to the class. The students help to compose a narrative about the book and Tubman's participation in the underground railroad. One student is chosen to write on the chart paper provided, but all students are writing the text on their white boards. Ms. Jacobs is monitoring the white boards and noting the abilities of the individual students as they write. She also supports the students' composing skills by making observations such as, "We've already started two sentences with "She," maybe we can think of another way to begin this sentence. Ms. Jacob's students can write entire sentences as they contribute to the interactive narrative, but she is helping them to make choices of interesting words, complex sentences, and literary forms in their writing.

A fascinating fact comes to light as the students are composing the story and discussing the book. When Ms. Jacob's asks the question, "Where does the underground railroad run?" a number of the students answer, "From Mexico to California." This revelation provides an opportunity for Ms. Jacobs to use a United States map to correct a misconception about historical information that she may not have learned if it had not been for the discussion generated by the interactive writing discussion.

The English language learners in the group are participating actively and finding great success in composing the story. Because a group is composing the story, the anxiety level is lowered considerably and the peer interactions make writing more enjoyable. The students learn that some of their peers are very good at finding interesting words to use, while others are more adept at deciding on good titles. They are learning to appreciate each other's unique contributions.

• •

CONCLUSION

Interactive writing involves the students in a thought process that is converted to writing. By discussing what they will write, and when and why conventions of writing are used, students are consistently reminded of the rules of writing and spelling in English. Students soon become more confident of their ability to transcribe their thoughts into readable English text because the teacher provides support by asking questions and reminding the students to think about the rules. The conventions and thoughts they practice writing as a groups are then transferred to their independent writing.

References

McMullan, K. (1991). *The story of Harriet Tubman, conductor of the underground railroad*. New York: Bantam Books.

Pinnell, G., and McCarrier, A. (1994). Interactive writing: A transition tool for assisting children in learning to read and write. In E. Hiebert & B. Taylor (Eds.) *Getting reading right from the start: Effective early literacy interventions,* pp. 149–170. Needham Heights, MA: Allyn and Bacon.

Suggested Readings

Button, K., Johnson, M. & Furgerson, P. (1996). Interactive writing in a primary classroom. *The Reading Teacher, 49,* 446–454.

Fountas, I., and Pinnell, G. (1993). *Guided Reading: Good first teaching for all children*. Portsmouth, NH: Heinemann.

LANGUAGE EXPERIENCE APPROACH

20

The language experience approach (Lee & Allen, 1963) is an activity-based writing lesson that helps students to see the connections between experiences, what is spoken, and the written language. The students participate in an experience such as a field trip, science, or art lesson. The teacher engages the students in a discussion of their experience and as they talk about what they did, the teacher models writing their words on large chart paper. The teacher demonstrates the connection between sounds and written letters by sounding the words out as she takes the students' dictation. The students are able to read the text because they participated in the activity and the written words tell what they said about their experience. For these reasons, language experience lessons are very appropriate for English language learners (Hernandez, 1997).

The texts that are created from language experience lessons are frequently used for rereading, creating books for the students to illustrate or use in reader's theater. Big books made by the students from a language experience text provide an opportunity for the students to work collaboratively as illustrators and make a contribution to the class library.

STEP BY STEP

1. Provide an active learning experience such as a field trip, science experiment, art lesson, or physical movement lesson. For individual students, language experience lessons are based on any experience the student wishes to share.
2. Seat the students so they can see the chart or chalkboard where you are writing. Engage them in conversation about the activity they have just experienced. Encourage them to use complete sentences as they describe the activity.
3. Record the students' descriptions of their experience. The recording reinforces their understanding of the oral to written language connection best if you follow this sequence:
   - Repeat the sentence to be written and then say it again one word at a time as you write it.

Publishing Format	Instructions
Parent newsletter	Language experience lesson is taught and text is used to share class activities with parents. One of the students illustrates the text. Note that it is a collaboratively written text and list the students who contributed.
Wall story	After the text is written, recopy it one sentence at a time onto large construction paper. Ask a different student to illustrate each page. Display the pages, in proper sequence, along a wall or hang from a display line in the room. After awhile the pages can be taken down and made into a big book.
Individual books	After the text is written copy it, one sentence per page, onto a master that can be folded into a book. Make photocopies of the pages. Help the students to fold them to make a small book, staple it together and have the students illustrate it.
Pocket chart game	As the text is dictated write the sentences on sentence strip paper, one sentence per strip. Mix the sentences up and have the students rearrange them in order. After awhile, cut the words apart and encourage the students to rebuild the original text or create a new one using the same words.
Walk on story	After the text is written copy the sentences, one sentence per page of construction paper. Have the students illustrate the sentences and then laminate the individual pages. The students read the text by spreading the pages out on the floor and stepping from page to page, reading as they walk.

Figure 20.1   Ways to Publish Language Experience Texts

- Have the students read the sentence along with you, pointing to each word as it's read.
- If sequence is important to the text, ask leading questions such as, "And then what did we do?"
- If the students are not dictating the sentences in proper sequence, you may want to record their sentences on sentence strips so that they can be rearranged in sequence after all the sentences are written.

4. When the entire text has been dictated, reread it aloud with the students reading along. Celebrate the vocabulary contributed by the students and give the students who dictated sentences a special pat on the back. Involve the students in deciding how they want to publish their text.

5. Provide time and materials for the students to use in creating a product from their dictation. Figure 20.1 shows ways that language experience texts can be published.

APPLICATIONS AND EXAMPLES

Ms. Chan's first graders are completing the planting of bean seeds they brought back from their trip to the farm. Ms. Chan asks the students to tell her how they planted their seeds.

"We got some dirt," says Lee.

Ms. Chan picks up her marker and says, "Let's write this down so we can put it in our newsletter this week. We (she sounds the letters as she writes them) got—some—dirt."

The students dictate sentences about their experience as Ms. Chan writes their words, sounding them out as they are written. When they are finished, Ms. Chan and the students read the sentences together.

"You did a nice job. We will put this story in the newsletter this week. Your parents will like to read about what you did. Do you want to do anything else with this story?"

"Can we make a book, and draw pictures?" asks Tia.

"Do you want to make a big book or little ones?" Ms. Chan asks.

"Big one!" the students reply.

Ms. Chan gets large pieces of construction paper, cuts the chart story apart and gives the students each a sentence to illustrate. She helps them to glue the sentences to the bottoms of their papers, under their illustrations. They put the book together with large metal rings and place it in the reading center. The students all enjoy stretching out on the floor to reread their book.

Mr. Mejas and his seventh graders are reading *The Giver* (Lowry, 1993). The students are reading a few chapters and then meeting with Mr. Mejas to discuss the book. As a part of the literature circles that meet once a week to discuss the chapters that have been read, each student dictates a favorite phrase or sentence selected from the text. The sentences are displayed on the bulletin board in categories marked, *Beautiful Language, Powerful Language, Suspenseful Language,* and *Descriptive Language.* Often Mr. Mejas has the students close their eyes to listen to the sentences the other students are sharing. Listening with their eyes closed helps them to decide where the phrase or sentence should be placed on the bulletin board. As Mr. Mejas writes the words on the sentence strips, the students help him to spell the words by sounding them out as he writes them. After the phrase or sentence is written they discuss other words that may be related to the words written such as *transport, transportation, transporter, transition,* and *porter.* Mr. Mejas feels that by relieving the students of the writing in this approach they are able to focus more on the meanings of the words and the cohesion of the text.

CONCLUSION

Language experience lessons support the development of English vocabulary, including the active participation and verbal interaction of students through the use of their personal experiences in the creation of a written text. Follow-up activities such as the publishing of the text for use in reading practice serves to provide low-stress reading support for students learning a new language. Seeing their own stories published and illustrated also provides motivation and validation for students. Language experience texts can be used in multiple areas of the curriculum and serve to strengthen the concept-language connections of all students.

References

Lee, D. M., & Allen, R. V. (1963). *Learning to read through experience* (2nd ed.). New York: Meredith.

Lowry, L. (1993). *The giver.* Boston: Houghton Mifflin.

Hernandez, H. (1997). *Teaching in multicultural classrooms.* Upper Saddle River, NJ: Merrill/Prentice Hall.

LANGUAGE FOCUS LESSONS

··

> ## SUPPORTS
>
> - ● Comprehensible input
> - ● Increased verbal interaction
> - ● Contextualized language
> - ● Reduced anxiety
> - ✔ Active involvement of the learner

··

L anguage focus lessons (Gibbons, 1993) are lessons in which the focus is on English vocabulary and usage, rather than the curricular content. These lessons may involve exploration of content such as math, science, or social studies, but the focus of the lesson is on the language being used rather than the content itself. The language selected for language focus lessons is based upon teacher observation and knowledge of the language forms and functions that give English language learners difficulty. Examples of appropriate language for language focus lessons are shown in Figure 21.1.

▶ STEP BY STEP

The steps in teaching a language focus lesson are:

1. Observe your students and take notes on the types of language that they tend to misuse. Plan time to work with small groups of students who have the same types of needs for direct instruction in language usage.
2. Gather realia, visuals, and ideas for hands-on demonstrations of the language usage to be taught.
3. Introduce the vocabulary and model its use, simultaneously using the language as you model. Give several examples for each term so that students can see when and how the language is used.
4. Give the students an opportunity to actually perform or model a hands-on movement or activity as they use the focus language.
5. Design an activity that allows you to observe the students' mastery of the focus language. If they do not connect the language to the actions correctly, repeat steps 3 and 4.

Language Form	Curricular Connections	Examples
Articles a, an, one, the, this, these	Words that indicate plurals, singular forms	Cloze activities, narratives with articles and numerical indicator left out, which might relate to any subject area.
Prepositional phrases, position words in, on, under, beside, in back of	Language arts, science, social studies	Using literature that shows position, such as *Rosie's Walk*. Math activities such as placing a certain number of things *beside* others or stacking things *on top of* others using number and position words.
Degrees of obligation must, may, might, could, should	Predictions in science, literature, class rules	Discussion of class rules in which situations are discussed, and student choices compared with rules that *must* be followed. Science experiments where hypotheses are being tested, students discuss what *might* happen. Problem-solving activities in which things that *could* be tried are listed and compared to things that *must* be done.
Comparison words smaller, larger, fewer, less, wider, narrower, taller, shorter, greater than, less than, equal to	Mathematics, describing in any subject area	Discussion of size of groups, or objects, attributes of anything being compared.
Content-related words	Mathematics, science social studies, reading	Use of content words in context. Scientific terms such as experiment, liquid, solid, gas, presented with realia, multiple examples.

Figure 21.1   Suggested Language Forms and Functions for Language Focus Lessons

APPLICATIONS AND EXAMPLES

Mr. Lee is concerned because his second graders often leave off endings of words both orally and in writing. He observes and notes the students who are doing this and plans a language focus lesson for these students. During math the next day, Mr. Lee gathers six students to do an activity with joining sets and writing story problems. Each student is given a laminated picture of a lake with large lily pads and small frogs in green and brown. He instructs the students to pick out fifteen green frogs and put them on the lily pads. He then says the following sentence, emphasizing the plural /s/ each time he says it, "There are fifteen brown frogs on the lily pads in the lake. Six of them jump into the water to cool off. How many frogs are left on the lily pads?" As the students count out the six frogs he asks, "How many frogs jump into the water?"

The students answer, "Six."

"Yes," says Mr. Lee, "Six frogs jump into the water."

Mr. Lee then asks each student to repeat the words, "Six frogs," emphasizing the final /s/.

"When you add /s/ to the word frog. It lets you know there is more than one frog. It is very important to pronounce the /s/. One thing you will notice is that when you add the /s/ to the end of the word frog, it sounds like a /z/. The 's' at the end of the words sometimes sounds like a /z/ but we still spell it with an 's'. We will make a chart of the words that sound like a /z/ at the end when we add 's' to them." Mr. Lee explains.

"We will put the word *frogs* in jail because the 's' doesn't follow the rules and sound like an 's' should sound." Mr. Lee writes the word *frogs* on a 3 by 5 card and puts it on a bulletin board that has bars on it like a jail cell. "We will putting other words in jail whenever we find that they are not following the rules. If you find any more words that are spelled with an 's' at the end but sound like /z/, be sure to tell me so we can put those words in jail."

Next, Mr. Lee has the students write the story problem about the frogs, emphasizing the writing of the "s" on the words *frogs* and lily *pads.*

"Mr. Lee, Mr. Lee!" calls Gustov. "We have to put *pads* in jail too! It sounds like a /z/, just like *frogs.*"

"Good for you, Gustov! You're a great word detective," says Mr. Lee as he hands Gustov a blank card and a marker. "Put that word in jail."

"Now, I want you to think of other word problems you can write using the frogs and the lily pads," says Mr. Lee.

After the students have a chance to write some problems, Mr. Lee has them read the problems aloud and the other students work them out using the frogs and the lily pad pictures. Once Mr. Lee sees that the students are adding the "s," both in speaking and in writing, he changes the focus of the lesson to the "ed" ending, using the same materials but emphasizing that the frogs already jumped into the water. Because the "ed" at the end of the word *jumped* sounds like a /t/ instead of /ed/, the children decide that *jumped* must also go to jail.

Jose says, "English is hard, Mr. Lee. There are a lot of rule breakers."

"This is very true," says Mr. Lee with a sigh. "But you are very smart and you will learn to speak English. Just look at the word jail if you need help with a rule breaker. Maybe we need to write the rule that each of the words breaks so we can remember. What should we say about *frogs* and *pads?*"

"Put they sound like /z/ when they should sound like /s/," suggests Arturo.

"What about *jumped?*" asks Mr. Lee.

"Put it sounds like /t/ when it should sound like /ed/," says Tomas.

"Let's put them in different cells!" Katey adds.

At the end of the lesson Mr. Lee teaches the students a signal he will use to remind them when they are leaving off endings in their oral speech and in their written work. The signal he and the students agree on is a pinkie finger touched to the end of the nose. The students and Mr. Lee practice giving this signal to each other to help them to remember to carefully pronounce ending sounds.

Mr. Lee knows that one lesson will not solve the problem of the dropped endings on words, but he will use the pinkie to the nose signal to remind the students to clearly pronounce the /s/ and /ed/ when they are speaking, and to add them in writing. He also signals toward the word jail board to help the students remember how to pronounce the endings.

As the year progresses, Mr. Lee plans to teach more language focus lessons and add the other sounds for the "ed" ending as he sees the need. The children, in the meantime, are looking for more words to put in jail.

1. All students must respect the rights and space of others.
2. When finished with work, students may choose activities from the time management chart.
3. When choosing activities, students must consider any distractions their activities might cause and move away from students who are still completing work.
4. All work should be completed neatly and must be turned in on time.
5. Students must keep their voices low and respectful, being careful to avoid noise that could interfere with the activities of others in the class.

Figure 21.2 Classroom Rules and Procedures

Ms. Karras plans to teach a language focus lesson with her sixth-grade English language learners who are having difficulty understanding words that describe the classroom rules. She plans a lesson in which they will review the rules and use examples to help the students understand the meanings of the words, *must, may, might, should, and could.* To teach this lesson, Ms. Karras will refer to the rules and procedures chart shown in Figure 21.2.

Ms. Karras poses questions basing them on the statements printed on the chart. As Ms. Karras and the students discuss each item, they make a "requirement line" on the chalkboard, placing each of the "requirement words" from the chart along the line according to its strength. The students decide that *must* is a very strong word that means, "every time, no question about it," and they place *must* at the far right of the "requirement line." They place *may* to the far left and discuss the word *could* in relation to *may.* They decide that *could* and *may* are about the same in strength. *Should* is discussed next. The students decide that *should* is not really as strong as *must* but in the classroom they are often used to mean "It's required. You have to do it."

The lesson continues this way until all the words are placed along the line according to their strength. Ms. Karras then asks the students to think of laws and rules from home and the community that would be examples of each of the words on the chart. Cher suggests, "My dad got a ticket because he didn't stop at a stop sign. Stopping at stop signs goes under *must.*"

"Great example!" Ms. Karras comments. "The laws are musts. Can you tell me why?"

"Because you can kill someone if you drive a car and don't follow the laws," states Cher solemnly.

"That's true, Cher." states Ms. Karras. "Can you think of an example for *might?*"

"If my mother has time after dinner, she *might* bake a cake," suggests Tina.

"Good example, Tina," says Ms. Karras. "She doesn't have to do it, it's just a possibility. Is there another word you can use in place of *might* in that same sentence?"

"If my mother has time after dinner, she *could* bake a cake," replies Tina.

"Does that mean the same thing?" asks Ms. Karras.

Figure 21.3 The Requirement Line and Sample Sentences

"Not really," comments Juan. "*Might* means she's thinking about it. *Could* means it's something she can do but maybe she's not even thinking about it."

"I think you've got it," says Ms. Karras. "Let's practice some more."

Ms. Karras gives the students cloze sentences written on sentence strips and asks them to take turns reading the sentences and decide which word from the chart completes the sentence best. After they decide on the best word, they have to explain their choice. When they finish this exercise, the chart looks like the one in Figure 21.3.

CONCLUSION

Language focus lessons are appropriate whenever the teacher identifies a mispronunciation or misuse of language that occurs consistently. The lessons can be used with individual students, small groups, or the whole class. However, it is important with young students or those just beginning to risk oral communication that the lesson not be allowed to interfere with communication. If a student mispronounces or misuses language but the message is clear, it is always important to respond to the request or message. The teacher should note the misuse and the speaker or speakers who misuse the language, and plan a language focus lesson to support the students in refining their use of English. Language focus lessons are most effective when they are presented in a positive way and the students are encouraged to practice the newly acquired skills in an authentic context.

References

Gibbons, P. (1993). *Learning to learn in a second language.* Portsmouth, NH: Heinemann.

Suggested Readings

Chamot, A., & O'Malley, J. (1994). *The CALLA handbook.* Reading, MA: Addison-Wesley.

Diaz-Rico, L., & Weed, K. (1995). *The crosscultural, language, and academic development handbook.* Needham Heights, MA: Allyn and Bacon.

LANGUAGE FRAMEWORK PLANNING

22

....

SUPPORTS

- Comprehensible input
- ✔ Increased verbal interaction
- ✔ Contextualized language
- Reduced anxiety
- ✔ Active involvement of the learner

....

Language framework planning (Gibbons, 1993) is a strategy in which the teacher identifies the language necessary for the students to be successful in a lesson and plans activities that support the use of the language in multiple functions. It is called language framework planning because the teacher creates a framework prior to the lesson that identifies the topic, activities, language functions, language structures, and vocabulary that will be a part of the lesson. In this way, language and content acquisition are both supported. The framework is shown in Figure 22.1.

STEP BY STEP

The steps in language framework planning are:

1. Identify the language objectives of the lesson to be taught. These objectives should relate to the functions of language and the sentence patterns and structures to be practiced as a part of the lesson. To identify these objectives ask yourself these questions:
   - What are the language demands of this particular lesson?
   - What are the language levels of the students?
   It is helpful to create a checklist on which you can record the functions the students use regularly so that you can structure lessons to give them practice in utilizing new functions of language in a variety of content areas. A language function checklist is shown in Figure 22.2.
2. Identify the language structures that are likely to give the students problems and plan to model their use early in the lesson. If you are keeping regular samples of the students' language, these records are extremely helpful in planning language lessons as shown in Figure 22.3.
3. Plan the sequence of the lesson by creating a chart like the one in Figure 19.1 in which the language functions, structures, and vocabulary are modeled and then practiced by the students as a part of the activity.

Topic	Activities	Language Functions	Language Structures	Vocabulary
Shape	Sorting attribute blocks by shape	Classifying Describing	They are all (shape).	Triangle Circle Square Rectangle
Size	Sorting attribute blocks by size	Classifying Describing Comparing Contrasting	These (shape) are all (size). This one is (smaller, larger).	Large Small Medium Smaller Larger Bigger Littler

Figure 22.1 Language Framework Planning for a Kindergarten Sorting Lesson

4. Plan a way to document the students' success in using the language in the context of the lesson and ways to build upon this lesson to give them additional practice in the use of the language functions and structures gained. Anecdotal records and checklists are both helpful in documenting this type of learning.

APPLICATIONS AND EXAMPLES

Language framework planning can be used at all grade levels and curricular areas to support language and content acquisition. For example, Mr. Gomez is planning a project using interviews to introduce his third-grade students to the ways in which information is gathered from primary sources or from people who experienced the events being studied. He wants his third graders to learn to conduct interviews, practice their oral language skills, and find ways to confirm information gathered in this format. He begins by reading several articles from the local paper concerning some recent decisions made by the city council, which will greatly restrict the amount of money being allocated to summer youth programs. The articles name the city council members who voted to lower the city's investment in summer programs. Mr. Gomez and the students list the names of the people who should be interviewed, including some of the people who lobbied for the continued allocation of funds for the summer programs. Mr. Gomez then begins to plan the language lessons that will help prepare his students to conduct worthwhile interviews. His language framework plan is shown in Figure 22.4.

By planning ahead, Mr. Gomez is prepared to provide the support the students need in order to successfully participate in the primary source project. He knows that many of his students have difficulty coping with academic language, particularly in production. As a result of this their participation in class is severely restricted. To counter this Mr. Gomez plans to model the language structures and allow the students to work together in small heterogeneous groups so that they can support each other in preparing their questions and interviews. Mr. Gomez also plans to encourage the students to work in pairs to conduct the interviews, requiring each of the students to ask some of the questions.

Student's Name _____ School Year _____

Social Functions Observed (date)

Social Functions									
Asking permission									
Asking assistance									
Asking directions									
Denying									
Promising									
Requesting									
Suggesting									
Wishing/hoping									
Academic Functions									
Classifying									
Comparing									
Giving/following directions									
Describing									
Questioning									
Evaluating									
Expressing position									
Explaining									
Hypothesizing									
Planning/predicting									
Reporting									
Sequencing									

Figure 22.2 Functions of Language in the Classroom

Adapted from Gibbons, 1993.

Roberto   January 23   Giving directions to Joey

Roberto and Joey are moving pieces around a game board. Roberto is telling Joey how to move his game piece. "No, put it by . . . put it by the tree." Joey places his piece beside the tree on the board. Roberto says, "No, not there . . . put it on the. . . ." He reaches over and moves the game piece under the tree. Joey says, "Oh, you meant UNDER the tree." Roberto nods.

Figure 22.3   Sample of an Anecdotal Record that Documents Language Needs

Topic	Activities	Language Functions	Language Structures	Vocabulary
History	Read article from the newspaper	Describing Reporting Sequencing	First the council . . . then	Council sequence words
Research	Brainstorming	Following directions Questioning Planning Reporting	When did you . . . ? Why did you . . . ?	Prioritize Allocate
Visuals	Planning/ creating a visual	Expressing needs Expressing plans Asking for feedback	I will need . . . . I plan to . . . . Do you think . . . ?	Labels for materials
Oral reports	Presenting research	Explaining Summarizing Asking questions	First, I . . . . I found . . . . Do you . . . ?	Interviewed Documenting

Figure 22.4   Mr. Gomez's Language Framework Plan for a Primary Source Project

Mr. Gomez is aware that several of his English language learners are talented in art and he will encourage the other students to enlist their help in preparing visuals to accompany their reports. He has high hopes for the success of this project and his hopes are rewarded.

Language framework planning is especially helpful with older English language learners. Planning to provide language models for meeting needs specific to academic assignments supports the participation and success of all students.

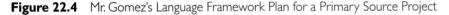

Ms. Brock is preparing a lesson for her middle school social science students to demonstrate how to prepare a project for History Day. Because her classes contain many English language learners she decides to prepare a language framework for the lesson. Her framework plan is shown in Figure 22.5.

As the students participate in planning their History Day presentations, Ms. Brock is able to observe and keep records of their use of the planning process and the language associated with the lesson. She can then plan subsequent lessons in which the students will have opportunities

Topic	Activities	Language Functions	Language Structures	Vocabulary
History	Show video of last year's event	Describing Evaluating Explaining	This student is . . . . How could this be . . . ? How could you . . . ?	Simulate Display Research
Research	Demonstrate the planning process	Sequencing Describing Explaining Planning Reporting Sequencing	First, you . . . . Next, you . . . . You must plan and document	Sequence words Describe Reenact
Practice	Students walk through a simple simulation	Describing Explaining Enacting Reporting Sequencing	I think that . . . . This happened first. This happened because	Predict Confirm Cause/effect Document

Figure 22.5 Ms. Brock's Language Framework Plan

to use the history language that they are acquiring in connection with hands-on lessons. Since Ms. Brock plans complete language framework lessons frequently, she decides that a simpler planning form is in order and adds a language planning section to her basic lesson plan format. She finds that this saves her time, but it also helps her to remember to consider vocabulary, language functions, and structures in all her lesson planning. Her basic lesson plan format is shown in Figure 22.6

Lesson Title _____ Date _____

Objective:

Language Objective:
Vocabulary Focus:
Language Functions to Model:
Language Structures to Model:
Materials:
Motivation:

Procedure:

Closure:
Evaluation:
Provisions for Individual Differences:
Target Students: Needs:

Lesson Reflection:

Figure 22.6   Language Framework Planning Add to a Basic Lesson Plan Format

CONCLUSION

Although language framework planning is time consuming, it provides a vital link to the difficulties many English language learners experience in content-area classrooms. When teachers observe English language learners who are not participating fully in classroom activities or are finding little success in their classroom interactions, attention to the language framework of the lessons may provide valuable clues for ways to better support these students in the classroom.

References

Gibbons, P. (1993). *Learning to learn in a second language.* Portsmouth, NH: Heinemann.

LEARNING CENTERS

23

Learning centers are places set up in the classroom where the students can engage in hands-on activities that allow them to obtain additional experience in using new skills, expand skills usage to more closely match their individual needs, and work cooperatively with other students. Learning centers are thus especially effective for meeting the needs of English language learners and other students needing expanded verbal interaction or hands-on practice to enhance their learning. See Figure 23.1 for suggestions of ways in which learning centers can be used in the classroom.

STEP BY STEP

The steps in implementing learning centers in the classroom are:

1. Identify skills that have already been taught in which the students need more practice. Set up places with materials that can be used for additional, authentic, and meaningful practice in the use of those skills.
2. Introduce the centers to the students, making sure that you demonstrate how they are to use the materials, what your expectations are for the activities, and how their work will be assessed. Display the rules and expectations in the centers so that the students understand that center work is a part of their assigned job and will contribute toward their course grade. The rules for moving from one center to the next should also be discussed and modeled. Rules about cleaning up materials before moving to the next center should be made clear.
3. Introduce a method for the students to use in documenting their participation in centers. This can be as simple as a list of names at the required centers, a contract form on which the students enter the names of the centers they will complete each day or a work folder in which they place all center work done each day. The students have to understand the requirements and the ways in which the center work will be assessed. Make your expectations very clear as to which centers are required and which are optional.
4. Whenever centers are changed, repeat the explanation and modeling steps so that the students understand what is required. Centers should be changed regularly so that students are challenged and provided with opportunities to practice new skills as they are taught.

Grade	Center	Description
Kindergarten	Counting Center	Students count objects and match object groups with numerals.
	Sorting Center	Students sort objects by beginning sounds (vocabulary development).
	Listening Center	Students listen to stories read on a tape recorder while they look at the book.
	Language Master Center	Students hear the name of an object read as a card with a picture of the object and the printed word is fed through the Language Master machine.
	Story Retelling Center	Students retell a story they have heard using small props made out of baked dough (see Story Reenactment chapter of this text).
	Letter Work Center	Students match capital and lowercase letters, which can be expanded to include pictures or objects whose names begin with the letters.
Primary	Word Work Center	Students build high-frequency words with magnetic letters or letter stamps.
	Pocket Chart Center	Students build sentences with word cards and place the sentences in the pocket chart. Can also be used to build compound words, contractions, match synonyms, antonyms, and word families.
	Computer Center	Students work cooperatively to use word processing software to write collaborative stories, problem-solving software to practice math and science strategies, and simple programming software to create graphics. (Practicing language as they collaborate.)
	Writing and Publishing Center	Students use materials at the center to write and publish stories, poetry, and informational books.
	Skills Center	After a skill (such as proofreading) has been taught, students practice the use of the skill in an authentic way. They can use proofreading marks to proof a story written by another student for the class newsletter, a letter written to be mailed, or stories written specifically to be edited.
	Literature Response	Students use this center to respond in double-entry journals, literature logs.
	Project Center	Students use materials in this center to create a project related to science (ex: a model), social studies (ex: a map), literature (ex: a diorama), or math (ex: props for a word problem), or any curricular area.
	Illustration center	Students use materials in this center to replicate the type of illustrations done by an illustrator they are studying such as Eric Carle (finger paint and collage materials) or Leslie Baker (watercolor).

Figure 23.1   Suggestions for Classroom Learning Centers   *(Continued)*

Grade	Center	Description
Upper elementary	Science Center	Students use materials in this center to replicate experiments demonstrated by the teacher.
	Observation Center	Students use this center to closely observe and write observations of nature, art, videotapes of performances in music, dance, and athletics.
	Theater Center	Students use this center to write scripts for scenes of their favorite books, enlist the help of peers to practice the scene, and then present it to the class.
	Editing Center	Students use this center to collaboratively edit student writing that is almost ready to be published. The center includes thesaurus, dictionaries, and English grammar texts.
Middle & high school	Logic Center	Student use this center to create "brainbenders," logic problems that can be solved by other students using props provided, or made by the students.
	Video Center	Videocamera, tripod, and tapes are available in this center so students can videotape scenes from literature, vocabulary role play, book commercials written by students, enactments of history, etc.
	Research Center	Encyclopedias, reference books, a computer with Internet access, are all available at this center to encourage student research on topics under study in the classroom.
	Multiple Intelligences Center	Seven different ways of studying a topic are presented in centers corresponding to Gardner's Seven Intelligences (soon to be expanded to nine). Students are encouraged to: • Write a song about the topic in the Musical Intelligence Center • Write a poem about the topic in the Linguistic Intelligence Center • Debate the topic with a peer in the Interpersonal Intelligence Center • Write in a personal journal about the topic in the Intrapersonal Intelligence Center • Write a logic or word problem about the topic in the Logical/Mathematical Intelligence Center • Draw a poster about the topic in the Visual/Spatial Intelligence Center • Choreograph a dance or mime in the Bodily/Kinesthetic Intelligence Center

Figure 23.1   continued

APPLICATIONS AND EXAMPLES

The third graders in Mr. Martino's class are learning to write friendly letters. Mr. Martino decides that he will introduce a series of learning centers that will enable his students to practice writing letters as well as to produce a class newsletter, which will give them authentic practice in writing in several domains. The centers Mr. Martino sets up in his classroom will support the letter-writing project and expand it so that the students get practice in writing letters for different purposes.

Mr. Martino begins by creating a life-sized mailbox out of a cardboard box that originally housed a washing machine. He sets up a **Mail Processing Center** in which the students must cancel the student-designed stamps on the incoming letters and place them in alphabetized letter cubbies labeled with the third-grade students' names. Mr. Martino also creates a mail cubby box for the kindergartners so his students can write to them also. The instructions in the mail processing center say, "Take the mail out of the mail collection box. Cancel the stamps using the mail cancellation rubber stamp. If anyone mailed a letter without putting a stamp on it, stamp it 'Return to sender' and place it in the mailbox of the person who sent it. Use the alphabetical sorting tray and sort the letters with canceled stamps alphabetically and then place them into the mail cubbies."

Mr. Martino has recently taught proofreading to his class and so he sets up a proofreading center and a class newsletter project that will be done on the computer. Students are encouraged to write articles for the class newsletter about class activities, activities with the kindergarten buddies, and any news about the students or families in the class. In addition to the news articles there will be a page of letters to the editor and letters to "Dear Anna," their class advice column, both of which will give authentic practice in writing friendly letters.

Mr. Martino sets up centers in which the news articles are to be written. In these **News Article Centers** he displays photographs of recent school and classroom activities and field trips for the students to write about. The instructions in the news writing centers say, "Write an article for the class newsletter about a news event in our classroom or school. Be sure to include the who, what, when, and where information about the event. When the article is completed, take it to the proofreading center to be proofread."

In the **Sports News Center** he places photos of the latest kickball and softball games, as well as trophies some of the students have won in recent little league games and swim meet competitions and brought in to share with the class. The instructions in this center say, "Write an article about a sports event in which you participated. Be sure to include who scored, what the final score was, who was playing, and when the event took place. When you finish the article, take it to the proofreading center to be proofread."

In the **Literary Review Center,** Mr. Martino places copies of books that he has read aloud recently as well as several books that the students are reading and discussing in literature circles. The instructions in this center read, "Write a book review for the class newsletter. Be sure to write about the parts of the book that make it interesting or exciting without giving away the plot. Include the author's name, the name of the illustrator, and any quotes you can get from people who have read the book. When your article is complete, take it to the proofreading table to be proofread."

At the **Letters to the Editor Center** the instructions read, "Write a letter to the editor about something you would like to see changed in our classroom or school. Be sure to tell why you want something changed and exactly what needs to be changed and how. Write the letter in correct friendly letter format and sign it. When you have finished your letter, take it to the proofreading center for proofreading."

At the **Dear Anna Center** the students can either write a letter to Anna or answer letters that other students have left at the center. The instructions in this center read, "In this center you may write a letter to Dear Anna about a problem you have and leave it to be answered OR you can choose a letter from the box of letters and write a response to it. Remember that the writer of the letter is expecting a helpful response. You do not have to sign your name to the letters you leave to be answered but you must sign them in some way like, 'Someone in a hurry,' or 'A friend with a problem.'"

Name _____	Date _____		
Work I accomplished today:		Completed?	Self-Rating
News article on _____		Yes No	1 2 3 4 5
Sports article on _____		Yes No	1 2 3 4 5
Letter to the editor on _____		Yes No	1 2 3 4 5
Letter to Dear Anna on _____		Yes No	1 2 3 4 5
Cartoon on _____		Yes No	1 2 3 4 5
Proofread _____ articles on _____		Yes No	1 2 3 4 5
Typed articles on _____		Yes No	1 2 3 4 5
Processed mail on _____		Yes No	1 2 3 4 5
Other reading or writing: _____		Yes No	1 2 3 4 5
Conference with teacher on _____			
Teacher comments: _____			
Plans for tomorrow: _____			

Figure 23.2 Mr. Martino's Daily Work Schedule

In the **Cartoons Center** the students are supplied with drawing materials and encouraged to draw cartoons to be included in the class newsletter. The instructions in this center read, "Draw a cartoon and submit it to the newsletter editor. Be sure to check your spelling before submitting it."

In the **Proofreading Center** Mr. Martino includes a poster showing the proofreading marks he has taught the class, some dictionaries, a thesaurus, and a grammar textbook. The instructions in this center say, "Work with a partner to proofread the articles. Use the dictionaries, thesaurus, or grammar books if you need them. Use the proofreading marks to show any changes that need to be made. Return the article to the author after it has been proofread."

In the **Computer Center** students type their article using a word processing program after the article has been proofread. The students work in pairs to help each other and once an article has been typed, it is saved on the newsletter file.

Mr. Martino takes his students through the centers, carefully modeling what is expected at each center. He shows the students how they cross their name off the list at each center as they work in the center and how they list their center work on the daily work schedule each day. See Figure 23.2 for a sample of the daily work schedule Mr. Martino uses to keep track of the centers the students are using and the quality of the work they are accomplishing.

The students in Mr. Tanaka's eighth-grade humanities class are discussing *The House on Mango Street* by Sandra Cisneros (1984).

"I don't know why people think it's such a great book," says Kara. "It's just a jumble of little stories. Some of the chapters are only a page long."

"What do you think makes a book a good book?" asks Mr. Tanaka.

"I think books are good for different reasons," replies Franco. "I like this book. What bothers Kara is just what I like about the book. It's like a whole lot of small pieces that tell you about her life—Sandra Cisneros's life. It's about people she knows and little stories about different people that are interesting."

"I guess that's what I don't like," adds Kara. "The people are ordinary. They're talking about ordinary things. I like books that tell about things I don't see every day."

"I don't think they're ordinary," says Franco. "They're interesting. They have things to talk about."

"What do you write about, when you write, Kara?" asks Mr. Tanaka. "Don't you write about the people you know and the things they do?"

"I guess that's why I don't write much," admits Kara. "I never think I have anything interesting to write about."

"We need to do some thinking about where our writing ideas originate. Maybe we should write some letters to authors and find out where they get their ideas," says Mr. Tanaka.

Over the next few weeks, Mr. Tanaka plans to teach a series of prewriting strategies to his students as they prepare to combine a personal writing study with a broad study of culture and its effect on the way people live, make decisions, and conduct their lives. Mr. Tanaka knows that most of his students identify with a certain ethnic group and define their culture in that way. He is hoping to help them see the many influences at home, at school, and in their communities that help the students to define themselves. The reading of *The House on Mango Street* is an introduction to this study.

In Sandra Cisneros's book one of the characters, Esperanza, writes poetry. She shares her poetry with an aunt who later dies, leaving Esperanza no one with whom to share her poetry. Mr. Tanaka discusses this character and her poetry with his class one day.

"How many of you have ever tried to write poetry?" he asks. No one raises a hand. "Well," Mr. Tanaka says slowly. "I think it's time we tried."

A soft moan is heard in the class. "I want to introduce you to some ways of writing poems," Mr. Tanaka says. "You might have noticed that the poems Esperanza writes don't rhyme. She tries to create a picture with words."

Mr. Tanaka begins the study of poetry forms by teaching the eighth graders how to write concrete poems where they write a sentence or two creating a visual image with words and then arrange the words on the page so they create a picture. He also teaches the class the formula for writing cinquain and diamonte poems. (See Figure 23.3.)

After he demonstrates and gives the class guided practice in writing poems in these three formats, Mr. Tanaka sets up a learning center where the students can gain extra experience in writing formula poems. He uses the word banks that the class has created in learning how to write formula poems and he places the words in pocket charts so that the students can rearrange them into cinquain and diamonte poems. Once the students have built poems in the center, Mr. Tanaka encourages them to recopy them on a single sheet of paper and leave them in the box at the learning center so that he can later bind the poems into a class poetry book. Mr. Tanaka reads the poems in the box each day and frequently asks permission to read them aloud in class. Sometimes the author asks him not to tell who wrote the poem and sometimes the poem is written in the student's home language. Mr. Tanaka shows appreciation for the students' efforts and gives them feedback on ways in which they can improve their poetry. He asks students to read and translate the poems for him if he can't read the language. See Figure 23.4 to see how Mr. Tanaka's poetry center is arranged.

As the study of writing and culture continues, Mr. Tanaka gradually teaches a number of skills and strategies to his students. As the lessons are taught, Mr. Tanaka sets up additional learning centers in the classroom to provide additional practice for the students. Before long, the students are all working in centers while Mr. Tanaka works with small groups of students on the projects they are creating. The centers he has created in the classroom provide Mr. Tanaka with time to give small-group instruction while his students are working on strengthening their writing and researching skills. The centers he has created in the classroom include:

- **The Poetry Center** where students create formula poems
- **An Internet Research Center** where students can search for information related to the culture project on which they are working

A cinquain is a five-line poem with lines written in the following arrangement:

Line 1:   a one word subject with two syllables
Line 2:   four syllables describing the subject
Line 3:   six syllables of action words relating to the subject
Line 4:   eight syllables expressing a feeling or a thought about the subject
Line 5:   two syllables describing or renaming the subject

An example of a cinquain written by a second grader:

Sneakers

smelly, dirty

jumping, turning, squeaking

They are so comfortable now!

grungy

A diamonte is a seven-line poem that is written in the shape of a diamond. This poetic form helps students to demonstrate their understanding of opposites. A diamonte poem is written using this formula:

Line 1:   one noun as the subject
Line 2:   two adjectives describing the subject
Line 3:   three participles (ending in "ing") telling about the subject
Line 4:   four nouns, the first two tell about the subject, the second two tell about the opposite
Line 5:   three participles telling about the opposite
Line 6:   two adjectives describing the opposite
Line 7:   one noun that is the opposite of the subject

An example of a diamonte written by a seventh grader:

Winter

Cool and crisp

Rushing, reading, cramming

Books, papers, ball games, beaches

Sunning, swimming, playing

Hot and sweaty

Summer

Figure 23.3   Cinquain and Diamonte Formula Poetry

Adapted from Tompkins, 1998.

- **A Webbing and Clustering Center** where students create prewriting webs or clusters to get them started in writing
- **An Art Center** for creating visuals to enhance the writing and presentations being prepared
- **An Unforgettable Character Center** where a different character from *The House on Mango Street* is highlighted each day. The students read the short chapter about a character and either create an illustration for the chapter read, or write a description of a character who is brought to mind by the Cisneros character and create an illustration for the new character. This center was added after a lesson on characterization and the four ways in which authors create characters, what they say, what they do, what they think, and how they look (Tompkins, 1998).
- **A Video Center** where the students create a short video to be used as a part of their project presentation. This video should represent a part of their culture which is difficult to depict without a visual image, such as typical verbal interactions, body language, personal space, or important artifacts. The video created in this center may be a simulation or a series of video clips made in the community or home, edited together using the simple editing equipment in the center.

Figure 23.4 Mr. Tanaka's Poetry Center

- **The Elements of Culture Center** where Mr. Tanaka selects a quote from Edward T. Hall's book *Beyond Culture* (1981) and posts it each day. The students are instructed to read the quote and respond to it by talking into the tape recorder at the center. They may work alone or in pairs and they may respond in English or their home language. After they have reflected on the quote of the day they are to include the quote and their reflection in their culture report in some way, as a visual, a part of a video clip, or in writing. The quotes Mr. Tanaka uses include thoughts like:

> It (time) is also tangible; they speak of it as being saved, spent, wasted, lost, made up, accelerated, slowed down, crawling, and running out. (p. 19)

> Modern education has left us with the illusion that a lot is known about learning, that real learning goes on in the school, and that if it doesn't happen in a school or under the aegis of a school (like the year abroad), it has no validity. (p. 35)

> Each culture has its own characteristic manner of locomotion, sitting, standing, reclining, and gesturing. (p. 75)

At the end of the month-long study, Mr. Tanaka's students have a new vision of culture and its place in shaping their beliefs and priorities. They discuss differences in culture with peers of their same ethnic background and discover that their assumptions are not identical. The learning centers have given them opportunities to expand their skills with practice over time. The students have had extensive experience in using the Web for research and they have all read and discussed two pieces of literature that have helped them to broaden their understanding of literature, poetry and culture, *The House on Mango Street* and *Beyond Culture*.

CONCLUSION

The use of learning centers in the classroom is a powerful way to encourage students to practice the new skills they are gaining. Centers should be carefully explained to students so that they understand what is expected of them as they use the center. Both behavior and learning expectations must be made clear in order for the centers to support learning.

Well-planned centers enable students to refine their skills, expand their uses of newly acquired skills, and create new and different ways to demonstrate their learning. In order to harness the power of learning centers in the classroom students must be encouraged to go beyond basic skill practice and find ways to be creative. Students should see their efforts recognized, valued, and celebrated if they are to expend maximum effort in learning center work.

References

Cisneros, S. (1984). *The house on Mango Street.* New York: Vintage Books (Random House).

Hall, E. (1981). *Beyond culture.* New York: Doubleday.

Tompkins, G. (1998). *Language arts: Content and teaching strategies* (4th ed.). Upper Saddle River, NJ: Merrill/Prentice Hall.

LEARNING STRATEGY INSTRUCTION

24

L earning strategy instruction (Gagne, 1985) is based on supporting the students to understand their own learning and to monitor the methods and results of strategies they use in reading, writing, discussions, and research. Learning strategy instruction is important in supporting English language learners to employ self-monitoring and self-help approaches in order to be successful in school (Chamot & O'Malley, 1994). Three areas of instruction are addressed in learning strategy instruction. All three of the areas are self-related. The learners focus on strategies they can use to improve their own success in school. The three areas of learning strategies included in learning strategy instruction are metacognitive strategies, cognitive strategies, and social/affective strategies.

Metacognitive strategies include having a plan for learning, monitoring the learning that is taking place, and evaluating how well content has been learned. **Cognitive strategies** include how to manipulate material mentally or physically in order to facilitate learning. **Social/affective strategies** include ways to interact with others or control your own emotions in ways that support your learning. See Figure 24.1 for descriptions of some of the strategies included in each category.

STEP BY STEP

The steps in teaching learning strategies are:

1. Select the strategy to be taught by thinking about the curriculum to be studied and the demands it will make on the learner. Plan to teach only a few strategies at first, giving the students opportunities to practice the strategies well before introducing new ones.
2. Develop students' self-awareness by having them reflect on how they approach a learning task. Remind them of the cooperative learning activities they have been involved with and what they have learned about their approaches to learning during the debriefing sessions. See Figure 24.2 for suggestions of additional introductory activities.

Activity	Description
Brainstorming	Students suggest ways they have used in studying material. No judgment is made. The list is made and then students can use the list to suggest learning tasks that would match well with the strategies suggested. The benefit of this activity is to introduce the idea that there are many learning strategies and students have choices in approaches.
Partner interviews	Students pair up and interview each other about the strategies they use for studying. After the interviews, each student describes one strategy shared by the partner.
Questionnaires	Teacher prepares a questionnaire about strategy usage, which the students fill out. The results are tabulated and used as a basis for a group discussion.
Task think-aloud	Students demonstrate a task, such as tying shoes, and think-aloud to demonstrate the strategies they use. After one student demonstrates the task think-aloud, a student who has a different approach is given an opportunity to demonstrate it.
Strategy list think	A list of strategies such as note cards, diagrams, webs, and oral review are listed on the board and students give suggestions as to the learning tasks that would be appropriate for their use. Example: Note cards don't work for studying for a spelling test but do work for preparing an oral presentation.

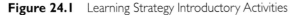

Figure 24.1   Learning Strategy Introductory Activities

3. Model the strategy you are teaching. Call the strategy by its name each time you model it. Explain how the strategy works to support the students' learning. Give examples of instances in which the strategy will be helpful.
4. Provide an opportunity for the students to practice using the strategy.
5. Hold an evaluation discussion. Ask the students to demonstrate how they used the strategy and what was difficult for them. Provide a self-evaluation tool, or scoring rubric, for them to use in evaluating their strategy use. See Figure 24.3 for strategy self-evaluation tools.
6. Have the students make strategy posters to display in the classroom, which explain the steps in the strategy use. Refer to those posters frequently when making assignments. Help the students to see that they have choices in strategies to use and that strategies can be used in many different contexts and learning tasks.

Metacognitive Strategies	
Planning	Preview the material in order to plan a way to organize it for use.
Organizing	Plan the method of study to be used. Parts of the material to be studied and the sequence of study is determined.
Selective attention	Focus on key words or concepts to be learned.
Self-management	Organize a plan for studying, including time and place.
Monitoring comprehension	Check your comprehension during reading or listening
Monitoring production	Focus on your speech or writing while it is happening.
Self-assessment	Plan ways to check on your learning through such things as learning logs, reflective journals, and checklists.
Cognitive Strategies	
Referring	Use research and resource materials such as dictionaries, encyclopedias, word walls, etc.
Classifying	Organize like materials together. Grouping the knowledge or concepts to be learned.
Note taking	Write down important information and key words to be learned.
Activating prior knowledge	Make connections between what is being studied and your experiences.
Summarizing	Review the main ideas either orally or in writing.
Deduction or induction	Look for patterns in order to use a rule or make one.
Imagery	Use mental or drawn pictures to aid in memory or understanding.

Figure 24.2   Categories of Learning Strategy Instruction and Their Descriptions

Strategy Use Rubric

Student's Name _____

Learning Strategy _____

Each time you use a learning strategy, place an **X** on the continuum to show how well you think you used it.

< – >

Poorly	OK	Well
I did not follow the steps well.	I did follow the steps. I didn't give it my full attention.	I followed the steps and was successful.

Strategies used this week:	Subject area:	Effectiveness
_____	_____	1 2 3 4 5
_____	_____	1 2 3 4 5
_____	_____	1 2 3 4 5
_____	_____	1 2 3 4 5

Figure 24.3   Learning Strategy Self-Evaluation Tools

APPLICATIONS AND EXAMPLES

Some of Ms. Hernandez's second graders are consistently failing their weekly spelling tests. Ms. Hernandez realizes that some of the students don't seem to have strategies to use in studying their words. She begins the learning strategy instruction by initiating a conversation with the students on Monday morning as she is getting ready to list the new words for the week.

"How are you studying the words for your spelling test?" Ms. Hernandez asks the class.

"I write the words on a big piece of paper and hang it on my bulletin board at home," replies Amanda. "I look at the words every day and spell them to myself."

"I make flash cards and use them to practice writing the words," says Carlos.

"Let's make a list of all the methods we use to study spelling words," says Ms. Hernandez. She writes *Make a poster* and *Make flash cards* on the chalkboard. As the students add suggestions, the list grows. When the students have exhausted their ideas for studying the words, Ms. Hernandez says, "I want to show you one way of studying the words that I used when I was in second grade. You may find it helpful."

Ms. Hernandez gives each student ten 3-by-5 cards. As she writes the new spelling words on the board, she spells them aloud and the students write them on their 3-by-5 cards.

"Now, let me show you how to use the cards," Ms. Hernandez says. "You look at one card at a time. You spell the word aloud as you look at the card." She then demonstrates with one word. "These, t-h-e-s-e, these."

"Next, you look at the word again, turn the card over and write the word." She demonstrates this step.

"You turn the card back over and check to make sure you spelled the word correctly. You repeat the spelling to yourself before you move on to the next card."

Ms. Hernandez then instructs the students to go through the procedure with their new words. While they are practicing, she walks around the room, stopping to give encouragement and to ask questions about the meanings of the words or to ask students to use a word in a sentence.

After their practice session, Ms. Hernandez gives the class a practice test. A number of the students get a perfect score on the test.

"How do you think this method works?" Ms. Hernandez asks the class.

"I think it works great!" says Erma. "I never got a hundred on Monday before."

"You will want to use this strategy several times this week to make sure you really know the words," Ms. Hernandez reminds the students. "I chose these words because they are words you often misspell in your writing so be sure to double-check your spelling of them in your writing this week, too."

Ms. Hernandez is supporting the students' use of learning strategies in response to a concern she has about their study strategies. She introduces the strategy by helping the students recognize that it is necessary to have a strategy for studying. She models one strategy and gives the students practice in using it. She then gives an evaluation exercise, the spelling test, and gives the students an opportunity to discuss their use of the strategy and how it works. She also relates the strategy to their assignments and why they would want to use the strategy.

••

Ms. Teale has a number of students in her eighth-grade math class who do not turn in homework on a regular basis. She devises a student questionnaire to determine the students' approaches to doing homework. Her questionnaire is shown in Figure 24.4.

Ms. Teale does an analysis of the results of her homework questionnaire, but before she shares it with the class she asks the students to predict what she found when she compared their responses on the questionnaire to their grades in the class. She puts the students into groups of three and asks them to discuss the questionnaire and which of the responses were most important in assuring that homework was done regularly and grades were good. Each group shares their predictions which are remarkably similar. The consensus is that doing homework regularly, at a set time and place, is most helpful.

Ms. Teale then asks the students to discuss the barriers they encounter in doing homework. They come up with a list of barriers:

no place to study
younger brothers and sisters interfere
television is always on
lack of motivation
after-school jobs

The students brainstorm ways to overcome the barriers to doing homework. Their suggestions include talking to their parents and finding a place in the house for them to do homework, setting up a schedule, asking that the television be turned off for a set amount of time each evening, and setting up a homework club so the younger siblings are all doing homework, too.

Ms. Teale does a time management demonstration where she demonstrates how she plans the ways she uses her time between the end of the school day and bed time. She gives each student a daily planning paper that divides the hours from 3 P.M. until 11 P.M. into half-hour segments. She leads the students through a planning activity in which they examine the ways they use their time and helps them to find an hour each evening in which they could do homework. Several of the students are surprised at the amount of time they spend watching television or talking on the telephone.

Ms. Teale provides a role-play activity where the students pair up and conduct a conversation as if they are talking to their family about the homework problem and giving suggestions as to how

Name _____

Please mark your answer to each question with an **X** placed at the appropriate place on the continuum or checklist.

1. I do homework assignments

< – >
Never   Sometimes   About half   Most of   Always
                                      the time   the time

2. I do homework

____ while watching TV or listening to the radio

____ at the kitchen table

____ in my room   ____ on my bed   ____ at my desk

____ right after school   ____ after dinner   ____ right before I go to bed

3. My parents ask me if I have homework

< – >
Never   Sometimes   About half   Most of   Always
                                      the time   the time

4. I feel the practice I get doing homework is

< – >
a waste   somewhat helpful   helpful   important   very important
of time

5. I feel the weight given to homework assignments in this class is

< – >
too much   about right   too little

Figure 24.4   Homework Questionnaire

it can be solved. The students practice sharing their daily planning sheets with their families and enlisting their support in implementing a homework hour for the family. Ms. Teale emphasizes how helpful this family approach will be to the younger students in the family.

At the end of the next week, Ms. Teale asks each of her students to write a brief reflection on the homework issue and whether or not their planning and family discussions were helpful. Those students who carried through on the assignment are asked to share their reflections with the class. Although she still has a few students not completing homework, Ms. Teale feels that the exercise was successful for several of the students. The number of homework assignments being submitted has increased and several of the students are sharing success stories involving their younger brothers and sisters.

CONCLUSION

Learning strategy instruction helps students to become more responsible for their own success in school. Teaching students how to monitor their own understanding and identify, plan, and implement ways to help themselves to understand and evaluate the effectiveness of the strategies being used supports their motivation to learn and their self-confidence.

Although study skills have been taught in school for a number of years, learning strategy instruction introduces the idea that students don't always learn in the same ways. The individual learning style and strong intelligences (see the chapter on Multiple Intelligences) become important in identifying strategies that work for each individual.

References

Chamot, A., & O'Malley, J. (1994). *The CALLA handbook.* Reading, MA: Addison-Wesley.
Gagne, E. (1985). *The cognitive psychology of school learning.* Boston: Little, Brown.

LEVELED QUESTIONS

25

....

SUPPORTS

- ● Comprehensible input
- ● Increased verbal interaction
- ✔ Contextualized language
- ✔ Reduced anxiety
- ● Active involvement of the learner

....

Leveled questions are used when teachers adapt the way they ask questions so that students can answer or respond to them according to their language acquisition stage (Krashen & Terrell, 1983). In order to level questions, the teacher must observe the students and note the way in which they interact in English. Once the teacher knows the level at which the student interacts in English, the questions the teacher poses to the student can be adjusted to assure the student's success in answering. This may involve the teacher using gestures, visuals, or slowing the speech slightly while asking the question. The teacher asks the question in a way that encourages the student to answer by pointing to a visual, giving a one-word response or a complete sentence or explanation depending upon the student's level of language acquisition. The teacher's role in using this strategy involves knowing the student's level of English acquisition and providing enough context in the question so that the student can respond, either verbally or nonverbally, with understanding and confidence.

STEP BY STEP

The steps in using leveled questions are:

1. Observe your students to determine their current levels of interaction in English. On a class list, indicate whether each student is at the preproduction stage, early production stage, speech emergent stage, or intermediate fluency stage. See Figure 25.1 for a description of students' English proficiency at each of these stages. This list will need to be kept up to date as you work with the students and observe their responses.

2. Determine which visuals, artifacts, or gestures you will need to make your meaning clear to the students whose understanding of English is limited. Gather these support materials to use during the presentation of the lesson and your questioning. Remember that English language learners feel more comfortable participating when they have ways to demonstrate their understanding with visuals and support materials.

3. Plan a series of questions that will help you to involve your students and determine their levels of understanding of the material you will be teaching. In the beginning it is helpful

Stage	Appropriate Expectations
Preproduction	Nodding, pointing, physically demonstrating
Early production	One or two word responses, making choices from given language samples (Is it a whale or a dolphin?)
Speech emergence	Phrase or short sentences (expect grammar errors)
Intermediate fluency	Longer sentences, fewer grammar errors

Figure 25.1 Appropriate Expectations for Students at Different Speech Stages

Adapted from Krashen & Terrell, 1983.

to plan a series of questions at different levels so that you can move around the room and use levels of questions for appropriate students without too much hesitation or confusion. See Figure 25.2 for suggestions.

4. Use the list of students and speech levels as a checklist to make sure that you are involving all the students in discussion and questioning and that you are adapting the levels of your questions to their changing language acquisition levels.

Stage	Question or Cue
Preproduction	"Show me . . . ." "Which of these . . . ?"
Early production	"Is it the _____ one or the _____ one?" Questions that can be answered with one or two words.
Speech emergence	"Did this happen at the beginning or at the end?" "What happened next?" "Where did you find the answer?"
Intermediate fluency	"How did you . . . ?" "What was the character trying to do?"

Figure 25.2 Appropriate Questions for Speech Stages

Adapted from Krashen & Terrell, 1983.

APPLICATIONS AND EXAMPLES

Leveled questions can be used at all grade levels and in all curricular areas. For example, in Ms. Chanis's first-grade class the children are using manipulative to join sets and build number sentences. As Ms. Chanis moves around the room observing the students at work and asking questions, she varies the way the questions are asked according to the language acquisition stages of her students. As she stops at Hnu's table she asks Hnu to show her a set of six objects. Because Hnu is functioning at the preproduction stage in English, Ms. Chanis asks, "Show me 6." Hnu quickly counts out 6 blocks and lines them up on her desk. Ms. Chanis says, "Yes! 1,2,3,4,5,6. You showed me 6." She points to the blocks as she counts them and smiles at Hnu.

By keeping her sentence short and using a sentence form that has been modeled during the lesson introduction Ms. Chanis is supporting Hnu's successful participation in the math lesson.

As Ms. Chanis moves to other students she adjusts her questions to the language stages of the children. She is keeping track of the students with whom she interacts by checking their names off on a checklist, which also helps her to keep track of the students' language stages.

Ms. Chanis asks an early production student to tell her how many objects are in the set on his desk. A speech emergence student is asked to give the number sentence for the set of two red blocks added to the set of four green blocks. An intermediate fluency student is asked to tell a story about a picture of a group of two pigs joining a group of four pigs wallowing in the mud.

Each leveled question is followed by a brief modeling of language to help support the students in incorporating more English speech into their verbal interactions. A student responds with one word and then listens as Ms. Chanis models the use of that one word in a short sentence. A student who responds with a short phrase will hear a confirmation that the phrase is correct, but then Ms. Chanis will scaffold that student's response by extending the phrase into a full sentence. Even in math, Ms. Chanis is aware of the need to continually scaffold language for her English language learners.

Leveled questions are appropriate at any grade level as long as there are students who need them in order to successfully participate in class interactions. In Mr. Burrow's ninth-grade class there are a number of English language learners who need to have leveled questions in order to participate in class discussions and questioning periods.

As Mr. Burrows reviews the Cuban missile crisis with his students, he wants to discuss the reason for concern at the time. Mr. Burrows structures a series of questions to help his students locate Cuba on the map and recognize the geographic proximity to the United States, which was the reason for concern.

To encourage participation by a preproduction stage student, Mr. Burrows says, "Show me the country of Cuba on the map." The student then uses the map in the classroom to point to Cuba.

Mr. Burrows asks an early production student to go to the map and look at it carefully. He then asks, "What is the name of the ocean or sea in which Cuba is located? Show me where you found that information on the map."

For a speech emergence student he asks, "How far is Cuba from the United States?" He follows up that question with a request to "Show Cuba and Florida on the map."

For an Intermediate Fluency student Mr. Burrows asks, "Why was President Kennedy so concerned about the build-up of missiles in Cuba in the early 60s?"

The discussion and questions continue, and the map is used to ensure that the students are able to understand the main points of the discussion. Mr. Burrows models English sentences as he points out the countries on the map and makes it clear that President Kennedy was concerned because the Soviet Union was building up missiles very close to American shores. Mr. Burrows then uses small ship pictures placed on the map to illustrate how the United States blockaded the approaches to Cuba and caused the Soviet ships carrying missiles to return home. Mr. Burrows is aware of the need to provide visuals to support his English language learners' comprehension of English, but he is also aware that their understanding of spoken English is better than their ability to produce English sentences. He finds ways to make himself understood and to actively involve all of his students.

CONCLUSION

The use of leveled questions in the classroom requires that the teacher know the stages of language development in which each student is functioning. It also requires that the teacher understand appropriate expectations of students in each stage of language development. Although this knowledge is vital it is not difficult information to obtain if the teacher is willing to observe the students carefully.

After gathering this knowledge and establishing a method for updating the information regularly, the teacher is ready to use leveled questions to ensure that each student in the class is provided with opportunities to participate fully. The effectiveness of this strategy stems from several sources. The students become more fully engaged in the lessons when their anxiety levels are reduced, their participation supports their understanding, and their self-confidence and language use increases. All of these factors contribute to the reduction of classroom management challenges as well.

References

Krashen, S., & Terrell, T. (1983). *The natural approach: Language acquisition in the classroom.* Oxford: Pergamon Press.

Suggested Readings

Diaz-Rico, L. T., & Weed, K. Z. (1995). *The crosscultural, language, and academic development handbook.* Needham Heights, MA: Allyn and Bacon.
Gibbons, P. (1993). *Learning to learn in a second language.* Portsmouth, NH: Heinemann.

MANIPULATIVE STRATEGIES

26

SUPPORTS

- Comprehensible input
- Contextualized language
- ✔ Reduced anxiety
- Active involvement of the learner

Manipulatives are concrete devices provided so that students can move them, manipulate them, to support their thinking and learning. Although they are most often used in math and science, they can be very helpful in supporting language understanding in other subject areas. For manipulatives to be used effectively the teacher must demonstrate their use, while simultaneously modeling the connection to academic language. Manipulatives can be concrete representations of the concepts being taught as in models of the human body, which can be disassembled for study, or non-representative manipulatives such as small wooden cubes used for counting and math calculations. The concrete representation manipulatives are often used to support the development of academic vocabulary, while the non-representative manipulatives are used to manipulate an abstract concept such as number. See Figure 26.1 for suggestions for using manipulatives.

STEP BY STEP

The steps in the use of manipulatives are:

1. Identify the concept to be taught and the parts of the concept that could be represented by a concrete object of some kind. Design a teaching plan that allows the demonstration of the concept using the manipulatives as examples.
2. Demonstrate the use of the manipulatives as you explain the concept to the students. Use the demonstration to connect the manipulative, the concept, and any new vocabulary. Model the way you expect the students to use the manipulatives.
3. Provide guided practice in the use of the manipulatives. Walk the students through the procedure to be used, demonstrating how to use the manipulatives and connecting the manipulatives to the vocabulary to be learned.
4. Give the students time to use the manipulatives independently while you circulate around the classroom observing, giving feedback, and scaffolding language usage.
5. Celebrate the students' demonstration of learning, again taking the opportunity to connect the manipulatives to the vocabulary and concepts learned.

Subject Area	Suggested Manipulative Use
Vocabulary	• Miniatures or wooden cut-outs of objects • Colored blocks to teach colors, singular, plural forms • Attribute blocks to teach shapes, sizes, texture, color • Dolls to teach body parts
Mathematics	• Beans for counters • Small props for acting out word problems • Geometric shapes cut into fractional parts • Colored linking cubes for building patterns • Measuring cups and containers for studying measurement
Science	• Human body models • Realia for experiments • Styrofoam balls and toothpicks for construction • Magnets, batteries, iron filings

Figure 26.1 Manipulatives That Might Be Used in Various Subject Areas

APPLICATIONS AND EXAMPLES

Mr. Sanchez is using story props to teach his first graders the use of a Venn diagram. Two hula hoops are laid on the floor and the students are sitting around them. In front of each student are three or four props from one of the two versions of *Stone Soup,* which the class has read together in the past few days.

"In the green hoop we will put the props from the newer version of *Stone Soup* (McGovern, 1968) that we read first," Mr. Sanchez says as he places the McGovern version of the book in the center of the green hoop. "In the red hoop we will put the props from the other version of the story," says Mr. Sanchez as he places the Brown (1947) version of the book in the center of the red hoop.

"Now watch what I am going to do," he says as he lifts one hoop and lays it so it overlaps the other one. "Now we have a section of the hoops that overlap. When you see two circles that overlap like this, it is called a Venn diagram. The part that overlaps is where we will put the props that show something that was the same in both versions of the story. Who has something that was in both versions of the story?"

Petra holds up a stone. Mr. Sanchez nods and smiles as he says, "Yes, Petra. There was a stone in each version. That's why it was called *Stone Soup*. Where should we put the stone?"

Petra smiles at Mr. Sanchez but makes no move to place the stone. Mr. Sanchez continues, "Put the stone in here, Petra," he says as he motions to the overlap in the hoops. "The stone was in the first story," he makes a circular motion to indicate the green hoop and points to the first book. "The stone was in the second story," he repeats the motion with the red hoop and the second book. "So we put the stone in here," he points to the overlap and Petra puts the stone in the correct place.

"Very good! The stone was in both stories," Mr. Sanchez smiles at Petra and points to both books.

The process is repeated with the students making decisions about the proper placement of each of the props in the Venn diagram. As they place the props the students talk about whether or not they were in both stories. When there is disagreement Mr. Sanchez urges them to look in the book. When all the props have been placed Mr. Sanchez pairs the students to work together on another Venn diagram. He gives each pair of students a large laminated piece of construction paper with a Venn diagram drawn on it. He gives each pair a set of pictures of the same set of props they have just used. The partners are to reenact the sorting of the props and recreate the Venn diagram they have just done as a class. The only addition to the task is a set of word cards that identify each prop. The partners must read the words and put them into the Venn diagram along with the props. There is a lot of conversation among the pairs, in home languages and English, as the students make decisions about the placement of the props and words. Occasionally a student will come to get one of the versions of the story to prove a point. As the pairs complete their work they raise their hands and Mr. Sanchez comes to them so they can read the words they have placed on the diagram and explain their diagram. Mr. Sanchez uses this time to reinforce word identification skills, their pronunciation of the vocabulary, and their correct use of the Venn diagram.

In this use of manipulatives Mr. Sanchez has used concrete manipulatives, the props. He then moved to semi-concrete manipulatives, the pictures. Finally, he provided abstract manipulatives, the words. He also used partner work to facilitate the use of home languages to communicate and solve problems and supported the students as they reported their results in English.

• •

Older students also benefit from the use of manipulatives in the classroom. As Ms. Yang's fifth graders are studying the human body, she provides a model of each of the systems of the body that contains removable parts so the students can take the model apart, closely examine the parts, and reassemble the model. They are completing a diagram of each system as a part of a human body notebook they are compiling.

Ms. Yang has put together groups of four students to work cooperatively to disassemble the model, use the parts of the model to help them label their diagrams, and then reassemble the model. The group works together to test each other on the names of the body parts and exactly where the parts fit into the system. Each group member must help the others to learn each of the body parts, where it fits in the model, how it is spelled, and where the label goes on the diagram in their notebooks. Everyone knows that the diagrams must be completed again on Friday as a test. Each group that has every member pass the test with at least an 80% will get extra recess time on Friday afternoon, so everyone is anxious to help each other learn. No one wants to be sitting inside studying for a human body retest while everyone else is outside playing on Friday afternoon.

• •

CONCLUSION

The use of manipulatives, whether they are real objects that help students to relate language to concepts or representational objects such as blocks, counters, or beans are often supportive to students' understanding. Presenting new concepts in a concrete way, before moving to semi-concrete representations such as pictures and finally to abstract symbols, helps students to make the gradual switch from the concrete to the abstract form of thinking. Manipulatives can be used in many ways, but careful thought should be given to connecting the vocabulary, concepts, and thought processes through demonstration, in much the same way vocabulary is introduced to infants. For example, "This is a cup. We drink from a cup," as the cup is being shown and demonstrated.

References

Brown, M. (1947). *Stone Soup*. New York: Aladdin/Macmillan.
McGovern, A. (1968). *Stone Soup*. New York: Scholastic.

MODELED TALK

27

SUPPORTS

- Comprehensible input
- Contextualized language
- ✔ Reduced anxiety
- ✔ Active involvement of the learner

Modeled talk (Herrell, 1999), the concurrent verbal explanation and physical demonstration of directions or concepts, is one of the simplest and most powerful strategies for use with English language learners. It takes some preplanning and practice but can soon become a habit for effective teachers. Modeled talk is the use of gestures, visuals, and demonstrations as explanations are made. Gestures and modeling provide examples for learners to follow and lowers their anxiety since they know exactly what to do because they have seen the directions or content modeled.

▶ STEP BY STEP

The steps in implementing modeled talk are:

1. Identify the lesson to be taught and the materials to be used. Think about what you plan to say to explain the lesson and the directions to the students. Prepare the materials you will be asking the students to use so that you have an example to show and, if necessary, examples in various stages of completion. Design gestures that will help the students to understand exactly what will be expected of them without having to rely on English vocabulary for understanding.

2. Practice your talk in front of a mirror to determine if your instructions, modeling, and gestures convey the message you want the students to understand.

3. Design a standard visual that will be used on a regular basis, if the lesson or directions require that the students follow a sequence of instructions, so the students become accustomed to looking for this visual for support in remembering the sequence. Simple, numbered drawings work well for this. A set of standard drawings, laminated and placed in sequence on the chalkboard, can be used again and again for different activities. A picture of a pair of scissors, for example, always reminds the students that the next step is to cut, while a picture of a crayon serves to remind them to color.

4. Review the steps the students are to take, after you have delivered your modeled talk. Use the visual you have created to reinforce the students' reference to them for support in remembering what to do. During the section of the lesson when the students are performing the activities you have explained, refer to the visuals whenever there is a question about what to do next so that the students practice the use of them. See Figure 27.1 for suggestions of props and visuals that support modeled talks.

Props	Visuals
Any textbooks to be used Scissors, tape, rulers, pencils, notebooks that will be needed Realia whenever vocabulary will be new Word cards for any new vocabulary to be written Maps, globes, manipulatives, examples of products to be made	Numbered charts showing sequence to be followed Diagrams showing a recap of directions given Standard illustrations for scissors (for directions to cut), crayon (for directions to color), pencil (for directions to write), computer (when it is to be used), ruler (for directions to measure), paintbrush (for directions to paint)

Figure 27.1   Props and Visuals to Support Modeled Talk

APPLICATIONS AND EXAMPLES

Ms. Milsovic is using modeled talk to explain the day's learning centers to her kindergarten class of English language learners. As she begins, she is sitting in a small chair as the students sit on the floor in front of her.

"When I play the music," Ms. Milsovic says as she points to herself and then briefly touches the play button on the tape player so the children hear a short section of the music they use as a signal to change activities, "you (indicates the children) will go to centers (she motions toward the centers)."

"First (she holds up one finger), you will go to the planning board." As she says this she signals for them to follow her to the planning board. The planning board is made of a large metal automotive drip pan. It has photographs of each of the centers attached by magnetic tape across the top of it and room for children's names on magnets under each of the center pictures.

"You will look for your name," Ms. Milsovic continues as she shows the children the name cards, which are not yet attached to the board. She reads a few of the names so the children understand what is written on the name cards.

"If Cher's name is under this center," she points to the picture of the art center, "he will go to the art center first." She motions for the children to follow Cher to the art center.

At the art center Ms. Milsovic shows the children exactly what they will do there. She demonstrates each step as she talks about it. On this particular day the children are studying about frogs and toads and they are using green paper plates to make frogs with long curled tongues. Ms. Milsovic shows them how to make the frog and posts a visual with drawings that demonstrate what to do first, second, and third. After she demonstrates, she refers to the visual and asks one of the children to tell her what to do at each step. See Figure 27.2 for an example of the visual Ms. Milsovic used.

Each center is carefully modeled and key English vocabulary is taught and practiced. When all the centers have been explained, the children and Ms. Milsovic return to the planning board and the names of the children are placed on the board so they know where do go first. Once this is done, Ms. Milsovic plays the music on the tape recorder which signals that it's time to move to centers. Since the children know what to do at each center and there are visuals available at each center to remind them, in case they forget, Ms. Milsovic is able to work with small groups of students at the writing center using interactive writing to teach them how to write words describing frogs. The children are secure in their understanding of what is expected of them.

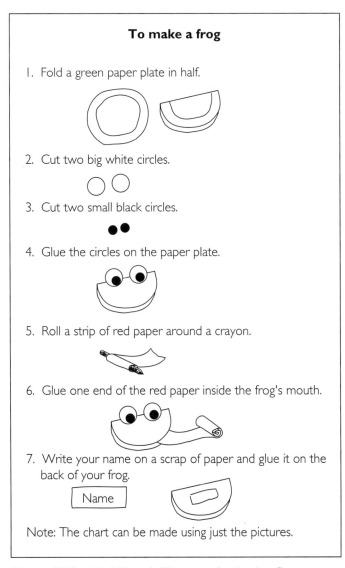

To make a frog

1. Fold a green paper plate in half.

2. Cut two big white circles.

3. Cut two small black circles.

4. Glue the circles on the paper plate.

5. Roll a strip of red paper around a crayon.

6. Glue one end of the red paper inside the frog's mouth.

7. Write your name on a scrap of paper and glue it on the back of your frog.

Name

Note: The chart can be made using just the pictures.

Figure 27.2   Ms. Milsovic's Directions for the Art Center

Ms. Delgado is demonstrating how to make four-corner books for her fifth graders who are always looking for new ways to celebrate the books they have read. Since the students will be making their books while Ms. Delgado is holding literature discussions, she wants to make sure that they know exactly what to do. She displays a poster that shows each of the steps in their assignment and then she gives a modeled talk demonstrating the steps in the process. Figure 27.3 shows the poster Ms. Delgado displays.

As Ms. Delgado demonstrates the making of a four-corner book, she refers to the steps listed on the poster. "First," she says as she points to the number one on the poster, "you fold a piece of paper like this." She demonstrates and then points to the drawing on the poster. Ms. Delgado writes a numeral one on the chalkboard and puts the sample she has started under the number one.

"Second," she continues, as she points to the number two on the poster, "you fold the paper in half, this way." She takes a premade sample which was completed in step number one, demonstrates step number two, and then points to the drawing on the poster, writes a numeral two on the chalkboard, and puts sample number two under it.

"Third," she says as she points to the number three on the poster, "you cut on the folds you just made." She demonstrates the cutting on an additional sample, makes a numeral three on the

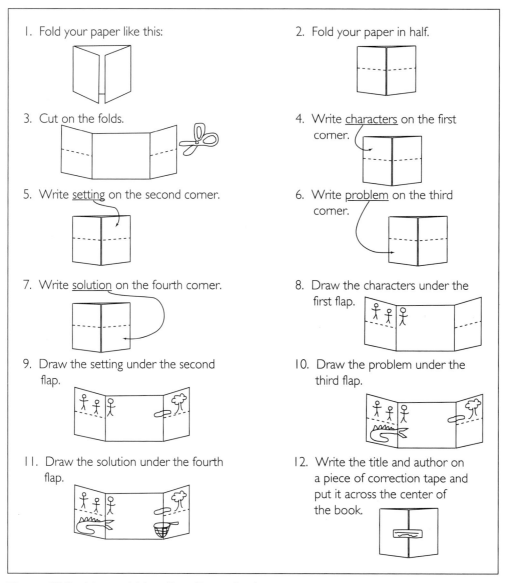

1. Fold your paper like this:
2. Fold your paper in half.
3. Cut on the folds.
4. Write <u>characters</u> on the first corner.
5. Write <u>setting</u> on the second corner.
6. Write <u>problem</u> on the third corner.
7. Write <u>solution</u> on the fourth corner.
8. Draw the characters under the first flap.
9. Draw the setting under the second flap.
10. Draw the problem under the third flap.
11. Draw the solution under the fourth flap.
12. Write the title and author on a piece of correction tape and put it across the center of the book.

Figure 27.3   How to Make a Four-Corner Book

chalkboard and puts sample number three under it. At this point she has a sample at each stage of the preparation sitting along the chalk tray for the students to examine if the need arises.

Next she takes a premade sample of the four-corner book she has just shown how to make and writes CHARACTERS on one corner. "You write the word *characters* on the first corner," she says as she demonstrates.

Ms. Delgado models each step, adding the word *setting* on the second corner, the word *problem* on the third corner, and the word *solution* on the fourth corner. She then lifts the flap on which the word *characters* is written and demonstrates the drawing of the main characters of her book and repeats the process with each of the four corners.

Last of all, Ms. Delgado takes a piece of wide correction tape and puts it across the middle of her four-corner book and writes the title and author of the book on it. As she does each of these steps she refers the students to the poster and leaves a sample on the chalkboard for them to examine as they are making their own books. Once she has completed the modeled talk, she puts the supplies out on a table for the students to use and calls a literature discussion group together. The rest of the class is busily engaged in making four-corner books and her group is not disturbed.

They know how to make their books and know they will have an opportunity to share the books after Ms. Delgado finishes working with her groups. This was explained to them as a part of the modeled talk—and it's on the poster.

● ●

CONCLUSION

Modeled talk is helpful in lowering students' anxiety because they know what is expected of them. It serves another important function when the teacher uses it consistently. English speaking students often learn how to model talk and use it when explaining procedures and concepts to English language learners in the classroom. Students' use of modeled talk to other students increases the opportunities for English language learners to interact successfully with their peers and it builds feelings of community within the classroom.

References

Herrell, A. (1999). Modeling talk to support comprehension in young children. *Kindergarten Education: Research, Theory, and Practice, 3,* 29–42.

MULTIMEDIA PRESENTATIONS

28

SUPPORTS

- Comprehensible input
- ✔ Increased verbal interaction
- Contextualized language
- ✔ Reduced anxiety
- ✔ Active involvement of the learner

Multimedia presentations (Diaz-Rico & Weed, 1995) involve the use of media such as audio and video equipment (VCRs, video disk players, video cameras), computers and related software and Internet sources to do research, publish, and make classroom presentations. In recent years the availability of computer multimedia technology, Internet access, and materials in multiple languages has greatly improved, making the use of these resources in the classroom more practical. The use of multimedia presentations with English language learners is especially important because of flexibility the approach lends in both teaching and learning. Students benefit when teachers use multimedia in presenting lessons because the media usage adds context to the language and the lessons. Students using multimedia to gain access to information in multiple languages are supported in their learning. When students use multimedia to present their research, writings, and projects, they can document and present their growing capabilities without the constraints encountered when making oral reports.

In the use of multimedia it is not just the finished product—the report or presentation—but also the processes of exploring, synthesizing, and summarizing that with technology creates opportunities for meaningful learning to take place.

The use of multimedia in the classroom presents some challenges for both teachers and students. In fact, a teacher without experience in this approach is sometimes overwhelmed with both the possibilities and the potential barriers. However, there are many resources available to teachers in the use of multimedia in the classroom. See Figure 28.1 for a partial list of resources for more information.

STEP BY STEP

The steps in implementing multimedia presentations are:

1. Model the use of multimedia by incorporating video clips, overhead projector, audio tapes, and other media as you teach. Emphasize how the use of the media allows you to visually or auditorally demonstrate as you teach. Before you ask students to use multimedia ap-

Books

Herrell, A. & Fowler, J. (1997). *Camcorder in the classroom: Using the videocamera to enrich curriculum.* Upper Saddle River, NJ: Macmillan/Prentice Hall.

Lewis, C. (1997). *Exploring multimedia.* New York: DK Publishing.

Serim, F., & Koch, M. (1996). *NetLearning: Why teachers use the Internet.* Sebastopol, CA: Songline Publications.

Articles

Harris, J. (series of articles). Mining the Internet. *The Computing Teacher.*
http://www.ed.uiuc.edu/Mining/Overview.html

Rogers, A., Andres, Y., Jacks, M., & Clauset, T. (1990). Telecommunicating in the classroom: Keys to successful telecommunicating. *The Computing Teacher, 17,* 25–28.
(On-line: http://www.gsn.org)

Educational Web Sites

Bilingual and Multicultural Education
Bilingual ESL Network www.redmundial.com/ben.htm
Culture Pages www.hut.fi/-rvilmi/Project/Culture/
CyberSpanish Website www.actlab.utexas.edu/-seagull/spanglist.html
Elementary Spanish Curriculum www.veen.com/Veen/Leslie/Curriculum/
International E-Mail Classroom Connections www.stolaf.edu/network/iecc/
NABE: Instructional Technology (ITSIG) www.redmundial.com/nabe/it.htm
National Clearinghouse for Bilingual Education (NCBE) www.ncbe.gwe.edu

Space Exploration
http://spacelink.msfc.nasa.gov/

High School Literature Studies
www.romeoandjuliet.com
www.boston.com/commonwealthshakespeare/
web.uvic.ca/shakespeare/index.html
the-tech.mit.edu/Shakespeare/

Figure 28.1 Resources for Teachers Interested in Multimedia in the Classroom

proaches give them experience in seeing the effectiveness of different media in the support of learning.

2. Introduce the different media slowly. Begin with one piece of equipment and encourage students to use it as they demonstrate learning. You might choose to begin with the overhead projector and transparency film by having cooperative groups work together to create a transparency that documents the work of the group. Give the students practice in standing in front of the class using the overhead to show their work. Give instructions as to where to stand and how to turn the projector on and off. Demonstrate how they can reveal one portion of the transparency at a time to show new information as it is discussed and how two or three transparencies can be placed on top of each other to create a graph or a more detailed visual.

3. Repeat the demonstration and use of different media as it is appropriate. Always review the reasons why equipment is used so students can begin to make wise choices about the media they may want to use to support their presentations, determining whether or not the use of media actually enhances the quality of the demonstration.

4. Allow yourself and the students time to practice with the equipment before using it for more formal presentations. When computers are introduced new users need time to explore them,

Grade Level	Project	Equipment/Access
Kindergarten	Story retelling	Overhead projector Transparency pictures
	Math presentations	Math manipulatives Overhead projector
Primary	Book talks (video book reports)	Video Camera, VCR, monitor
	Publishing books	Computer with software for word processing & illustrating (Children's Writing & Publishing Center)
	Research on the Internet	Computer with Internet access, listing of websites which the teacher has previewed.
Above Third	The sky's the limit!	Computer with Internet access
		Writing and publishing software
		Hyperstudio
		Video productions
		Computer programmed presentations using professional presentation packages such as Powerpoint
	Classroom connections projects	Internet projects connecting classrooms across the nation. (http://www.gsn.org)
	Space exploration projects	Internet projects related to space travel & exploration
	http://spacelink.msfc.nasa.gov/	

Figure 28.2 Suggestions for Multimedia Projects

their functions, and possibilities. When introducing the Internet system, new users, teachers, and students alike will need to see the procedures for gaining access and the web site addresses clearly displayed so they can practice logging on, gaining access, and searching for information until they are comfortable with the sequences.

5. Pair computer users by computer experience, with a more experienced user supporting a new user. Don't overlook the more experienced user as a classroom resource. Often students have a lot of expertise to share with teachers and other students. Be sure to include

training for the more experienced users so that they are aware of the importance of "talking the new user through the procedure" and NOT jumping in to do it for him.

6. Assign a presentation that requires a multimedia element and support the students in developing their presentations. Gradually require more sophisticated media use. Start with media with which the students are comfortable and gradually add different possibilities as the students become more familiar with equipment, software, and usage. Encourage partner work in the beginning so that more experienced users of technology can provide support for new users. See Figure 28.2 for suggestions of multimedia projects.

APPLICATIONS AND EXAMPLES

Ms. Grundbrecher's second graders are busily engaged in a project entitled *Farm to Market*. Because their school is located in an agricultural area, the district encourages the study of the production of food, how it is harvested and transported to market, and the interdependence of farmers, food processors, and distributors.

The students are familiar with the Macintosh computer because they use it regularly to publish their writing. For this project Ms. Grundbrecher introduces them to Kid Pix, a computer program that allows them to create graphs and illustrate their research. The students are using a "stamp" option, which has a large library of pictures, to illustrate their reports.

For this introductory unit using computer technology, the students will use the library and a few Web sites already selected by the teacher to gather their information. They start with the area of the country where they live and the foods that they see growing in the fields. They widen their search to determine the different foods that are grown in the rest of the state and finally research agriculture in other states. They then create a graph using the stamps from the Kid Pix program to illustrate the variety of foods grown in the United States.

After identifying the wide range of food grown across the country, the class begins to look at transporting the food from place to place. Again using the Kid Pix stamps, the students create a map which visually represents the journey of the crop and the many different people who are employed to make it possible for the food to be available.

Ms. Grundbrecher is lucky enough to live in an area where she can take the students to visit the fields, a processing plant, and a distribution center. After all the research the second graders have done they are very knowledgeable visitors. They ask important questions about the types of transportation used to deliver the food, where is goes, and how long it takes to get there. The foreman at the processing center is very impressed and asks one of the students how they know so much about the processing and distribution of food.

"We researched it on the Internet," the smiling seven-year-old replies.

Mr. Bateman's tenth-grade chemistry class is discussing possible uses for chemistry in real life. Yolanda is interested in becoming an astronaut and asks, "Why do I need to study chemistry if I want to be an astronaut. I can't see any use for it in space."

"That's an interesting question, Yolanda," replies Mr. Bateman. "I was just reading about a service provided by NASA where students can read articles about the space program and even have their questions answered by astronauts and engineers associated with the program. Let's start a list of questions that we would like to have answered."

Mr. Bateman uses a large sheet of butcher paper and creates a KWL chart. "Let's first talk about what we know about the space program and then we'll generate some questions we want to have answered. We'll use the textbooks and on-line resources to try to find answers first, and then create a list of questions for the engineers and astronauts at NASA."

The students list all the information they have about the space program and when they are finished they realize that what they know is mostly related to the launch procedures that they view on television. They really have little knowledge about the actual experiments that are being done in space or what scientific knowledge is being gained through the launches.

Mr. Bateman has contacted NASA on-line and has received a copy of the teacher's guide that accompanies the NASA "Live from . . ." series. Through this introduction to the NASA programs the students interact with scientists through the NASA question/answer repository, where a number of their questions are answered. The students find that by reading information about research goals, viewing photos on-line, and searching for actual data gathered from shuttle flights and other NASA projects they are gaining a much broader understanding of all the different types of research being conducted through the space programs.

As it becomes obvious that the NASA research connection will be an ongoing study, Mr. Bateman is realizing that several of his students are spending a lot of time in the chemistry labs and computer stations working on projects that stem from the NASA teaching materials and the Internet connections. Yolanda is no longer the only student interested in the space program.

"Mr. Bateman, did you know that the space program uses engineers, chemists, biologists, data analyzers, doctors, veterinarians, and a whole lot of other types of scientists? I never knew that so many different jobs were involved in the space industry," Joseph says.

"It's an exciting program. The American public knows very little about all the inventions and medical benefits we have gained from the research," replies Mr. Bateman.

"Well, if they'd just get on the Internet they'd know," replies Joseph. "It's all on there."

• •

▶ CONCLUSION

Multimedia presentations in the classroom support students in conveying information to their peers. The use of visuals of many types helps students and teachers to connect vocabulary and meaning, making their reports more interesting. The use of the computer, VCR, camcorder, and other technology in the classroom is appealing to students and serves as motivation to be more innovative in completing assignments. The use of the Internet in the classroom introduces some challenges, however. Just as in researching from more traditional materials, students will need instruction in giving credit and citing sources. They may be tempted to simply download reports from the Internet, therefore, specific guidelines will need to be set and monitored in the classroom setting.

NASA Web Page:
http://quest.arc.nasa.gov/interactive.html

To send an e-mail message for information about future projects use:
listmanager@quest.arc.nasa.gov
Leave the subject line blank and in the message body write:
subscribe sharing-nasa

References

Diaz-Rico, L., & Weed, K. (1995). *The crosscultural, language, and academic development handbook*. Needham Heights, MA: Allyn and Bacon.

Kid Pix Deluxe (version 4.1), NOVATO, CA: Broderbund (www.broderbund.com).

Power Point, (version 7.0), Redmond, WA: Microsoft, (www.microsoft.com).

MULTIPLE INTELLIGENCES STRATEGIES

29

> ### SUPPORTS
>
> - Comprehensible input
> ✔ Increased verbal interaction
> ✔ Contextualized language
> - Reduced anxiety
> - Active involvement of the learner

Multiple intelligences (Gardner, 1993) are the ways in which people are smart—the modes in which they process information effectively. While traditionally teachers have taught only two intelligences in the school setting (linguistic and logical/mathematical) there have been at least five additional intelligences well researched and documented, and others are currently being documented. Although all people possess all intelligences at varying levels, it is helpful for teachers to present content material through a variety of intelligences in order to make the information comprehensible to all learners. It is equally important to encourage students to demonstrate their understanding of content in a format consistent with their strong intelligences. Using knowledge of multiple intelligences and being flexible in planning instruction and assessment is one way of supporting students to be more successful in the classroom. Using knowledge of multiple intelligences strategies is especially beneficial to English language learners since allowing them to learn and demonstrate their understanding in the mode in which they are most confident serves to lower the affective filter and boost their self-esteem and motivation. See Figure 29.1 for an explanation of the seven intelligences currently documented.

STEP BY STEP

The steps to implement the use of multiple intelligence approaches for teaching and assessing are:

1. Introduce the concept of multiple intelligences to your students. Depending on their ages you might use the actual labels for the intelligences, the definitions and examples, or simply talk about people being smart in different ways, while using the "body-smart," "people-smart," and "self-smart" labels to help them understand the concept. Explain that knowing more about the way you learn is one way to help yourself to do better in school. Tell the

Intelligence	Definition
Bodily/ kinesthetic	Body-smart, sports-smart, hand-smart—the person has the ability to move through space effectively, learns well with movement, can imitate movements easily.
Intrapersonal	Self-smart—the person understands his/her own ways of knowing and learning, is in tune with his/her own needs.
Interpersonal	People-smart—the person reads others well, works well in groups, interacts effectively with other people.
Linguistic	Word-smart—the person manipulates words and language easily, understands what is read, enjoys verbal interactions.
Logical/ mathematical	Number-smart, Logic-smart—the person manipulates numbers and/or logic easily, understands the logical connections among concepts.
Musical	Music-smart—the person expresses himself/herself easily in rhythm and melody, sees patterns and music in all endeavors.
Visual/ spatial	Picture-smart—the person sees pleasing visual/spatial arrangements around him/ her, has the ability to learn and express with visual arrangements, art, and beauty.

Figure 29.1   Multiple Intelligences and Their Meanings

Adapted from Gardner, 1993, and Armstrong, 1994.

class that you will be giving them some choices in the way they study and the way they show you that they are learning.

2. Assume that the students in your classroom have a variety of intelligences and plan your lessons and assessments to allow the students a choice in the way they study and the way they document their understandings. See Figure 29.2 for suggestions on how to allow this flexibility.

3. Observe your students during the first few times that you allow them choices in their mode of studying and/or documenting their learning. Keep track of the choices they make and talk to them about their preferences and the ways in which they would choose to spend their time. You might also want to have them take the informal MI Assessment Survey found in appendix A. Build a system in your classroom in which the students have choices on a regular basis.

4. Provide some ways for the students to evaluate their own work and the choices they make about the ways in which they do the work. A self-evaluation rubric is helpful in teaching the students to self-monitor and evaluate their own comprehension and production in different learning and assessment modes. See Figure 29.3 for a suggested self-evaluation tool for multiple intelligence activities.

Intelligence	Teaching	Assessing
Bodily/ Kinesthetic	Introduce motions Encourage role playing Allow movement	Have the students show, not tell Encourage the use of role play to document learning Encourage the use of mime, dance, the invention of physical games to document learning
Intrapersonal	Give opportunity for self-teaching, computer tutorials, Internet, programmed learning	Use self-evaluation rubrics Allow the person choices in ways to best show the learning Encourage the use of self-made multi-media reports
Interpersonal	Encourage group work Celebrate group skills Teach pieces and encourage reciprocal teaching	Encourage group reports Use group evaluation reports Evaluate the products of the group, holding all members responsible
Linguistic	Give reading/follow-up Encourage additional reading/ writing	Use written response activities Oral reports Dialogue journals, learning logs
Logical/ mathematical	Quantify instruction Relate instruction to logical constructs Relate instruction to math/ logic puzzles	Have student design a math or logic game that shows what has been learned Have student design "mind-benders"
Musical	Teach with rhythm, rap Relate instruction to songs, poetry	Have student demonstrate understanding by writing a rap or song
Visual/ spatial	Teach with visuals, charts, drawings	Have student make posters, charts, illustrations, dioramas, constructions

Figure 29.2 Teaching and Assessing Through Multiple Intelligences

Adapted from Gardner, 1993, and Armstrong, 1994.

Name _____   Date _____

Activity _____   Intelligence _____

My understanding of the content of this activity is:

< – ->

very   slight   about average   better   outstanding
minimal   than normal

I think that my understanding was affected by:

_____ my background knowledge   _____ the way in which the material was
                                                      presented

To understand the material better, I will need:

_____ nothing, I understand   _____ more practice (in same mode, in
                                                      another mode)

_____ another presentation of the content (in same mode, in another mode)

My ability to convey my understanding in this activity was:

< – ->

very   slight   about average   better   outstanding
minimal   than normal

I think that my performance (demonstration of understanding) would have been improved by:

_____ a different choice of response   _____ more practice

I chose to demonstrate my understanding through:

_____ writing   _____ drawing/graphics   _____ music   _____ math

_____ role play   _____ dialogue   _____ personal discussion

_____ group project   _____ other _____

A better choice for me might be:

_____ writing   _____ drawing/graphics   _____ music   _____ math

_____ role play   _____ dialogue   _____ personal discussion

_____ group project   _____ other _____

Figure 29.3   Self-Evaluation Rubric for Multiple Intelligences Activities

APPLICATIONS AND EXAMPLES

The students in Ms. Barry's second-grade class are reading versions of Cinderella stories and comparing them. Ms. Barry has chosen *Jouanah, a Hmong Cinderella* (Coburn & Lee, 1996) as the focus book of the week because so many of her students are from the Hmong or Hispanic cultures and the book is available in Hmong, Spanish, and English. After she reads the book aloud to the class, Ms. Barry suggests that the students might want to do some activities focusing on the book in literacy centers this week. Because she has read so much about multiple intelligences, Ms. Barry has decided to set up seven centers, each allowing the children to interact in a way unique to one of the intelligences. The centers Ms. Barry sets up are:

- *Listening Center* (Linguistic Intelligence), where the children listen to the story in either Spanish, English, or Hmong and look at the pictures in a copy of the book written in the language of choice.

- *Music Center* (Musical Intelligence), where the children listen to a tape of Hmong music and dress up in traditional Hmong festival clothes. Older Hmong students are invited to teach traditional Hmong dances to Ms. Barry's children at this center.
- *Games Center* (Bodily/Kinesthetic Intelligence), where the children play traditional Hmong games as they are played at Hmong festivals similar to the one attended by Jouanah in the Cinderella tale.
- *Tape-recorder Center* (Intrapersonal Intelligence), where the children respond to the Hmong Cinderella story on tape, telling about their favorite part of the story or what they would have done if they had been Jouanah.
- *Story Reenactment Center* (Interpersonal Intelligence), where the children work in groups, using props from each of the Cinderella stories they have read to reenact the plots.
- *Pattern Center* (Logical Mathematical Intelligence), where the children complete pattern strips based on intricate traditional Hmong patterns similar to the ones shown in Jouanah's festival clothes in the Hmong Cinderella story. Once the patterns are completed, they are used as borders for the bulletin board where the products from the art center will be displayed.
- *Art Center* (Visual/Spatial Intelligence), where the children draw the features and create costumes for male and female paper dolls, which will be added to the bulletin board depicting the festival where Jouanah and Shee-Nang met in the story. The children are also encouraged to create other pictures to be added to the bulletin board.

Ms. Barry encourages the children to use the centers for the entire week. They must keep track of the centers they visit and rate their enjoyment and the work they do in each using a self-evaluation rubric similar to the one in Figure 24.3. At the end of the week, Ms. Barry reflects on the choices the children made in their center use and she talks to the class about what she has noticed, "Some of you tried to work in each of the centers this week, others went to only two or three. Why do you suppose that happened?"

"Some of them were more fun," says Tong quietly.

"It's OK Tong," replies Ms. Barry. "I didn't say everyone had to go to all the centers. What you say is true. Some of you found some of the centers to be more fun than others. Why do you suppose that is true?"

"Well, I didn't do the patterns because they looked very hard," says Sia.

"We like to do things we can do well," smiles Ms. Barry. "That is true. We are all better at some things than others. Which center did you like best, Sia?"

"I like the story reenactment center. I like to tell the stories with my friends," says Sia shyly.

"Yes, I know you like to work with your friends," replies Ms. Barry. "We are all different and that's why we need to have different ways of learning. Did you all learn a lot about the Hmong Cinderella story by working in the centers?"

"My mother said that the Hmong men used to steal their brides just like Shee Nang did in the book," says Mia with wide eyes.

"My mother said that, too!" adds Hou. "She says my dad stole her from her family."

"Were they mad?" asks Jerry.

"No, they expected it to happen. He stole her but it was OK," replies Hou. "It's a tradition."

"What's a tradition?" asks Jerry. And from there the discussion continued. The class was very interested in the different wedding traditions and the students vowed to go home that night and learn more about wedding traditions in their own culture.

• •

Mr. Yoshino's eleventh-grade literature class has been engaged in a project in which they are being encouraged to read classic tales they missed reading in their childhood. Each student has identified the children's literature that they most enjoyed as children. Mr. Yoshino has shared some of the classic tales from Japan and others have brought in favorite tales they read or heard told in their homes. If a written version of the story is not available the students have been busily transcribing the oral tales for future generations. Mr. Yoshino is very pleased with the students' work and wants to plan a culminating activity to celebrate their explorations into cultural literature.

"I would like for you to share some of your work with the elementary students next door," begins Mr. Yoshino. "I think that some of them have never heard some of the stories you have discovered, and I would like for us to find ways to get the younger students excited about literature the way you have."

"I have been reading about something called multiple intelligences which talks about how people have multiple ways of knowing and learning, and I would like for you to think about a way that you could share your favorite story with the younger children. Let's brainstorm some of the things we might do," Mr. Yoshino says as he turns to the chalkboard.

"I think my story needs to be reenacted," says Marin. "But I will need to have other people to help me do it."

"That's fine," replies Mr. Yoshino as he writes *Reenactment* on the board. In just ten minutes time the class has created a list that includes:

- Reenactment
- Mime
- Puppet show
- Interpretive dance
- Student involvement
- Read-aloud with finger puppets
- Rap
- Skit
- Storytelling with costumes
- Story told in song
- Show with children taking parts

"This looks wonderful," says Mr. Yoshino as the class appears to be running out of ideas. "If you think of anything you want to add to the list, feel free to add it. I want you to begin to work, either alone or in groups, to plan your presentations. I will talk to the principal at the elementary school and set up a date for our presentations. What shall we call them?"

"Why don't we call it a Literature Festival?" asks Frederick.

"Good idea. Any other suggestions?" asks Mr. Yoshino.

"I like Frederick's idea," says Janine. "We can set it up like a festival and have some booths where the children can be actively involved in dressing up and being a part of the action. Other places they can just sit and listen."

"That sounds like a good plan, since we are trying to support the use of different intelligences and ways of learning," adds Mr. Yoshino. "Who wants to form a cooperative group?"

"I need some players for my reenactment," says Marin. "But first I need to develop my script. May I work on that first?"

"Sounds like a good plan," says Mr. Yoshino. "Does anyone need a cooperative group to start work today?"

Soon the room is full of busy noise. Some of the students have begun to work in cooperative groups, dividing the responsibilities among the members. Others, like Marin, will need a group later but have to do some individual work first. A few have chosen to do a solo presentation and are busily planning how they will do it. Everyone is actively involved.

CONCLUSION

The use of multiple intelligences strategies supports the students' learning of new materials because it allows them to use the processing systems in which they integrate knowledge most effectively. By providing multiple ways for the students to demonstrate their understanding, their confidence in their own abilities is fostered and their anxiety is reduced.

References

Armstrong, T. (1994). *Multiple intelligences in the classroom*. Alexandria, VA: Association for Supervision and Curriculum Development.

Coburn, J., & Lee, T. (1996). *Jouanah, a Hmong Cinderella*. Arcadia, CA: Shen's Books.

Gardner, H. (1993). *Multiple intelligences: The theory in practice*. New York: Basic Books.

PARTNER WORK

Partner work (Meyers, 1993) is a form of cooperative learning that is particularly effective with English language learners because of the opportunities for verbal interaction and support it provides (Diaz-Rico & Weed, 1995). In partner work the teacher pairs two students to accomplish a learning task. They are given specific instructions and expected to accomplish a process or product to share with the group or with other pairs. Suggested formats, learning tasks, and pairing schemes for partner work are shown in Figure 30.1.

STEP BY STEP

The steps in implementing partner work are:

1. Decide the purpose of the partner work to be done before you assign the pairs. If language development is one of the main purposes of the pairing, make sure one of the partners can provide a strong English model.
2. Model the task to be done. Choose one student to act as your partner for the demonstration and walk through the steps to be done. List the tasks on a chart or chalkboard to serve as a reminder of the steps in the process and the expectations of what will be accomplished.
3. Circulate among the pairs during the activity, giving them feedback on the way they are working together and communicating. Support pairs who are struggling by entering into their interactions, modeling strategies they can use to get the task done.
4. Provide an opportunity for the pairs to share their process or product with another pair or the whole group. Celebrate their accomplishments and review the language they were able to use.

APPLICATIONS AND EXAMPLES

Mr. Santiago's second graders are listening intently to his reading of *Wilfred Gordon McDonald Partridge* (Fox, 1985). When he finishes reading the book he reviews the story by creating a flip book labeled *Beginning, Middle,* and *End.* He asks the students to tell the things that happen at

Format	Learning Tasks/Procedure	Pairing Scheme
Think-pair-share	Group discussions, literature studies, problem solving reviewing of content materials for tests. Teacher presents question or task. Students think about their responses and then share and discuss their responses with their partner.	One strong English model
Buddy read	Reading of content material, challenging text. One student reads, the other listens or takes notes. They stop periodically to discuss and create a graphic organizer for study.	One strong reader
Research interview	Content material in science, social studies, and any informational writing. Students do individual research on a topic or aspect of a topic. Partners interview each other to gain the knowledge obtained by their partner. When sharing with another pair or whole group, each partner reports the material learned from the partner. The original researcher has the responsibility of monitoring the report by the partner to guarantee its accuracy.	Equal partners or one strong reader
Conversation role play	Oral language development, adjusting to social situations, situational vocabulary. Partners role play certain social situations such as a birthday party, a job interview, meeting new people at a non-family party. Appropriate language is introduced by the teacher in advance and the partners pretend to be a part of the social situation. After a while pairs are combined into groups of four and the partners must introduce each other to the new pair, providing appropriate information they have gained by the initial conversations.	Equal partners
Convince me	Problem solving tasks in science or math. Teacher presents a problem to be solved. The students work independently to find innovative solutions to the problem. The students are then paired to try to convince each other of the viability of the two solutions or to combine their solutions to make a better solution. They then meet with another pair and the foursomes must decide on and present their best solution to the whole group.	One strong English model

Figure 30.1 Formats, Learning Tasks, and Pairing Schemes for Partner Work

the beginning of the story. As they mention the elements in the beginning of Mem Fox's wonderful book, he reviews them, "We meet the characters, Wilfred Gordon, Miss Nancy and the other old folks at the home. We learn about the setting, that Wilfred Gordon lives next door to the old people's home. We learn about the problem, that Miss Nancy has lost her memory." As he talks about the elements, Mr. Santiago lists *Characters, Setting,* and *Problem introduced* under *Beginning* on the flip book. Mr. Santiago repeats the process for the *Middle* section of the flip book and writes, *Problem gets worse, Characters are developed.* Under *End* on the flip book, Mr. Santiago writes *Problem is solved.* His flip book now looks like the one shown in Figure 30.2.

Mr. Santiago now asks each student to think about a memory they have that they could write about. He gives them time to think and jot some notes about their memories. Next, Mr. Santiago asks Erina to come up front and act as his partner so he can show the students what they will be doing next.

"I have written some notes about my memory. I will use my notes to tell you my story. As I tell you my story, I want you to take notes on this flip book labeled *Beginning, Middle,* and *End.* You are to take notes about my story because you will help me to decide if I need to add anything to my story so that it will be more interesting. You will also be watching to see that I have included all the important parts of my story."

Mr. Santiago then tells his story and Erina writes the names of the characters by the word *Characters* on the *Beginning* section of the flip book. As he tells about the setting she writes a few words by *Setting* and writes a few words by *Problem introduced* as he tells about the problem. Erina continues to take notes as Mr. Santiago completes the telling of his story.

"Now that I have told my story to Erina, I want her to look at her notes to see if I have left out any important parts. Erina, what do you think?"

"I don't have any notes in the *Middle* section under *Characters are developed.* I think you need to tell me some more about the characters in the middle of the story to make it more interesting."

"Good, I can do that when I actually write my story inside the flip book. That will be the next part. For now we need to work in pairs to tell our stories to our partners. Then they can take notes and help us to make sure we have all the parts to make our stories as interesting as Mem Fox's story about Wilfred Gordon."

Mr. Santiago gives the students time to think about their stories and jot some notes. Then, he pairs the students up, making sure that there is a strong English speaker in each pair. The partners tell their stories to each other, creating the *Beginning, Middle,* and *End* notes on the cover of the flip books. Once everyone has told their stories and received feedback from their partners, they get to work actually writing the stories in the flip books. They know exactly what to write now that they've told the stories and received advice from their partners.

Partner work is a valuable strategy in many areas of the curriculum. It gives students confidence to tackle tough assignments by interacting and collaborating with another student.

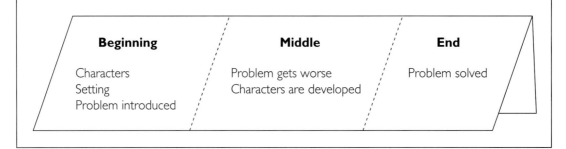

Figure 30.2 Mr. Santiago's Flip Book

1. Look at the loft diagram.
2. Decide which materials you will need to build the loft and how much of each material will be needed.
3. Figure the cost of the materials using the price list in the catalogue. Try to find ways to save money and cut down on waste.
4. Double-check your math.
5. Prepare a presentation and diagram to show how you did your calculations.
6. Decide how to present your plan to the class.
7. Practice your presentation.

Figure 30.3   *Steps in the Planning Process*

Ms. Tucker's sixth graders are learning to use multiplication and division to solve real-life problems. She has brought in a diagram of a loft that she wants to build in the classroom and catalogues from a local hardware store that lists prices on building materials. She explains to the class that she would like to build the loft in the classroom so they will have a quiet place to read when they have finished their work each day. The students smile when they see the diagram of the loft with its comfortable beanbag seats and colorful posters.

"I want each of you to look through the catalogues and use the diagram to figure out how much money we need to raise to buy the materials to build the loft," Ms. Tucker explains. "There are several choices of materials that we can use. Some of the boards are more expensive than others. Some of the boards come in different lengths, so we need to figure out which length to buy so that we don't waste too much lumber."

"You will be working with a partner to determine your plan for buying materials and the total cost of materials if we follow your plan. After your planning time, you and your partner should work together to practice a presentation and make a picture of some kind to show the class so that the whole class can vote on which plan we will use."

"You will need to work closely with your partner to double check all your math. Also, make sure you haven't forgotten any materials like nails, paint, or paint brushes."

As Ms. Tucker is reviewing the steps in the partner work, she lists the steps the students must take to accomplish their task. Her list is shown in Figure 30.3.

As the partners begin to work, Ms. Tucker moves around the room listening to the active verbal interactions, making suggestions and giving encouragement. Some of the pairs have chosen some unusual materials for their loft. She can't wait to hear their presentations.

CONCLUSION

Partner work can be used in many ways across the curriculum. By pairing students to support one another in the successful completion of the task or to review materials and prepare for an assignment, the students are given opportunities to interact verbally, practice relating facts and concepts, monitor each other's understanding, or provide home language support. English language learners can be paired in several different ways depending on their stages in English acquisition. If a student needs home language explanations, then a perfect partner for that student is another student who shares the same home language and who is also more fluent in English.

If an English language learner is fairly fluent in English but needs more practice in speaking and writing English, then a good English speaking role model makes a good partner. Partners can also be used to create bilingual books and labels, versions of favorite literature in various languages, or illustrated books using partners with strengths in writing and illustration. Partners can be used in math and science by pairing students with strengths such as writing and science or art and science.

References

Diaz-Rico, L., & Weed, K. (1995). *The crosscultural language and academic development handbook.* Needham Heights, MA: Allyn and Bacon.

Fox, M. (1985). *Wilfred Gordon McDonald Partridge.* Brooklyn, NY: Kane/Miller Books.

Meyers, M. (1993). *Teaching to diversity: Teaching and learning in the multi-ethnic classroom.* Toronto, Canada: Irwin Publishing.

PEER TUTORING

3|

SUPPORTS

- Comprehensible input
- Increased verbal interaction
- ✔ Contextualized language
- Reduced anxiety
- Active involvement of the learner

Peer tutoring (Thonis, 1994) is a strategy in which a student who has already achieved certain skills, works with a classmate to help him/her to acquire the skills. It differs from partner work because partners work together, sharing the responsibilities. Peer tutoring is effective with English language learners for several reasons. A peer who has mastered a higher level of proficiency in academic skills and English usage can often support learning by explaining the assignment in the student's first language or modeling what is expected. The peer tutoring situation often serves to lower anxiety for the learner because questions can be answered more readily on a one-to-one basis because the students are less likely to be inhibited. Questions can even be answered in the home language when the students come from the same language background. Peer tutoring also serves to provide the tutor with positive feelings of self-esteem and accomplishment as his/her tutee gains knowledge and English proficiency.

STEP BY STEP

The steps in implementing a peer tutoring program are:

1. Identify students who are having difficulty in specific academic areas and who would benefit from one-to-one tutoring.
2. Identify students who have proficiency in these academic areas and who could provide tutoring for other students. Provide training to the peer tutors in:
   - How to pose questions that support thinking
   - How to break the task into manageable pieces
   - When to explain in the first language
   - How to support English vocabulary development
3. Match the students who need tutoring with peer tutors considering such things as gender, home language, and personality.
4. Confer with both members of the team—as a team and individually—to celebrate achievements, solve problems, and answer questions. If the team works well, continue to place the students together. Change the teams for various skills instruction.

151

APPLICATIONS AND EXAMPLES

The fourth graders in Mr. Yamada's class are all busily engaged in reading/writing workshop as Mr. Matthews, the principal, enters the classroom. "I have a new student for you, starting tomorrow," Mr. Matthews says with a smile. "I have just finished talking to his foster mother. He's a new arrival from Bosnia and I know you have a student who came to us from the same area last year."

"I'm glad you let me know ahead of time," replies Mr. Yamada. "I can get Peter ready to serve as a peer tutor. What is his name?"

"His name is Vladimir," smiles Mr. Matthews. "His new family is calling him Vlad. He's only been in the country for a few days."

Mr. Yamada has a short talk with Peter about being a peer tutor. Peter is very excited about having a friend from his own country. "When will he be here?" asks Peter.

"He's due to start school tomorrow," replies Mr. Yamada. "Go on up to the office to talk to Mr. Matthews, though. Maybe he will give you Vlad's phone number so you can talk to him before he starts school. He might feel more comfortable coming tomorrow if he knew he'll have someone here who speaks his language."

"Great idea!" says Peter as he heads for the office.

When Peter comes back he's smiling broadly. "I talked to him and he's going to play on our soccer team. He plays goalie and we sure need one. They always make me play that position and I hate it."

"What else did you find out about him?" asks Mr. Yamada.

"He wants to be called Vladimir, not Vlad. He's good in math. He likes to read, but he doesn't read English well. His English is way better than mine was when I came last year. We really didn't talk in English, much," Peter says sheepishly.

"That's OK, Peter. You'll be helping him to learn English, but I don't want either of you to forget your native language. It's good that you can practice together."

Mr. Yamada and Peter worked together each morning for a few minutes making sure that Peter knew what was expected of him as a peer tutor. Peter and Vlad sat next to each other and Peter was encouraged to explain assignments to Vladimir anytime he needed help. While Mr. Yamada worked with small groups of students, Peter would tutor Vladimir and help him to understand the main concepts being taught. Peter quickly learned how to give a brief review of any explanations Mr. Yamada gave, supporting Vladimir with English translations or first language explanations. Vladimir was very proud of his growing abilities in English and Mr. Yamada had to chuckle whenever the soccer team played. The whole team, no matter what their home language, shouted encouragement to each other in Croatian.

Ms. Bartell's seventh-grade pre-algebra class is studying motion problems. Ms. Bartell is trying to use as many concrete examples as possible since she has so many English language learners in the class. A number of her students are trying very hard, but they are having a lot of problems with the difficult concepts of train or planes heading in opposite directions and their likelihood of passing each other or crashing. On top of the challenge of the math concepts, Ms. Bartell is aware that the English language is interfering with comprehension.

"I need some peer tutors for my math students," Ms. Bartell says one day in the faculty lounge. Some of the language in the more advanced word problems is really causing difficulties."

Across the room Mr. Flores looks up from his newspaper and asks, "What are the students' home languages?"

Ms. Bartell looks startled, as if she really hadn't expected a response to her plea. "Most of the students are Spanish speakers," she replies.

"Why don't we set up a tutoring center after school. I have some advanced Spanish students who will be taking the College Advanced Placement Exam in Spanish at the end of the year and they could use some conversational practice. They're all seniors and pretty bright kids. Could you use them?" he asks.

"Yes! Yes! Yes!" Ms. Bartell practically shouts. "Can we set up a meeting so I can review them on the math concepts and teach them some tutoring strategies?"

"I think we can arrange that. I'd want some ways to support their Spanish conversation as a part of the deal. Maybe we should work together on this," Mr. Flores says.

The next day Ms. Bartell discusses the idea with her pre-algebra class and they seem to be interested. "You mean we'll be tutoring seniors in Spanish and they'll be tutoring us in math?" asks Lorenzo.

"Mainly, they'll be tutoring you in math," smiles Mrs. Bartell. "But, Mr. Flores wants them to have some Spanish conversational practice as a part of the deal."

Ms. Bartell and Mr. Flores meet the next day to set up a peer tutoring program and decide on the priorities and time line. See Figure 31.1 for their plan of action.

CONCLUSION

Peer tutoring is a highly effective practice for English language learners. It provides an opportunity for verbal interactions in both English and the home language, when tutors are matched by home language. It provides authentic verbal practice in English because of the shared responsibility for studying an academic assignment. Both students benefit from the activity because the tutor is building confidence and self-esteem, learning organizational skills, and refining his/her academic understandings. The peer being tutored gains practice and confidence in verbal and written English and opportunities to have lessons clarified in a less stressful setting.

Guidelines:

All students must agree to participate at least two afternoons a week.

One teacher will monitor on Mondays and Wednesdays, the other on Tuesdays and Thursdays.

Tutor and tutee must agree on a schedule and stick to it unless they mutually agree to change.

Tutor Training:

Ms. Bartell will

- train the math tutors, review their math concepts and provide any ongoing training needed as the content changes.
- provide any materials she wants the tutors to review.
- expect monthly reports from the tutors.
- assess any tutees who feel they are ready to discontinue tutoring.

Mr. Flores will

- prepare any materials he wants discussed as a part of the peer conversations in Spanish.
- conduct any training for the Spanish conversations that he deems necessary.

Schedule:

3:00–3:45   Math Tutoring (may be conducted in Spanish, English or any combination)

3:45–4:15   Spanish Conversations (reciprocal vocabulary building—English and Spanish)

Figure 31.1   An After-School Peer Tutoring Plan

References

Thonis, E. (1994). The ESL student: Reflections on the present, concerns for the future. In K. Spangenberg-Urbschat & R. Pritchard (Eds.), *Kids come in all languages: Reading instruction for ESL students*. Newark, DE: International Reading Association.

PERFORMANCE SAMPLING

32

SUPPORTS

- Assessment appropriate for use in planning lessons based on the needs of the individual student

Performance sampling is a form of authentic assessment where the student is observed in the process of accomplishing academic tasks and is evaluated on the way in which the tasks are done. The word *authentic* indicates that the tasks the students are asked to do are very similar or identical to actual tasks that students routinely accomplish in the classroom setting, unlike more traditional forms of assessment, which tend to be very unlike everyday classroom activities.

Performance samples are well named because the teacher observes a sample of the student's performance in a given academic task. Examples of the types of tasks used in performance sampling are:

- Working a mathematics problem that involves reading the problem, setting up an approach to finding a solution, and finding a reasonable solution
- Responding to a writing prompt by webbing a short piece of writing, writing a draft of a written piece, working with a peer to elicit feedback on the draft, revising the piece, and working with a peer to edit the piece for mechanics and spelling
- Researching a topic in social studies and documenting the information gained by completing a data chart

Performance samples are documented in several ways. The teacher might write an anecdotal record of the observation (see Chapter 3, Anecdotal Records). The teacher might design a scoring rubric and evaluate the student's performance on the rubric (see figure 32.1 for an example). The teacher might design a checklist and evaluate the student's performance on the basis of the items on the checklist. (See Figure 32.2 for an example of a checklist that might be used in this way.)

Performance sampling is a particularly appropriate form of assessment for English language learners because their approach to academic tasks is observed and documented and their assessment is based on their ability to perform the task rather than their fluency in English, which is sometimes the case in more traditional forms of assessment (Hernandez, 1997).

STEP BY STEP

The steps in performance sampling are:

1. Decide on the academic area to be assessed and choose a task for the students to perform that will demonstrate their understanding of the content that has been studied. Design an observation instrument such as a rubric or checklist (see Figures 32.1 and 32.2) or structure an anecdotal record that will itemize the abilities documented by the student.
2. Set up a schedule so that you can observe all the students within a reasonable amount of time.

5   Exemplary Performance
     The student:
              planned the task in an outstanding way
              followed the plan to achieve a high-level product
              proofread and corrected all errors
              produced a unique product

4   Strong Performance
     The student:
              planned the task
              followed the plan to complete the product
              proofread and corrected the majority of errors
              produced a good product

3   Acceptable Performance
     The student:
              performed the task to an acceptable end
              corrected some errors
              showed some understanding of what was required

2   Weak Performance
     The student:
              showed some confusion about what was expected
              left out some important steps in the process or didn't finish the task completely
              failed to correct errors

1   Very Weak Performance
     The student:
              showed only minimal understanding of the task
              completed a very small portion of the task

0   No Performance
     The student failed to complete the task

Figure 32.1   Example of a Scoring Rubric for Performance Sampling

_____ The student read the problem.
_____ The student made an attempt to find a solution to the problem.
_____ The student demonstrated planning to devise a solution.
_____ The student followed the plan created.
_____ The student found a solution to the problem.
_____ The student found multiple solutions to the problem.
_____ The student evaluated the solutions found and recognized the most unique or viable one.
_____ The student was able to communicate viable reasons for his/her choice of solutions.
_____ The student was able to explain the methods used in finding the solution to the problem.

Figure 32.2   Example of a Checklist for the Assessment of Performance Sampling

3. Gather materials and set up the task so that you can observe the students and document their performance. Plan an assignment for the rest of the class to do so that you will be able to observe without interruption.

4. Observe the students, complete the observation instrument, and give them feedback on their performances.

APPLICATIONS AND EXAMPLES

Mr. Juarez' first graders have been working on basic addition facts using manipulatives and word problems. He has been using counters in the shape of bears to demonstrate how to solve addition problems with missing addends. Since the students have been practicing this skill for several weeks now, Mr. Juarez is anxious to see how automatic their responses are when asked to solve addition problems with missing addends. Mr. Juarez gathers some counting bears and a clay cave that he has used for demonstrations and he sets up a schedule so that he can observe some performance samples each day for a week. He plans to observe four students a day so that he can observe all the students in his class by the end of the week.

Mr. Juarez gets the students started in learning centers so that he can observe without being disturbed. He sets up the materials he will use at a table in one corner of the room so he can keep an eye on the whole class while he works with one student at a time. He plans to observe as the students each solve five missing addend problems. He will observe to determine:

1. Does the student need to use the counters to solve the problem, or does the student have an automatic response to the problem that indicates memorization of addition facts?

2. Does the student use the counters in an effective way so that a correct solution is found?

3. If the student has difficulties with the problem, is it because of problems in counting, in understanding what to do, or confusion with math concepts?

4. How does the student approach the problem? Is the approach one that shows a plan, or is it a random approach?

Once Mr. Juarez knows exactly what approach he will use and the questions he will ask, he calls the first student over to the table. "Antonio, I want you to show me how you find the answers to some math problems. If there are three bears and two of them are still asleep in the cave, how many are awake?"

Antonio takes three counters, places two of them into the cave and points to the remaining bear, saying, "One."

"Very good, Antonio. Now what if there are five bears and two of them are asleep in the cave. How many were awake?"

Antonio picks up five bears, puts two of them in the cave and answers, "Three," very quickly.

Mr. Juarez is beginning to see a flaw in his planning. "Can you find the answers without using the bears?" he asks Antonio. Antonio nods, indicating "yes." "That's OK," Mr. Juarez says. "If you can tell me the answer without using the bears, you don't have to use them. If you need to use them you can."

"OK," responds Antonio.

"What if there are seven bears and five of them are in the cave asleep. How many are awake?" asks Mr. Juarez.

Antonio says, "Two," almost before Mr. Juarez finishes the problem.

Mr. Juarez gives Antonio two more problems and then writes a brief anecdotal note that says,

11/30 Antonio Flores. Antonio used the counters to quickly find the correct answers to $2 + \underline{\hspace{1cm}} = 3$, and $3 + \underline{\hspace{1cm}} = 5$. He did them so quickly I suggested he could try to do the problems without using the counters. He was able to complete the next three problems without hesitation. He was confident and didn't need to use the manipulatives.

Mr. Juarez called the next child to the table to be assessed.

• •

Mr. Vang teaches seventh-grade social science and wants to assess his students' understanding of the procedures that have been taught for logging on to the Internet and doing a basic search for information on a given topic. He uses the checklist that the students have been given as his assessment instrument and takes a few minutes at the end of each class period to observe a performance sample of a few students. He asks the student to log on and search for a topic. He has a long list of topics from which to choose so he doesn't have to repeat himself too frequently. In addition to the logging-on and searching tasks he is also observing the students' keyboarding skills to see if any of them need to take a typing class the next semester. The performance sampling takes very little time but reveals several students who haven't mastered the basic skills or are having difficulty with keyboarding. Mr. Vang calls together the group that needs a refresher on Internet and suggests that they plan to come in after school for a few days and get some extra practice.

"We are going to be using the Internet very heavily within the next few weeks, and you'll need to be able to log on and get your searches done efficiently or the rest of the students will become impatient with you," Mr. Vang says. He passes out the log-on checklist and suggests that the students study it well. "I'll be here after school every day this week. I want to see you come in and practice your logging-on and searching procedures until you're confident that you can do them efficiently. I'll recheck you when you feel that you're ready, but I'd like for it to be before the end of the week. Those of you having difficulty with keyboarding need to practice at home." Mr. Vang hands out some laminated keyboard diagrams. "I know practicing on a cardboard keyboard is not the same as the real thing, but it will help you to find the keys more quickly, so practice," he says.

As the students leave the room, Mr. Vang is already thinking about his next performance sampling, which will be on the efficient use of search descriptors. He's pleased that he was able to assess the students in an authentic way with very little time invested.

"I think this will really help us to use the Internet more effectively," Mr. Vang thinks to himself.

• •

▶ CONCLUSION

Performance sampling is an effective way of assessing students' skills and understanding in an authentic way. Because the students are asked to perform rather than simply answer questions, the teacher is able to observe and identify the areas in which the student is able to do the work and the areas in which further instruction or practice is necessary. Performance sampling is particularly appropriate for English language learners because their performance is less dependent on their ability to convey information in English. The teacher can ask questions in a way that allows the students to use gestures, manipulatives, actions, or drawings to demonstrate their understanding. See chapter 25, on Leveled Questioning, for further suggestions on the use of questions for various stages of language acquisition.

References

Hernandez, H. (1997). *Teaching in multicultural classrooms.* Upper Saddle River, NJ: Merrill/Prentice Hall.

PORTFOLIO ASSESSMENT

33

SUPPORTS

- Assessment appropriate for use in planning lessons based on the needs of the individual student

Portfolio assessment refers to a system for gathering observations, performance samples, and work samples in a folder or portfolio; analyzing the contents of the portfolio on a regular basis; and summarizing the students' progress as documented by the contents of the portfolio (Herrell, 1996). Often students are involved in making selections of work to be kept in the portfolio. Students are also involved in the review and summarization of the work, setting goals for future work, and sharing the contents of the portfolio with parents (Farr & Tone, 1994).

This approach to assessment is particularly appropriate for English language learners because it allows assessment based upon actual sampling of the students' work and the growth they are making with less dependence on scores on standardized tests, which are often very difficult for English language learners to understand (Hernandez, 1997). Portfolio assessment allows the students to demonstrate their content knowledge without being so dependent on English fluency. The focus in this approach to assessment is celebration of progress rather than focus on weaknesses.

STEP BY STEP

The steps in implementing portfolio assessment are:

1. Decide what curricular areas you want to include in the portfolio and obtain baseline work samples, performance samples, or observations for each student, in each area to be included.
2. Explain the portfolio system to the students, stressing their active involvement in the selection of materials to be included in the portfolio. Also explain the use of baseline samples and the fact that future work samples will be selected to demonstrate the students' progress. Involve them in setting up the portfolio and labeling the samples of work that will be used as baseline samples.
3. Establish a schedule of observations and performance and work sampling that will serve to document periodic checks on the students' progress and provide updated samples of their work.
4. Schedule periodic conferences with the students and their parents to review the contents of their portfolios, celebrate their growth, and involve them in setting goals for themselves.

APPLICATIONS AND EXAMPLES

Mr. Zepeda's third graders have just begun the school year. Mr. Zepeda is busily assessing them in reading, writing, math, and science. He is planning to use portfolio assessment in his class this year and he wants to get baseline data so that he knows where the students are functioning and can begin to group them for instruction. He has listened to the students read individually and taken a running record of their reading so he can analyze it for strategy use. He has tested their sight vocabulary and their mastery of math facts. Today he is having the students write a friendly letter so he can determine their spelling development and their ability to express themselves in writing.

As soon as Mr. Zepeda finishes gathering the baseline data he schedules individual conferences with his students. As the rest of the class works on plans for their first literature project, Mr. Zepeda talks to Amanda about the baseline assessments.

"Amanda, I want to talk about the testing we have done so far this year. You did very well on the reading assessments. What would you like to work on in reading this year?" asks Mr. Zepeda.

"I don't know," responds Amanda. "I like to read. I'd just like to have time to read in school."

"We will have time to read every day this year, Amanda. What kinds of books do you like to read?" asks Mr. Zepeda.

"I like to read the *American Girl* books and other series about girls my age," answers Amanda.

"We will be doing a lot of reading for information this year. In third grade we start to learn to do research and read books to learn more about different subjects. Since you've enjoyed the *American Girl* books, you probably know a lot about different periods of history in America. I hope you will begin to branch out in your reading and try some new kinds of books. Does that sound like something you could do?" Mr. Zepeda asks.

"I guess so, just as long as I still have time to read my chapter books. They're fun to read," answers Amanda.

"I think you'll find that you have time for reading both types of books. We'll also do a lot of writing. How do you feel about your writing?" asks Mr. Zepeda.

"I'm OK in writing," shrugs Amanda. "We didn't do much writing last year."

"What kinds of things do you like to write?" asks Mr. Zepeda.

"I mostly just write in my journal. I've never done much of any other kind of writing," responds Amanda.

"I think you'll find that the kinds of things you've been writing in your journal can be expanded into stories and maybe even books," suggests Mr. Zepeda.

Amanda smiles, "I'd like to learn how to write books."

Mr. Zepeda has similar conferences with each of his students. After each conference he writes a few notes in his teacher's log so he can keep track of the interests of his students and encourage them to read and write more in the areas of their interests. He also sets up a schedule so that he is collecting material for the portfolios on a regular basis. He encourages the students to select work for their own portfolios as well.

Six weeks later Mr. Zepeda is getting ready for parent conferences. He passes out the students' portfolios for them to arrange the contents in sequential order.

"As you arrange the materials in your portfolios, I want you to select the one piece of work that you feel best about. Write a one page note to your parents explaining why you are proud of that piece of work and what you learned from doing it," suggests Mr. Zepeda. "If you would like to come along to the conferences, it's OK," he adds. "We're not going to be discussing anything secret. You are welcome to come. We will be looking at the work in your portfolios and talking about how you are doing. I'd like for you to be a part of those conversations."

"Can you write a note saying it's OK?" asks Tito. "My dad won't believe I am invited to come."

"That's a good idea," responds Mr. Zepeda. "I guess we should start calling them parent, student, and teacher conferences." See Figure 33.1 for Mr. Zepeda's system of building portfolios.

Each student has a folder.

The folder contains:

Writing samples   Anecdotal records   Photos

Periodic running records in reading   Periodic math assessments

Records of the books the student has read

A complete writing project including prewriting, drafts, and final, published copy

A summary of the student's progress   Goals set and accomplished

Figure 33.1   Mr. Zepeda's Portfolio Assessment System

Ms. Melo's junior homeroom class is getting ready for parent conferences. They have their portfolios out to select their best work. Each marking period Ms. Melo has them select their best work to share with their parents. Ms. Melo encourages the students to prepare a short presentation for their parents, reviewing what they see as their major accomplishments during each marking period.

"We have done this so much this year," says Addid. "I feel like I could do it in my sleep."

"That's very good," smiles Ms. Melo. "This practice will serve you well when you interview for college admission or a job. We don't practice this kind of thing enough and when you have to talk about your strengths and goals, some of you are at a loss as to what to say. I want this to be comfortable and automatic for you."

"I didn't know you had to interview for college," says Kara. "I though you just applied."

"Some colleges don't have you interview. But some of them do. Sometimes it's not for admission into the college, but there will always be things you want at the college that will require interviews," says Ms. Melo.

"What do you mean, things we want?" asks Gustav.

"Well, things like work-study jobs, fraternities, or positions on the school newspaper," says Ms. Melo.

"Oh, those things," smiles Gustav, who is the editor of the high school newspaper.

"Some of the colleges are even having students bring their high school portfolios to the interviews," adds Krista.

"Most of our high school friends don't even have a portfolio," says Germain. "I think Ms. Melo is the only homeroom teacher who has her students do them."

"My English teacher has us keep a portfolio for English class," says Sasha. "I just pick work from that portfolio for my overall portfolio for Ms. Melo."

Ms. Melo adds, "I know that not everyone is keeping portfolios, but if I'm going to have conferences with your parents I need to know how you're doing in all your classes. Your parents can't always get around to all your teachers on parent conference night."

"I see that as a good thing," quips Michael.

"Who, exactly, don't you want them to see, Michael?" grins Shiela.

"Sorry I mentioned it," says Michael sheepishly. "My dad will know exactly who to go see when he sees my portfolio. I'm not doing too great in . . . ."

"Chemistry!" the whole class adds.

"I guess your secret is out, Michael," smiles Ms. Melo. "Now what are you going to do about it?"

"I guess I need to start going to homework club for some tutoring," Michael says.

"Why don't you write your dad a note to that effect and set a chemistry goal in your portfolio?" asks Ms. Melo. "I'd include that goal in your portfolio presentation, too."

"I have to put it in writing?" asks Michael with a shocked expression.

"I think your dad will take it more seriously if you do. He'll know that you really intend to do it," responds Ms. Melo.

"I guess you're right," says Michael as he gets out a piece of paper and starts to write.

Two nights later Michael makes his portfolio presentation to his parents. He shows them his history project proudly and tells all the things he's learning about the American revolution. When asked what piece of work he's most proud of, he slowly removes the note committing to Homework Club for chemistry tutoring. "This may seem to be a strange thing to be proud of," says Michael, "but it's the hardest thing I've ever had to commit to." Michael's parents seem very pleased with the note about his commitment to attend homework club for help in chemistry. "We knew you weren't doing well, but you didn't seem to be concerned. We're glad to see that you're ready to buckle down. I'm afraid Michael doesn't always take school too seriously," says Michael's dad.

"Michael is a very bright young man. He hasn't had to study too hard to get good grades in the past," says Ms. Melo. "I think he's just beginning to realize that he needs to develop better study habits if he's going to do well in college."

"I'm amazed that you know him so well," says Michael's mom. "You only have him for one subject."

"That's true, but I review all his subjects through his portfolio. Michael is not shy about talking about himself," Ms. Melo smiles.

"Well, we're very glad you are putting some pressure on him," adds Michael's dad. "He needs to get serious."

"Oh, I think he's made that decision for himself," responds Ms. Melo. "Homework Club is a big step."

CONCLUSION

Portfolio assessment is a powerful way to involve students in the evaluation of their own work and begin to set goals for themselves. Teachers and students select work samples to include in the portfolio and the work is used as a basis for conferences between students, teachers, and parents. Because work samples, photos, video, and audio tapes can be included in a portfolio, students who have strengths in intelligences such as music or art can demonstrate their abilities in authentic ways. It is important to note that a portfolio is an assessment tool only when the samples and artifacts included in the portfolio are used for discussion, planning, and goal setting.

References

Farr, R., & Tone, B. (1994). *Portfolio performance assessments.* Fort Worth, TX: Harcourt Brace.

Hernandez, H. (1997). *Teaching in multicultural classrooms.* Upper Saddle River, NJ: Merrill/Prentice Hall.

Herrell, A. (1996). Portfolios and young children, a natural match. *Kindergarten Education: Research, Theory, and Practice, 1,* 1–10.

Tripp, V. (1991–1999). *The American Girl Series.* Walnut, CA: Pleasant Co.

PREDICTABLE ROUTINES AND SIGNALS

34

> ## SUPPORTS
>
> - Comprehensible input
> - Reduced anxiety
> - ✔ Active involvement of the learner

Predictable routines and signals in the classroom are among the easiest strategies to implement and yet extremely important in reducing the anxiety of English language learners (Krashen, 1982). Because English language learners do not always understand everything that is said in the classroom, having set patterns, routines, and signals helps them to relax and not worry as much about being able to follow the sequence of events and activities during the school day. If they know what to expect they can use more of their energy focusing on the instruction and less focusing on what they will be expected to do next. Routines that can be set and predictable include such things as the sequence of the subjects to be taught, places within the classroom where certain things are stored and accessible to students, a certain spot on the chalkboard or bulletin board where reading or homework assignments are posted, a daily list posted that gives the routine in sequence, hand or flashing light signals that indicate the close of one activity and the beginning of another. See Figure 34.1 for a list of predictable routines and signals that support English language learners in the classroom.

STEP BY STEP

The steps in implementing predictable routines and signals are:

1. Set up your room with certain areas designated for group activities, free reading, and partner work. Establish these areas with the students by modeling their use and asking questions like, "Will you work with other people in this area?" or "Where will you sit if you want to read a book by yourself?"
2. Establish a set place for students to turn in assignments, pick up needed materials, keep their bookbags, lunchboxes, and other personal belongings. Model putting these things in the established places.
3. Model each new routine as it is established and be careful to maintain the routines once they've been established. Anytime a student shows confusion about a classroom routine or expectation, determine if a set routine would lessen the student's confusion.
4. Be consistent about modeling as you give directions. For example, "Take out your math book," should be accompanied by you holding up the math book. "Open to page 21," should be modeled and *page 21* should be written on the board. Modeling, gestures, and demonstrations are all vital ways to contextualize instructions. **Be consistent!**

Routine	Use	Benefit to English Language Learners
Morning sign in	A way of taking role and indicating lunch count	Students feel a part of the class and that their presence is valued
Set activity at the beginning of the school day	A way to engage students immediately. Such things as journal writing, reading library books, tasks such as watering plants, sharpening pencils are appropriate.	Students know what to do immediately. Have a chance to share their evening in writing, sign up to share journal entries, or chat briefly with peers and teacher.
Set place in the room where certain activities occur	Students move to certain areas for group lessons, review, sharing orally	Students know what to expect when moved to a certain area
A list of the day's activities and approximate times are posted in the same place each day	Helps students get their assignments in order and know which books to get out, when homework will be collected	Students have a visual reminder of the day's activities, less reliance on oral directions
Consistent use of modeling and contextualizing of oral directions	Helps students to follow directions	Students waste less energy wondering what to do next
Use of hand signals, light signals	Helps student to redirect their energies, know when activity changes are coming	Students alerted to upcoming events, drawing to a close of activities and events
Posting of assignments, page numbers, long-term assignments, homework	Helps students stay on task	Students are aware of expectations
Set place to submit assignments and get materials	Fosters reliability and self-reliance	Students are aware of expectations

Figure 34.1   Predictable Routines and Signals in the Classroom

APPLICATIONS AND EXAMPLES

Mr. Castles' kindergarten students know exactly what to expect when he starts singing, "Time to clean up." They immediately begin to put their materials away. They seem to shift into high gear when they see their teacher pick up a book and go to sit in the rocking chair. They all know it's story time. They quickly clean up and go sit on the carpet. They love to hear Mr. Castle read stories.

Mr. Castle has a set of predictable routines and signals that he uses with his five-year-olds. They know that when the light on the overhead projector comes on Mr. Castle wants them to quiet down. He has several songs that he sings to give them signals about changing activities and he always puts notices to go home on top of the bookshelf by the door. If Mr. Castle forgets to give out the notices, he hears from 20 five-year-olds, "You forgot to give us our notes!"

Ms. Newsome teaches high school economics. A number of her students are English language learners so she has set up study partners for them. Ms. Newsome uses a simple routine to signal to her students when an assignment can be done with the study partners. She writes the names of both partners on the top of the assignment page when she determines that the assignment can be done in collaboration. When she feels that the assignment is one that her English language learners can handle on their own, she doesn't write the names on the assignment paper. Ms. Newsome has established a set routine that also serves as a signal to her students as to when collaborative work is acceptable. She also has some lessons that she puts on tape and the English language learners are instructed to use the listening station to listen to the tape and follow the directions step by step. Her English language learners know when she wants them to move to the listening station because Ms. Newsome simply hands a tape to Joaquin, which signals that it is his job to go by and tap the others on the shoulder. Ms. Newsome doesn't have to say a word.

CONCLUSION

Predictable routines and signals save a lot of time in the classroom because a short signal or standard routine lets the students know what is expected of them. The signals and routines also serve to lower students' anxiety and help them to feel that they are fully participating members of the classroom community.

References

Krashen, S. (1982). *Principles and practice in second language acquisition*. Oxford: Pergamon Press.

Suggested Reading

Diaz-Rico, L., & Weed, K. (1995). *The crosscultural, language and academic development handbook*. Needham Heights, MA: Allyn and Bacon.

PREVIEW/REVIEW

35

SUPPORTS

- Comprehensible input
- Contextualized language
- Reduced anxiety
- ✔ Active involvement of the learner

Preview/review (Lessow-Hurley, 1990) is a teaching strategy usually associated with bilingual classrooms where a teacher or instructional aide gives a preview of the lesson in the students' home language. The lesson is then taught in English and the material is reviewed in the home language to assure content understanding. This same strategy can be adapted to an English-only classroom by using realia, visuals, gestures, and vocabulary instruction as a part of the preview—making reference to the support materials during the actual lesson, and then reviewing and explaining the content of the lesson to the students using the support materials. Preview/review is especially effective in facilitating content knowledge acquisition because of the contextualization of the academic language through the use of realia and visuals. See Figure 35.1 for suggestions of appropriate support materials and activities for preview/review lessons. Also see Chapter 2, Advance Organizers, for additional suggestions.

STEP BY STEP

The steps in a preview/review lesson are:

1. Plan your lesson, identifying key concepts and vocabulary. Gather any realia, visuals, or support materials that will help the students to understand the concepts and vocabulary needed to comprehend the lesson.
2. Introduce the important vocabulary and key concepts during the preview section of the lesson using the support materials. The focus in this section of the lesson is NOT on actually teaching the lesson, but on making the students familiar with key vocabulary and concepts.
3. Teach the actual lesson, referring to the support materials and key vocabulary whenever possible.
4. Review the key vocabulary and concepts, encouraging the students to demonstrate understanding by referring to the support materials.
5. Create a bulletin board or learning center that allows the students to practice the key concepts further through use of the support materials used in the lesson.

Realia	Visuals	Activities
Foods Household objects Animals Costumes of the period Music of the period	Transparencies made from photos Magazine pictures Line drawings Art prints Maps	Role playing Illustrating Sorting and labeling Lesson word walls Reader's theater Creating display boards Creating board games

Figure 35.1   Support Materials for Preview/Review Lessons

APPLICATIONS AND EXAMPLES

To prepare her second graders for a field trip to the zoo, Ms. Allen brings in photographs of zoo animals. She introduces the animals to the students using the photographs and creates a chart by displaying the photographs, listing key information about each animal such as the names used for the baby animals, the type of food eaten by the animal, and the animal's natural habitat.

A map of the zoo is displayed in the classroom and Ms. Allen teaches a lesson on asking questions and gathering information during the zoo trip. Each student is given a clipboard with information sheets about each animal they will see. The class brainstorms questions they will ask the zoo guides about the animals and the students practice taking notes on their information sheets.

As a review of the lesson the students refer to the photographs of the animals and practice asking questions about them. The students are given individual zoo maps and they place the names of the animals they will see in the proper places on the maps. As they note the locations on the maps, they refer to the photographs and key information on the charts they have made.

The day of the zoo trip the students ask questions and note the answers on their information sheets. When they return to the classroom the next day they use their zoo maps and information sheets to add new information to the charts about the animals.

The students learned a lot about the zoo and the animals because they were prepared to ask questions during the field trip. By having the students practice asking questions, determining where they will locate the different animals at the zoo, and preparing them to take notes about the animals, Ms. Allen has given them an opportunity to fully benefit from their field trip. The students learned the vocabulary, language structures, and key concepts they would encounter on their trip.

Ms. Warren uses a preview/review approach to introduce vocabulary and historical settings to her high school English students prior to studying literary works. Prior to studying *The Great Gatsby* (Fitzgerald, 1925), Ms. Warren familiarizes her students with the music and art of the roaring 20s. She uses transparencies of great art to familiarize her students with costumes of the period, plays music of the period, shows film clips from newsreels of the day, and engages the students in role playing to act out the vocabulary they will encounter in their reading.

During the reading of the literature Ms. Warren stops whenever necessary to refer to the transparencies or role playing they did to make connections between the preview activities and the passage being read.

As a review, the students are asked to refer to the support materials or role playing to answer questions related to the literature being studied. The students are also asked to role play certain passages from the work in order to share their understanding of the motivations and emotions of the characters. Small groups of students are assigned short passages of the work to reenact and then that passage and key vocabulary are discussed.

CONCLUSION

Preview/review is an especially effective strategy because it helps motivate students to learn. The preview part of the lesson not only prepares them by introducing vocabulary but, when done well, creates an interest in the topic to be studied. The review section of the lesson gives the teacher an opportunity to make connections, correct misconceptions, and engage students in a celebration of their accomplishments.

References

Fitzgerald, F. S. (1925). *The great Gatsby*. New York: Scribner/Simon and Schuster.

Lessow-Hurley, J. (1990). *The foundations of dual language instruction*. White Plains, NY: Longman.

REALIA STRATEGIES

36

SUPPORTS

- Comprehensible input
- ✔ Increased verbal interaction
- Contextualized language
- ✔ Reduced anxiety
- ✔ Active involvement of the learner

Realia is a term for real things, concrete objects, that are used in the classroom to build background knowledge and vocabulary. Realia is used to provide experiences on which to build and to provide students with opportunities to use all the senses in learning. While using realia in the classroom is not always possible, it is usually the best choice if the student is to learn all they can about a topic. Realia allows the student to see, feel, hear, and even smell the object being explored. If the real thing is not available, the teacher must move down the continuum from the concrete (real thing), to a replica such as a model, to a semi-concrete object such as a photograph or illustration. However, each move down the continuum causes the loss of some sensory information that could be helpful in comprehension. See Figure 36.1 for suggestions of classroom realia that are helpful in the presentation of powerful learning experiences.

STEP BY STEP

The steps in implementing the use of realia are:

1. Be aware of opportunities to include realia in lessons as you plan. Preread any stories to be read aloud or used for reading instruction to identify any vocabulary that may be unfamiliar to the students and locate realia that will be helpful to their understanding.

2. Begin to collect items that can be stored in the classroom and organize them so that they can be easily accessed for instruction. Plastic tubs or large clear plastic bags are often used for this purpose. Some items will be used with only one theme or book and should be stored with the theme materials or book. Yard sales and end-of-season sales at craft stores are good sources of realia for classroom use. Parents can often be helpful in locating and supplying useful items.

3. Collaborate with other teachers at your school or grade level to build a library of realia that can be shared for major theme studies. Locate local merchants, farmers, and other resources for the loan of large items such as farm equipment or animals.

4. If it's too large to move and your students' learning would benefit by experiencing it, take a field trip. Give your students the opportunity to really understand what they are studying.

Category	Realia	Uses
Household items	Eating utensils, kitchen appliances (from different cultures), miniatures such as household furniture, old-fashioned items no longer commonly seen	Active experiences, vocabulary development, role playing, story reenactment, prereading activities, oral language practice, story problems in math
Food	Fruit, vegetables, unusual items unfamiliar to children; many plastic food items are now available for classroom use.	Sensory experiences, vocabulary development, acting out stories, grammar activities (singular, plural)
Clothing	Different kinds of hats, gloves sweaters, jackets, boots, any examples of ethnic clothing to support understanding	Vocabulary development, story reenactment, writing support, oral language practice
Literacy materials	Books, magazines, newspapers, encyclopedia, reference books, checkbooks, bank books	Role play, vocabulary development, easy access for research, exposure
Farm or occupational items	Rakes, plows, harnesses, tools, baskets, hay, nails, models of barns, silos, scarecrows, wagons, farm carts	Prereading activities, role playing, vocabulary development, knowledge of size and weight
Flowers and plants	Examples of flowers and plants being studied or read about; unusual plants such as large sunflowers, pumpkins	Vocabulary development, sensory experiences, size comparisons
Animals	Classroom pets, house pets, farm and zoo animals, birds	Sensory experiences, vocabulary development
Crafts	Knitting, crocheting, tatting, sculpting clay, potter's wheel, spinning wheel, loom	Vocabulary development, role playing, sensory experiences, prereading activities
Ethnic items	Piñatas, chopsticks, wok, tortilla press, tea sets, clothing	Vocabulary development, cross-cultural experiences

Figure 36.1 Realia for Powerful Learning

APPLICATIONS AND EXAMPLES

Ms. Castaño has found a beautiful little bilingual book, which she wants to use with her third graders. Many of her Hispanic students speak very good English now but the parents are concerned that they are losing their fluency in Spanish. Ms. Castaño is always looking for ways to encourage the use of their primary language. The book she has found, *My Mexico—México Mio* (Johnson, 1996) is a collection of poetry in English and Spanish. Many of her third graders will be able to read both the English and Spanish versions of the poems and there are many opportunities for active lessons and vocabulary development in both languages.

As Ms. Castaño prepares her lessons for the next week she also gathers realia to support the students' understanding. Her school is near a little park where she will be able to take the students on a walk to see an adobe wall like the one described in the poem "Adobe Brick." Maybe she can even talk her father into coming to school and demonstrating how to make adobe bricks.

Ms. Castaño has a broom in the classroom and she finds a huge plastic cockroach given to her as a joke years ago that she will use with the broom for the students to reenact the poem "I am Cucaracha." She's smiling to herself now as her preparations for the use of this lovely little poetry book begin to get exciting.

Ms. Castaño knows of a market where she can buy some gourds to use in making maracas as described in the poem "Gourds." She knows that her friend Marcella will be glad to bring her loom to school so the children can practice weaving as they read "I Saw a Woman Weaving." After that experience she can teach the children to weave paper placemats and maybe one of the mothers will come to school to make tortillas as a culminating activity on Friday. She picks up two ears of corn to take to school so the children will understand how the tortilla flour is made.

Ms. Castaño makes a list of new vocabulary that will be learned this week and is pleased to see many new Spanish and English words on the list. Her native English speakers will be learning a lot from this week's poetry unit, too.

Mr. Millar's sixth graders are exploring survival skills through a combined literature and science study based on several survival stories, *My Side of the Mountain* (George, 1959), *Island of the Blue Dolphins* (O'Dell, 1960), *River Rats, Inc.,* (George, 1979), and *Hatchet* (Paulsen, 1987). The students are working in groups to explore the realia they have found or had relatives send to them from the areas in which the stories took place. In some cases they have been able to actually taste the berries and boiled twigs that the characters in the books had to eat to survive.

Mr. Millar has contributed some of the realia used in the study, like some of the more primitive tools that are no longer readily available. In other cases the students have used some of the raw materials described in the books to actually construct the tools and cooking utensils made by the characters in the stories. Now that the students have all read one of the survival stories, they are comparing the survival strategies used in each of the books.

"Most of the tools they made in the stories depended a lot on the wood and stone and other materials that were available in the area," observes Johan.

"That is very true," agrees Mr. Millar. "What else was affected by the location of the story?"

"The problems they had," replies Susana. "Survival in the Canadian wilderness is very different than survival on a Pacific island."

"I thought it was interesting that they had different plants that they used for medicine," adds Teresa.

"The botany books we looked at listed a lot of plants that were edible or used for medicinal purposes," says Jacob. "I never knew that you could eat boiled twigs either."

"They sure don't taste too great," grins Teresa.

"What could you eat if you were stranded around this area?" asks Mr. Millar.

"Twinkies from the Minute Market," jokes Susana.

"No, seriously," says Mr. Millar. "Are there any local plants you could eat?"

"My grandmother says they used to eat dandelion salad," suggests Johan. "We could try that. We have a lot of dandelions growing in our yard."

"See if you can get her recipe," smiles Mr. Millar. "We're going to take a survival hike in a few weeks so we need to research the plants that we may have to eat. Mr. Smithson, the botanist at the college, is coming along just to make sure we don't poison ourselves. We will also have to gather indigenous materials from the woods to use as tools and cooking utensils. We have some research to do before we go, though. All we will carry along is a supply of water and some very basic tools like the stone and wood hatchets and a first-aid kit."

The students looked at Mr. Millar with a wide assortment of expressions, from excitement to apprehension.

CONCLUSION

The use of realia in the classroom supports student learning in a wide variety of ways. Introducing real objects that can be seen, felt, and manipulated serves as a powerful way to connect vocabulary to real life. The use of realia is motivating to students because they can actually use the real objects in the way in which they are intended to be used. Realia introduces an authentic hands-on nature to many lessons. The use of real objects conveys meaning in a way that no photograph or illustration can. There is no confusion over the size, weight, texture, or smell of an object, fruit, vegetable, or tool when the real thing is present. In some cases it becomes important to provide several objects in order to see the range of possibilities, such as several different kinds of apples or tiny sunflowers to be compared with the huge examples seen in certain parts of the world. The teacher can be extremely innovative in the use of realia as demonstrated in chapters 15 and 17 in this text.

References

George, J. (1959). *My side of the mountain*. New York: Dutton.

George, J. (1979). *River Rats, Inc*. New York: Dutton.

Johnson, T. (1996). *My Mexico—México mio*. New York: G. P. Putnam's Sons.

O'Dell, S. (1960). *Island of the blue dolphins*. Houghton Mifflin.

Paulsen, G. (1987). *Hatchet*. New York: Aladdin Paperbacks/Simon and Schuster.

RECIPROCAL TEACHING

37

Reciprocal teaching (Palincsar & Brown, 1986) is a reading strategy in which students take turns teaching small sections of text. It is usually done in small groups. All students initially read a section of the text. One student begins by summarizing a section of the text and questioning the others about the meaning of the section. Any difficult parts are identified and discussed and then predictions are made about the next section to be read. The students take turns summarizing and questioning until all sections of the text have been read, summarized, and discussed.

This strategy is recommended for use with English language learners because of the potential for supporting comprehension in small group interactions and the active use of learning strategies. Support from the group in explaining and discussing in the student's first language is a positive factor that can be added by making sure that students with the same home language are put in groups together. It is important, also, to make sure that each group contains at least one student who is a strong speaker and reader of English.

STEP BY STEP

The steps in implementing reciprocal teaching are:

1. Identify a section of text that has some difficult vocabulary or concepts. Plan a lesson where you model the steps in reciprocal teaching and relate them to learning strategies that support comprehension of the text. (See Chapter 24, Learning Strategies Instruction, for more information.)
2. Explain to the students that they will work in small groups helping each other make sense of the information they will be reading. Form a small group of students to work with you in demonstrating the approach. Start by giving everyone in the small group a paragraph of text that contains some difficult vocabulary or concepts and ask them to read it silently.
3. After the group has finished reading silently, briefly summarize the content of the material and pose questions to students in the group. Model and identify literal questions (simple recall), inferential questions (finding unstated meaning), and critical questions (calling for higher-level thinking).
4. Identify any difficulties in understanding the text that you or any member of the group experience and relate the identification and exploration of those difficulties as "comprehension monitoring." (See Chapter 18, Interactive Read Aloud.) Ask the group to suggest ways

in which they overcame the difficulties as they were reading. As they suggest possibilities, remind the group that they are using cooperative learning strategies when they share solutions in a groups like this.

5. Make a prediction about what you think will happen in the next section of text, identify the strategy as "predicting" and relate it to making inferences. Give the group the next paragraph to read silently and encourage a student to be the next reciprocal teacher.

6. Post a chart that reviews the steps to be taken. Divide the class into groups and encourage them to take turns teaching the materials to one another. See figure 37.1 for an example of a reciprocal teaching chart.

Step	What to Do	Learning Strategy
Group formation	Form a group of students to read cooperatively. Choose the sequence of reciprocal teachers (students).	Cooperation
Read	Each member of the group reads the first section of the text to him/herself.	Silent reading
Summarize	The first student summarizes the section just read.	Summarizing
Question	The first student questions other members of the group moving from low-level to high-level questions.	Literal Inferential Critical Questioning
Identify	The first student identifies any area of text that presented difficulty to any member of the group.	Comprehension monitoring
Problem solving	The group discusses possible solutions or strategies that could be used.	Cooperation
Prediction	The first student makes a prediction about what is likely to happen in the next section of text.	Predicting Inferring
Read	The group reads the next section silently.	Silent reading

Figure 37.1   Steps in Reciprocal Teaching

The whole procedure is repeated with the second student in the group leading.

APPLICATIONS AND EXAMPLES

The fifth graders in Ms. Tobias' class are moving from their study of Australia into the exploration of the aborigine tribes and their ways of communicating. Ms. Tobias wants them to read *The Cave Painters* by Percy Trezise (1988) because it gives such a comprehensive look at the wide variety of terrain in Australia and the different cultures that are represented by the aborigine peoples. She knows the text is challenging, not because of the content, but because of the unusual proper names and so she decides to do two things. First, she will preteach some of the proper names and second, she will encourage the students to work in cooperative groups and do reciprocal teaching to support one another in the reading of this "tough text."

Ms. Tobias divides the students into cooperative groups of five students each and gives each student a number. She reminds the groups of their past experiences with reciprocal teaching and quickly reviews the steps on the chart in the room (see Figure 33.1). Each student is given a copy of the book and each group is given a large map of Australia with instructions to plot the locations of the various tribes that are described in the book.

As the groups get started, Ms. Tobias wanders around the room listening to the discussion. Because she has tried to put the less fluent English speakers into a group where there is another student with the same home language, there are a lot of side discussions in Spanish and Punjabi in the groups. The students seem to be doing a lot of group problem solving, and she hears some references to the videos of Australia, which she has shown in the past few days.

After the groups have finished reading and discussing the book, Ms. Tobias calls the whole group together to review the process and talk about the history of the people that was recorded in the caves. The group also adds a number of new words to the Australian word wall. The students were especially fascinated by the different foods that were described in the book.

"They talked about poison yams, Ms. Tobias," says Richie. "I never knew yams could be poisonous."

"That was a surprise to me too," Ms. Tobias exclaims. "I knew mushrooms could be poisonous. I'd never heard of poisonous yams."

"You never tasted the ones my mother makes," quips Sammy.

Ms. Tobias smiles, "I'm going to tell her you said that."

"Can we make some cave paintings like the ones in the book, Ms. Tobias?" asks Jennifer. "I think they would look nice on the walls for Parent's Night."

"Good idea, Jennifer," replies Ms. Tobias. "Maybe some of you could write a script about the travels of the aborigines. I think there is a lot to learn about Australia. There were a number of new animals, plants, and foods mentioned in this book that we need to research."

"I'll get on the Internet and see what I can find," offered Simon.

"Great idea!" smiles Ms. Tobias. "The rest of you look things up in the books we checked out from the library. Let Simon know if there's anything you can't find and maybe he can locate the information on-line. Let's make a list of the things we want to research."

Mr. Wishon's eighth graders are studying the U.S. Constitution. They are trying to understand the process the constitutional congress went through in writing the Constitution and the nature of the government that it created. Mr. Wishon has divided the class into cooperative groups and they are getting ready to read the Constitution for the purpose of understanding two things: 1) How the constitution has changed over the years, and 2) What was built into the original document that has allowed it to remain in place over 200 years with all of the changes that have taken place in American society.

Mr. Wishon walks the groups through the first round of reciprocal teaching with the preamble and Article I. Since Article I includes ten sections, Mr. Wishon has an opportunity to model a number of different levels of questions. He lists them with examples of questions he asks at each level. See Figure 37.2 for the chart that Mr. Wishon creates.

First the class walks through Article I with Mr. Wishon asking the questions and the small groups discussing them. Then the groups begin the reciprocal teaching process on their own, with students taking turns with the summarizing and questioning.

Once the reciprocal teaching groups have explored all seven articles, Mr. Wishon conducts a group discussion where the class reviews the things they know about the original Constitution and its contents. They note the date of the signing, then Mr. Wishon has the groups open their social science books and use reciprocal teaching to read what the book has to say about the Constitution.

"It's sure a short description for such a long document," observes Martina.

"Yes, it is," agrees Mr. Wishon. "That's why I wanted you to read it thoroughly. I'm sure there are a number of citizens in this country who really never read it as thoroughly as you have today. Now what I want to do is look at the amendments and the history of why they were added. Who notices something about the dates of the amendments?"

"They started amending it almost right away," notes Brian.

Type of Questions	Examples
Literal (Knowledge) Identification and recall	Who . . . ? What . . . ? When . . .? Where . . . ? How . . . ?
Comprehension Selection of facts and ideas	Tell in your own words. What is the main idea . . . ?
Application Use of facts, rules	How is _____ an example of _____? Why is _____ important?
Analysis Separating the whole into parts	What are the main elements of _____? How does _____ compare or contrast to _____?
Synthesis Combination of ideas into a new whole	How could you design a _____? What might happen if you combined _____ and _____?
Evaluation Developing opinions, judgments, decisions	Do you agree with _____? How would you decide to _____?

Figure 37.2   Levels of Questions and Examples
Adapted from Chamot & O'Malley (1993).

"Yes, it was only three years later," smiles Mr. Wishon. "Why do you think that happened?"

The discussion continues with the students actively involved in thinking, reading their textbook, and discussing the amendments and what they change in the original document. The group seems to have a good understanding of the process involved in amending the constitution and the discussion shows that they comprehend the importance of each of the amendments. Sometimes Mr. Wishon asks one of the students to translate for others when the language gets complicated. Everyone seems to be very interested in the lesson.

CONCLUSION

Reciprocal teaching supports student learning in several different ways. It encourages students to self-monitor for understanding. It requires the use of key vocabulary in explaining concepts. It encourages collaboration and group support in making sure that each member of the group fully understands the lesson.

Reciprocal teaching may require some adaptations for English language learners depending on their levels of English development. Some English language learners may not be ready to take a role as teacher but can serve in another capacity, perhaps as monitor of understanding, translator for other English language learners, or lister of key vocabulary words. Members of the group may have to adjust the questioning procedures so that the English language learners can draw pictures, point, or read aloud from the text in order to answer questions. These strategies should be modeled for the groups and students should be aware that they are responsible for supporting each member of their group in understanding the text.

References

Chamot, A., & O'Malley, J. (1993). *The CALLA Handbook: Implementing the cognitive academic language learning approach*. Reading, MA: Addison Wesley.

Palincsar, A. S., & Brown, A. L. (1986). Interactive teaching to promote independent learning from text. *The Reading Teacher, 39,* 771–777.

Trezise, P. (1988). *The cave painters*. Auckland, NZ: Harper Collins.

REPETITION AND INNOVATION

SUPPORTS

- ● Comprehensible input
- ✔ Increased verbal interaction
- ● Contextualized language
- ✔ Reduced anxiety
- ✔ Active involvement of the learner

Repetition and innovation is the use of a piece of text in several different ways to reinforce the understanding of it and the gradual integration of the vocabulary and concepts into the speaking and writing vocabulary of the students. The text is introduced and explored in multiple modes with the students finally rewriting the text to create an innovation on the original. This approach is especially effective for English language learners because they have multiple opportunities to revisit both the text and the vocabulary in multiple learning modes. See Figure 38.1 for suggestions of innovations that can be used for this strategy.

STEP BY STEP

The steps in implementing repetition and innovation are:

1. Choose a book that you and the students will enjoy rereading a number of times. With repetition and innovation you will be revisiting the same text several times and the book should have some interesting vocabulary and action or it will become boring. A book with a pattern or obvious structure makes a good choice for this kind of activity. If necessary, have the book read in the students' first language(s) before reading it in English.
2. Explore the structure of the story. If it is a circular story focus on the fact that one thing leads to another and stress that as you read. If the story has a beginning, middle, and end, emphasize that as the book is read. Try to help the students understand the structure and the relationship of the events to the structure.
3. Explore the pattern or structure of the book by having the students do some substitution of words using word cards in a pocket chart. Have them change words within the pattern or structure of the book until they can substitute words and make meaningful patterns on their own.
4. Using the pattern that you and the students have practiced on the pocket chart, have students write and illustrate a sentence on a single sheet of paper and then sequence the pages to make a class book. Read the book together, practicing the vocabulary and the pattern orally.

Format	Description
Pocket chart stories	Build stories using the pattern or structure from the focus book. A sentence frame is used with word cards and key vocabulary from the focus book.
Wall stories	The students retell the story and individual pages are written on large pieces of construction paper. The pages are hung from clothesline across the room or attached to the wall in sequence so the students can read the story using a pointer. When the wall story is taken down it is made into a class big book.
Shape books	A cover and pieces of paper are cut into the shape of an animal or object that corresponds to the topic of the writing. The innovation is written and published as a shape book.
Circular stories	A story that begins and ends in the same place is published in a circular shape (see Figure 38.2)
Three-part books	Stories that have a distinct beginning, middle, and end are published in a three-part book format (see figure 38.2).
Story quilts	Stories are written on individual pieces of paper which are decorated as quilt squares and tied together with yarn (see figure 38.2).
Formula poems	Students publish poems in different formats. (See figure 23.3 in the Learning Centers Chapter of this text for additional suggestions.)
Videos	Students write scripts as innovations on their focus book and the enactments of the scripts are videotaped.
Puppet plays	Students write scripts as innovations and the scripts are performed as puppet plays.

Figure 38.1 Suggestions for Innovations

5. Depending upon the structure of the book, write an innovation such as a circular chart (for circular stories); a three-part book for beginning, middle, and end stories; or an accordion book for cumulative stories. (See Figure 34.2 for illustrations of these book forms.) Involve the children in supplying the key vocabulary for the innovation either by doing the writing interactively (see Chapter 19, Interactive Writing), or by taking their dictation.

6. Create another innovation or new version of the same book in another format using the same pattern or structure. This time you could create a wall story using large sheets of construction paper, or a story quilt with individual pages of the book tied together with yarn to form a large quilt. (See Figure 38.2 for illustrations of these publishing formats.) By this time the students should be thoroughly familiar with the pattern, structure, and vocabulary.

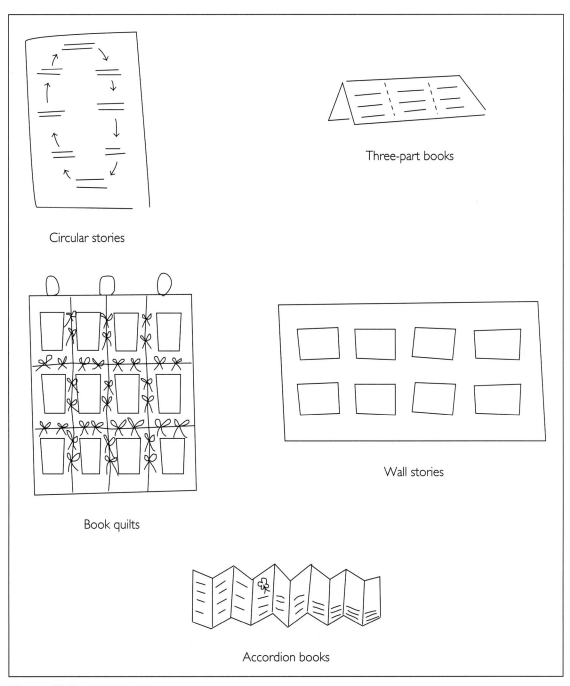

Figure 38.2 Publishing Formats

APPLICATIONS AND EXAMPLES

Ms. Leonard's first graders are sitting quietly listening to *If You Give a Mouse a Cookie* (Numeroff, 1985) read in Hmong by the bilingual aide. They are watching the pictures carefully and answering questions in Hmong about what the mouse might want next.

After they hear the story in their home language, Ms. Leonard helps them construct a chart of the sequence of things the mouse wanted using realia that she has brought from home. Ms. Leonard uses this time to review the English names for the household items—straw, scissors, broom, tape, etc. That day at the learning centers, the students sequence the pictures from the book and match the pictures to the real items as one of their activities.

Ms. Leonard has also provided drawings of the household items on Language Master cards for the students. They can practice sequencing the cards so they are in the same order as the story and they get to hear the English words as they slide the cards through the Language Master.

The next day Ms. Leonard uses the pocket chart to display the sentence frame, "If you give a(n) __(animal)__ a __(noun)__, he will want a __(noun)__." Using the words from *If You Give a Mouse a Cookie,* the students build sentences by adding word cards to the sentence frame. Ms. Leonard and the students read the sentences aloud after they are built. At the end of the lesson Ms. Leonard and each of the students write their favorite sentence interactively on a sheet of paper and the students illustrate their sentences.

The third day, Ms. Leonard starts the morning showing the students the book she put together from the sentences and illustrations they made the day before. They read the class book together and the students smile broadly when their pages are read. Ms. Leonard then shows them a large sheet of butcher paper on which she has drawn the mouse from the story with blank lines in a circle all around him.

"We are going to try to remember all the things the mouse wanted in the story and write the words on the blanks," says Ms. Leonard. "Do you think you can do that?"

"Yes!" the students declare confidently.

Ms. Leonard has one student at a time help her to write the words in the correct sequence on the blank lines. They have no problem remembering the sequence, the English words, and in most cases the spelling of the English words.

The final innovation on this story is started that day with the students writing about another demanding animal. They decide to write about a pig and all the things he wanted, starting with some mud—and ending with some mud. They are very excited when Ms. Leonard tells them that Laura Numeroff, the author *If You Give a Mouse a Cookie,* has also written a book about a pig. Her new book is called *If You Give a Pig a Pancake* (1998). Ms. Leonard then reads the book to the students.

The word wall in Ms. Avelar's fourth grade is covered with words they have learned in their literature studies over the past few months. The students often use the word wall to find a word to make the stories they write more interesting. Ms. Avelar is planning to do an in-depth study of the parts of speech with the students based on Ruth Heller's series of books, which each focus on a part of speech in an innovative way.

Ms. Avelar begins the study with the reading of *A Cache of Jewels and Other Collective Nouns* by Ruth Heller (1987), which focuses on nouns. The students join Ms. Avelar in finding all the nouns on the word wall and they review the meanings of the nouns as they move the word cards from the word wall to the pocket chart. As the students arrange the nouns on the pocket chart Ms. Avelar asks, "How can we arrange the words so that we will be able to find them easily?"

"In alphabetical order!" the students answer in chorus.

"Of course. That's the easiest way to find them. But suppose I want you to do something different with the words this week?" Mrs. Avelar asks. "Suppose I want you to make different groups of nouns. One group would be nouns with only one syllable. The next group would be nouns with two syllables. The next with three syllables. Could you do that?"

"Of course we can," the students nod.

"You can still put them in alphabetical order within each group," adds Ms. Avelar. "Then you will be able to find them more easily."

Once the students have completed the sorting of the nouns into syllable groups, Ms. Avelar then says, "Let's just look at the two-syllable nouns that we have found." She reads down the list: *apple, auto, baby, bottle, butcher, candle, candy,* and so on.

"Let's see if we can think of some more two-syllable nouns for our list. We will want to have a nice variety of them for the project we are going to do this week," Ms. Avelar says.

The students add *taco, pizza, sneakers, jacket, pumpkin,* and *catsup* to this list.

"Now I want you each to take one of these little booklets and write one of the two-syllable nouns at the top of each page. After lunch we will work on a new category of words," says Ms. Avelar as she passes out booklets to each of the students.

After lunch Ms. Avelar reads the Ruth Heller book on adjectives, *Many Luscious Lollipops* (1989). After practicing as a group, the students work in cooperative groups, adding a list of adjectives to each noun in their booklets. They are able to add some very unusual adjectives working in the group setting. Some of the students have asked Ms. Avelar if they can prepare a second booklet in Spanish and she has given them permission to do that. Several of the students who have asked permission to prepare the Spanish booklets are not native Spanish speakers and this pleases Ms. Avelar.

On the third day of the project, Ms. Avelar introduces verbs and the students practice the actions of the verbs they find on the word wall. Ms. Avelar reads *Kites Fly High* (1988), Ruth Heller's book about verbs, and the class brainstorms additional verbs to add to the word wall.

"I now have a hard job for you," says Ms. Avelar. "I want you to think of verbs for each of the nouns in your word booklets. For instance, the first noun in your booklet is *apple*. What can an apple do?"

"That's really hard, Ms. Avelar," says Tino. "An apple just sits there."

"That's good, Tino. Write *sits,*" smiles Ms. Avelar.

"Oh! I get it," says Tino with a grin.

After the students work in cooperative groups to write verbs for each of their nouns, Ms. Avelar introduces them to the pyramid poetry format. "We are now going to use the words we have been collecting into a poem that looks like a pyramid. The title of the poem is a noun," says Ms. Avelar.

"Let's pick one of our nouns to use as an example," suggests Ms. Avelar.

"Pizza!" says Gretchen.

"Good one," confirms Ms. Avelar and she writes *pizza* on the chalkboard. "Now we need two words that describe the word pizza."

"Hot and spicy," says Tomas as he licks his lips.

"Great!" says Ms. Avelar as she adds the line to the poem. "The next line has three words and uses verbs that tell about what the noun does. This is a hard one."

"The students all turn to the page in their booklets with the word *pizza* at the top and start reading action words.

"I've got it!" beams Nikki. "Steaming, bubbling, tempting."

"That's good," says Ms. Avelar as she adds the line to the poem. "So far we have:

Pizza
Hot, spicy.
Steaming, bubbling, tempting.

"Now we need a complete, five- or six-word sentence about pizza," adds Ms. Avelar.

"How about, 'I like pepperoni, mushrooms, and cheese'?" suggests Tyrone with a smile.

"That sounds great," says Ms. Avelar as she adds the line to the poem.

"Now we need one more complete sentence using six to ten words about the pizza," smiles Ms. Avelar.

"Oh, I know!" suggests Nikki. "Let's call Pizza Hut on the telephone right now!"

"That's it," says Ms. Avelar and she writes Nikki's sentence on the board under the other lines.

"Let's read our poem," suggests Ms. Avelar. The whole class reads together.

Pizza

Hot, spicy.

Steaming, bubbling, tempting.

I like pepperoni, mushrooms, and cheese.

Let's call Pizza Hut on the telephone right now!

"Can you guess why it's called a pyramid poem?" asks Ms. Avelar.

"It looks like a pyramid," responds Tyrone.

"That's true," says Ms. Avelar. "That's why you have some lines with four or five words and some with six to ten words. You need to choose the number of words you need to make each line a little longer than the one before it. It has to form a pyramid shape. Now, you know what I want you to do next," smiles Ms. Avelar.

"Write poems!" shouts the class.

"Yes, I want you to write pyramid poems. You may write by yourself or with a partner. You may write in English or in Spanish. You may write with paper and pencil or on the computer," says Ms. Avelar. "Use the word booklets to help you. Does anyone need a partner?"

The students move close to their partners and some go to the computers to write. Several students go to tables away from the others to write by themselves, but everyone is busily engaged in writing poems using their word booklets.

CONCLUSION

Repetition and innovation strategies provide students with multiple opportunities to learn new concepts. The choice of repetitions and innovations should be based on observation of the students' understanding of the concepts being presented. Each repetition or innovation should build on the last so that the students are experiencing gradually more difficult applications of the concepts. These activities are especially supportive of English language learners because they see multiple definitions and uses of the new concepts and vocabulary they are using.

References

Heller, R. (1987). *A cache of jewels and other collective nouns*. New York: Grosset and Dunlap.

Heller, R. (1988). *Kites fly high*. New York: Grosset and Dunlap.

Heller, R. (1989). *Many luscious lollipops*. New York: Grosset and Dunlap.

Numeroff, L. (1985). *If you give a mouse a cookie*. New York: Macmillan/McGraw Hill.

Numeroff, L. (1998). *If you give a pig a pancake*. New York: Macmillan/McGraw Hill.

Tompkins, G. E. (1996). *Language arts content and teaching strategies*. Upper Saddle River, NJ: Macmillan/Prentice Hall.

REPORTING BACK

SUPPORTS

- ● Comprehensible input
- ● Increased verbal interaction
- ● Contextualized language
- ✔ Reduced anxiety
- ✔ Active involvement of the learner

Reporting back is a strategy used to support students in bridging the gap between spoken and written language (Gibbons, 1993). This strategy can be used as a follow up after any active learning experience. The students describe their experience, using vocabulary that is connected with the experience so that the rest of the class has a clear understanding of the materials and sequence of actions that were used. The students then write their reporting back summary to be included in the class daily news, or their daily learning log. See Figure 39.1 for suggested activities appropriate for reporting back.

▶ STEP BY STEP

The steps in using the reporting back strategy are:

1. Prepare the students for an active learning experience by giving directions for the activity and modeling what is expected. Follow up your demonstration by saying, "After you finish your activity, you will report back to the class describing what happened. For example, if you were reporting back to the class on the experience just demonstrated, you would say, 'I opened the jar of red paint and I opened the jar of blue paint. I took an eyedropper and used it to draw up some of the red paint and dropped two drops of red paint into the plastic cup. Next, I used the eyedropper to draw up some blue paint and put two drops of blue paint into the plastic cup. I took a toothpick and swirled the two colors together in the cup. When they mixed together they turned into purple paint. I learned that red and blue paint mix together to make purple paint.' After you finish your activity, you and your partner need to decide what to say when you report back to the class."

2. After explaining the procedure to the students, list the steps on the chalkboard or on a chart. The steps might be:

   1. Mix your two colors together in the cup.
   2. Make a list of the steps you use.
   3. Practice reporting back with your partner.
   4. Ask for help if you need it.

3. During the activity, circulate throughout the classroom, reinforcing the vocabulary being used and scaffolding language by verbalizing what you see going on. For example, as one

Curricular Area	Activity	Adaptation
Art	Create a summer art activity book for younger students by trying out art projects and then writing step-by-step instructions of how they were done.	Computer use; photos or drawings to accompany text
Dance	Create a dance to demonstrate the connections between movement and content area study, research dance in various cultures and historical periods, present an oral summary of the research along with the dance created.	Videotape the presentations; create a book describing the research done and the connections found
Theater	Research and write a play related to a period of history, such as the American Revolution, Civil War, World War II, "Roaring Twenties."	Publish the scripts along with the reports on the research done
Language arts	Research and write informational books. Require the students to report back on their research along with the steps they used in writing and illustrating the book.	Publish the books along with pages from their learning logs describing the process used to research; write and illustrate it, including any collaboration they did
Science	Use experiments as a topic for writing a children's science activity book for younger students to use as summer science activities.	Add diagrams, photos, and learning log examples to the book
Social studies	Teach the students to write anecdotal records as they observe interactions among people in public places such as the school cafeteria or the local mall. Focus on describing body language and facial expressions as well as clothing and physical attributes.	Add drawings of the situations

Figure 39.1   Suggested Activities for Reporting Back

pair is dropping paint into the cup you might say, "You are dropping the paint into the cup. I see you dropping one, two, three drops of yellow into the cup."

4. After the activity, give the pairs time to practice their reporting back dialogues. Then, ask each pair of students to report back to the group. This works best if each pair has a slightly different task. In the color mixing activity each pair might have different colors or different numbers of drops to use so that the reporting back stays interesting and nonrepetitive.

5. After each pair reports back, list important words that they used on the chalkboard and celebrate their use of interesting and important vocabulary. Emphasize the role the vocabulary plays in helping the audience to visualize exactly what the pair did.

6. After completing the reporting back, students write their report back and use it either as news items for the class daily news or as daily entries in their learning logs.

APPLICATIONS AND EXAMPLES

Ms. Christensen's sixth-grade students are creating a class Rosetta stone and then using the alphabet they inscribe on the stone to write messages in hieroglyphics as a part of their study of ancient Egypt. The Rosetta stone is created as a class project, but the individual messages are transcribed by pairs of students writing in clay using sticks as styluses.

Ms. Christensen has modeled the use of the Rosetta stone to create her message and how the stone must also be used to decipher other messages. She has left the instructions for the activity on a chart in the room, but it is also written in hieroglyphics. She models her reporting back to the class with the directions, "Tell us what you did, step by step. Be sure to use words like *first, second,* and *next* so we can follow the sequence of what you did."

After the pairs complete their messages and report back orally, they write their messages in their social science learning logs, along with their translations and step-by-step descriptions of what they did.

Ms. Christensen has provided an activity that emphasizes the difference between casual spoken language between working partners, more formal spoken language used for class reports, and written language. As a closing activity she engages the students in a discussion in which they compare the types of things they said to each other while they were working on the messages, the kinds of sentences they used when they reported back orally, and the sentences they wrote in their learning logs. They also discussed the vocabulary they used in the more formal reporting back and writing. The students decided that the language used in the formal oral presentations was more like the language used in the writing in the learning logs than the language they used while talking to their partners. One student said, "When I was working with Jonathan, I used a lot of words like, *this* and *that* because we were pointing to objects and talking about them. When I talked about the objects in the reporting back, I had to use the names for them and say what I was doing instead of just doing it."

Ms. Carlson is an art teacher at Johnson Junior High. Johnson has an extremely diverse population of students and the school has established a school-wide goal of developing students' oral and written language. Ms. Carlson has decided to use reporting back as a strategy after each project, requiring the students to write descriptions of their projects and how they were made. This month, the classes are using clay to create three-dimensional figures showing their favorite recreational activities.

Ms. Carlson demonstrates the use of clay to make a tennis player in position to serve the ball. She then reports back to the students, modeling the use of sequence words to describe her step-by-step procedures. She uses the reporting back sequence to model the problem solving she had to do in order to create a sculpture that showed the arm and racket extended into the air. Using the overhead projector, Ms. Carlson then demonstrates how she will transcribe her oral reporting into her art learning log. She also includes a photo of her sculpture in her learning log.

The students spend about a week completing their sculpture. They work on their reporting back assignments and practice in partners while the slower sculptors are finishing their projects. Ms. Carlson invites Mr. Gobel, the principal, to come in to hear the reporting-back presentations and view the sculpture. Mr. Gobel is very impressed with the art, the descriptive ways the students found to describe the steps they used, and the problem solving they were required to use. He suggests they repeat the process for their parents the night of parent conferences.

CONCLUSION

Reporting back provides a step in the learning process that is frequently overlooked. It requires the students to use the lesson-related vocabulary to review the steps that were used in completing the assignment. It provides a direct connection between instruction and language.

English language learners are supported, when necessary, by being encouraged to use visuals that illustrate the steps and supply the vocabulary so that they have a scaffold when they report back to the teacher or the class.

References

Gibbons, P. (1993). *Learning to learn in a second language.* Portsmouth, NH: Heinemann.

Suggested Readings

Hernandez, H. (1997). *Teaching in multicultural classrooms.* Upper Saddle River, NJ: Merrill/Prentice Hall.
Peregon, S., & Boyle, O. (1993). *Reading, writing, and learning in ESL.* New York: Longman.

SCRIPTING

40

SUPPORTS

- Comprehensible input
- Increased verbal interaction
- Contextualized language
- Reduced anxiety
- ✔ Active involvement of the learner

Scripting (Lozanov, 1982) is a strategy that prepares English language learners with sample language interactions or situational dialogues appropriate for upcoming events. These sample language interactions, called *scripts,* are presented and practiced prior to the students encountering the situation when the scripts will be needed. Preparing and practicing scripts in advance of events is supportive of the learner because it lowers anxiety and builds confidence in the ability to communicate in English.

In order to use scripting the teacher must be able to identify or create opportunities for verbal interaction and engage the students in verbal and role play so that the students understand the situation in which the script is appropriate and practice delivery of the basic script as well as several possible alternate responses to ensure communication. Preparing the students for alternate responses sometimes involves the preparation of a ready-made template, which students can use in their own particular situation. The students do this by filling in the slots in the template with specific information in order to communicate. Suggestions for possible scenarios for scripting experiences are shown in Figure 40.1.

STEP BY STEP

The steps in using scripting with students are:

1. Identify a situation where a script will be helpful to English language learners or other students. Carefully plan the normal verbal interactions that would occur in the situation and write the words in the form of a short dialogue. Duplicate the script for the students.
2. Explain the situation to the students and enlist one student to walk through the script with you. Read the script with the student, acting out the physical actions that will normally be a part of the situation such as opening the door, pulling out a chair, or motioning for the other person to walk ahead of you. Be sure to emphasize that people's responses may not be exactly the same as the words in the script and the importance of listening to their responses. Provide some practice in listening to people's responses and choosing alternative words as appropriate. This step involves the analysis of possible responses by the teacher and providing practice for the students in which the teacher emphasizes the importance of listening to the speakers' response and choosing among the possible dialogues according to the direction the interaction takes. See Figure 40.2 for an example of dialogue with alternate responses.

Situation	Scripting Needs
Greeting classroom visitors	One person should de designated (students take turns); what to show, how to explain, how to introduce teacher, students, visitor; when to interrupt teacher, where to take the visitor at the end of the visit
Celebration visits to principal	What to say to the school secretary; how to introduce yourself and talk about why you're there
Field trips	What to expect, any special protocol, when talk is appropriate, when quiet is expected; special terminology needed
Parent nights at school	What is expected of each student; individual assignments as far as explaining the curriculum, classroom routines, providing commentary
Any situation where certain behavior or language is expected	The actions, language that is expected

Figure 40.1 Suggestions for Scripting Activities

A student prepared is a student empowered, relaxed, and ready to learn.

You ask, "How are you today?"

1. If the response is, "Fine, thank you."
   You say, "I'm happy to hear that."
2. If the response is, "Not too good."
   You say, "I'm sorry to hear that. Are you sick?"
3. If the response is, "OK."
   You say, "Oh, is something wrong?"
4. If the response is, "Wonderful, I'm having a great day!"
   You say, "That's great! What has happened to make it a wonderful day?"

Figure 40.2 A Dialogue with Alternate Responses

3. Pair the students and encourage them to practice the use of the scripts as they play the roles. Begin the practice with English language learners paired with more fluent speakers of English. The first few times English language learners encounter the situation and use the script they may be more comfortable with a more fluent English speaker's presence for support as long as the more fluent speakers understand their roles as backup supporters in case the script is forgotten or the communications don't follow the normal course of events.

APPLICATIONS AND EXAMPLES

Ms. Casias' first graders are preparing for their Mother's Day tea. They have drawn portraits of their mothers and written short descriptions of them. Ms. Casias plans to have the students read their descriptions and then ask the mothers if they can find their portraits on the portrait wall.

The students have made cookies and tea, carefully measuring ingredients and following recipes. The day before the tea Ms. Casias gives the students a copy of a script they will use when a mother is escorted from the office into the classroom and another short script that gives the students practice in introducing their mothers at the tea. The first script says,

"Hello, my name is _____ . I will take you to Ms. Casias' room. Please come with me." (Open the office door for the mother and motion for her to go first through the door.)

"I will show you the way to the room. We are very happy that you are here." (Walk to the classroom slowly so that the mother can walk with you.)

After the mothers arrive and everyone is served tea and cookies, the students will use the second script. (Student stands and motions to his/her mother as she is introduced)

"My name is _____ and this is my mother, _____ . I would like to read something I have written about my mother," Students read the descriptions they have written about their mothers and then say to their mothers,

"Can you find your portrait on the wall?"

(The mothers identify their portraits and the descriptions are placed under the portraits after the mothers identify them.)

As the mothers leave be sure to say, "Thank you for coming to our tea."

Ms. Casias arranges a section of the room to look like the furniture arrangement in the office and the students practice the first script. The fluent English speakers play the parts of the mothers and the English language learners practice greeting a mother and bringing her to the classroom. Once the mothers have all arrived in the practice session the chairs are placed in the same way they will be arranged for the tea and the students practice introducing their mothers. Because some of the mothers do not speak English some of the students practice introducing their mothers in English and their home language. Several of the students are able to read their descriptions in English and then translate them into the home language. For the students who need help with the translation the school primary language tutors will be available to help at the tea.

The day of the tea Ms. Casias takes time to practice the scripts before tea time and the students are all smiles as they serve as official greeters and later make introductions. The day after the tea the class talks about the tea and Ms. Casias decides that she will continue to ask students to go to the office to greet and escort visitors to the classroom. They seem to enjoy this experience.

Mr. LeBeau is taking his tenth-grade government class to the state capital on the train. After they arrive in the capital they will observe a legislative session and visit the local legislators in their offices. The students have prepared questions that they will ask the legislators during the scheduled interviews. Mr. LeBeau has prepared a script for the students so they will follow the proper protocol while entering the offices and participating in the interviews. Each group has a group leader who will keep the group together and make sure that everyone has an opportunity to ask questions.

Mr. LeBeau stages a practice session the day before the trip so that everyone has a clear idea of the sequence of events. They walk through the procedures of boarding the train and learn who their group leaders are. Mr. LeBeau even practices the short walk from the train station to the capitol building, discusses expected behavior, and gives the students time schedules so they understand exactly what will be expected of them.

The students are given scripts illustrating the language that should be used when entering the offices of the legislators, and they are given instructions about their behavior in the offices and the government buildings. They practice entering the offices in small groups with a designated leader and a back-up leader in case one is needed. One of the students plays the part of the receptionist in the office and the groups practice the proper behavior and sequence of events that is likely to occur during the interviews. The students are given some possibilities of different scenarios just in case the script is not followed exactly. The groups all practice asking and answering questions.

The students seem confident that they are prepared for the field trip. They all arrive nicely dressed and carrying notebooks for their interviews. On the way home at the end of the day Mr. LeBeau asks them how things went.

"It was almost like you sent them the scripts, Mr. LeBeau," says Marisea. "I knew exactly what to expect."

"You forgot one thing, though," adds Helia. "I didn't know what to say when they asked us if we wanted coffee."

"Well, did you want coffee?" asks Mr. LeBeau, smiling.

"I said, 'No thank you,'" answers Helia. "I didn't know how I would hold it, drink it, and take notes."

"Well, 'No thank you' was the right thing to say then," Mr. LeBeau assures her. "Sometimes you have to go without a script. But, you knew what to do."

CONCLUSION

Scripting provides English language learners with language they will need to use in a variety of situations. This strategy serves to reduce anxiety when students are placed into unfamiliar situations or being asked to use new language structures. Once students are confident that they can fall back on the scripts, they will find that they are more relaxed and can begin to communicate more freely. The scripts remain in their memories as back-up words, just in case.

References

Lozanov, G. (1982). Suggestology and suggestopedia. In R. Blair (Ed.), *Innovative approaches to language teaching*. Rowley, MA: Newbury House.

SHARED READING

41

SUPPORTS

- ● Comprehensible input
- ✔ Increased verbal interaction
- ● Contextualized language
- ✔ Reduced anxiety
- ● Active involvement of the learner

Shared reading (Holdaway, 1979) is a strategy that teachers use to read books, charts, and other texts with students when the text is too difficult for the students to read independently. Students and teacher read the text aloud together. Even when the students cannot read along with the teacher they are hearing the words pronounced as their eyes follow the text. In the primary grades large books with big print, called big books, are used with small groups of students so that everyone can see the illustrations and text (Depree & Iversen, 1996). Shared reading can also be done with multiple copies of small books, poetry charts, song lyrics, or any text as long as students and teacher can all see the words (Tompkins, 1997).

Using shared reading with English language learners is appropriate because the teacher has opportunities to use illustrations to support vocabulary development, to use think-aloud strategies to teach problem-solving approaches, and to integrate verbal interactions to support comprehension (Gibbons, 1993). When using shared reading with English language learners it becomes especially important to build background knowledge and experiences that help the students to understand the meaning of the text. The skills and strategies that can be taught through shared reading are shown in Figure 41.1

▶ STEP BY STEP

1. Introduce the book or text. When using a book, examine the cover and predict from the illustrations on the cover. Encourage the students to talk about experiences they have had that relate to the topic of the book, chart, or poem.
2. Read the book or other text aloud, tracking the words as you read so the students can read along. Use a pointer to make sure the students are looking at and saying the word with you. They may not know all the words, but they will hear you pronounce them as you point to them.
3. Stop at appropriate times to discuss what is happening or to predict what will happen next. Use the illustrations to help support understanding of vocabulary. Ask students to point to parts of the illustrations to show comprehension of words or events in the story. Involve the students in acting out movement words and story events to reinforce meaning.
4. Encourage students to talk about the story. Go back through the book and ask them to talk about what happened on each page. This is a chance for the students to practice oral language and incorporate new vocabulary into their retelling of the story.

Guided Reading Applications	Example
Word boundaries	"Frame the word *caps* in this sentence."
Left to right progression	"Point to the words with the pointer."
Punctuation uses	"How would you say this sentence?"
Word meaning	"Show me the dahlias in the picture."
Illustrations/story meaning	"How did you know he was scared?"
Cueing systems—visual, meaning, syntax	"How did you know the word was *monkeys?*" "Show me the picture that shows you what that word means." "Would we say, 'The boy went jeans'?"
Reading with expression	"How would he say that?"
Fix-it strategies	"How would it start if the word were lantern? Read it again."
Use of context for meaning	"Read the part that helps you understand what the word *flourish* means."
Reading for cohesion links	"Read the part that tells you that he heard the noise after he went to bed."
Reading to confirm	"Read the part that tells you why he was angry."

Figure 41.1 Skills and Strategies to Teach through Shared Reading

5. Reread the book or text several times, tracking with a pointer. Encourage individual students to take turns reading a page or refrain aloud, use the pointer or turn the pages.
6. After students have read the text several times, they can read small copies of the book or text independently or illustrate their favorite part of the story and write about it.

APPLICATIONS AND EXAMPLES

Ms. Baker and her kindergarten students are doing a shared reading of *Caps for Sale* (Slobodkina, 1968). Before they read the book, Ms. Baker shows the students some hats and caps. They talk about the difference between a hat and a cap. They examine the different caps and talk about the shape and color of each. Ms. Baker reminds the students of the *Curious George* stories (Rey, 1941) that they have read together and tells them that they will meet some more monkeys in the book they will read today.

When Ms. Baker reveals the cover of the book, Jana exclaims, "I see the monkeys!" and hops up to point to them.

"Yes," Ms. Baker says, "there are monkeys in this story. The title of the book is *Caps for Sale: A Tale of a Peddler, Some Monkeys, and Their Monkey Business.* That's a long title. What do you think it means?"

"The man in the tree is selling caps." suggests Kevin.

"You are right, Kevin!" says Ms. Baker. "He sells caps." She points to the peddler on the cover. "He is called a peddler. A peddler sells things."

"What do you think it means when it says, a tale of a peddler, some monkeys, and their monkey business?" asks Ms. Baker.

"My dad says 'No monkey business!'" says Curt. "He says that when he wants us to be good."

"Yes, monkey business is being silly, like monkeys," says Ms. Baker. "We will see what monkey business is when we read the book." Ms. Baker opens the book and begins to read, pointing to the words as she read them. When she gets to the refrain, "Caps! Caps for sale!" she encourages the students to read with her. When she gets to the part where the monkeys imitate everything the peddler does, she has the students act out what the peddler and the monkeys do. She stops to have the students predict several times during the story, and she points to pictures as she says words that might be unfamiliar to the students. They are all very involved in the reading of the story.

After Ms. Baker and the students read the story several times, she gets the caps out again and shows the students how to stack them like the peddler in the story did. The caps and several copies of the book are placed in the dramatic play area, where the students are told that they can act out the story later. Ms. Baker suggests that one person can pretend to be the peddler and others can take the parts of the monkeys.

"If you forget what comes next in the story, the books will be there to help you," says Ms. Baker. "Just look at the pictures and the words in the book and you will remember what happens next."

Ms. Baker often uses big books in her kindergarten classroom. The large illustrations help her to teach new vocabulary. She finds that her English language learners follow along with the rest of the students as they read the books and enjoy using the language from the books to retell the stories.

• •

Ms. Moua uses shared reading with the English language learners in her sixth-grade class as they read *Charlotte's Web* (White, 1952) together. The students each have an individual copy of the book. Ms. Moua introduces the new chapter by having the students review what has happened in the story so far.

The first day the students look at the cover of the book and predict what they think will happen. After they read the first chapter they act out the events of the morning at the Arable farm—with students taking the roles of Fern, Wilbur, Mr. and Mrs. Arable, and Avery. The second day they discuss the chapter from the previous day before they read the second chapter.

"I think Avery's going to do something mean to the pig," predicts Josef.

"No! He's not mean," insists Manuel. "He'll help his sister take care of the pig."

"No! He wants a pig too," reminds Graciel.

"Let's read and find out," suggests Ms. Moua.

The students read the second chapter of the book—stopping to discuss the meanings of words—act out some words, and reread for fluency when they stumble over words. Ms. Moua models the fluent reading of passages and then has the students repeat the passage, reading along with her. When the group finishes reading the second chapter, Ms. Moua has them list the events in the story so far. Ms. Moua takes their dictation and writes the sentences on sentence strips, placing the sentence strips in order in the pocket chart. The students and Ms. Moua reread their dictated story together. After the shared reading the students copy the sentences onto pages of a blank booklet Ms. Moua supplies for each student and they illustrate each page. Ms. Moua knows these students have no books at home to read. After this activity they will each have a copy of their retelling of *Charlotte's Web,* complete with their personal illustrations. One of their illustrated books is shown in Figure 41.2.

• •

Figure 41.2   An Illustrated Retelling of a Shared Book

CONCLUSION

Shared reading is used across grade levels for many purposes. For emergent readers shared reading is a way to model concepts about print such as reading from left to right, starting on the left page before reading the right-hand page, and the purpose of punctuation marks. For older readers, shared reading is a strategy used to support fluency, vocabulary, and comprehension. By reading books together students can see comprehension strategies modeled at the point in reading at which they are needed. Teachers have a chance to demonstrate what they do when they come to difficult words or concepts. Follow-up activities to shared reading enable teachers to provide projects that strengthen involvement with the book, such as retellings, simulation journals, or illustration opportunities. It is with these shared readings and follow-up projects that teachers and students achieve a shared literary understanding.

References

Depree, H., & Iversen, S. (1996). *Early literacy in the classroom: A new standard for young readers*. Bothell, WA: Wright Group.

Gibbons, P. (1993). *Learning to learn in a second language*. Portsmouth, NH: Heinemann.

Holdaway, D. (1979). *Foundations of literacy*. Auckland, NZ: Ashton Scholastic.

Rey, H. A. (1941). *Curious George*. Boston: Houghton Mifflin.

Slobodkina, E. (1968). *Caps for sale: A tale of a peddler, some monkeys, and their monkey business*. New York: Harper Collins.

Tompkins, G. (1997). *Literacy for the 21st century*. Upper Saddle River, NJ: Merrill/Prentice Hall.

White, E. B. (1952). *Charlotte's web*. New York: Harper and Row.

SKILLS GROUPING

SUPPORTS

- ● Comprehensible Input
- ✔ Increased verbal interaction
- ✔ Contextualized Language
- ✔ Reduced anxiety
- ● Active involvement of the learner

S kills grouping (Gibbons, 1993) is the act of arranging students in groups based on their need for instruction in a specific skill. Skills grouping is done for a short period of time, usually for only a few lessons, and is effective only when the groups are based on the teacher's knowledge of the language and skill levels of the students. The criterion for grouping is based on teacher observation of a specific instructional need. This greatly enhances the delivery of comprehensible input because the lessons are planned to scaffold learning at the students' present level of functioning (Krashen, 1985).

Skills groups tend to be heterogeneous as far as reading levels and overall academic functioning are concerned. A skills group might consist of students reading on a range of levels. Skills groups consist of students with a specific instructional need, for instance, a group of students who are not using quotation marks correctly or a group of students who need instruction in solving math problems involving fractions. Skills groups are used effectively in the teaching of language usage, reading, language arts, and mathematics skills.

▶ STEP BY STEP

The steps in implementing skills grouping are:

1. Set up a method for observing and documenting students' language levels, learning, and classroom performance. See the anecdotal records and performance sampling sections in this text for suggestions.
2. Frequently review the records you keep of the students' levels of functioning and needs for instruction and look for commonalities on which to base instruction. Form skills groups based upon these commonalities.
3. Design a lesson to teach the skill for which the group has a common need. Explain the skill, model it, and give the group opportunities to practice using the skill under your guidance. As a follow-up to the lesson give the students an authentic task that requires the use of the skill just taught. Observe the students' use of the skill in the assigned task. Celebrate with the students who are using the skill effectively and plan another lesson focusing on the same skill for the students who need more instruction. See Figure 42.1 for the cycle used in forming and teaching skills groups. Note that the skills groups are very flexible because

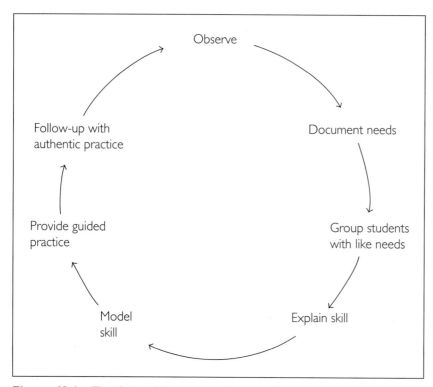

Figure 42.1   The Cycle of Forming and Teaching Skills Groups

future groups are formed on the basis of need. The students who achieve the objective of the lesson are not included in the next group of students reviewing the skill.

APPLICATIONS AND EXAMPLES

The fourth graders in Ms. Bersarian's class are writing simulation journals as they read their core literature books. They are taking the point of view of one of the characters in the book they are reading and writing in a journal each day as if they were the character. Their task is to write in the journal as if they had been a part of the action in the portion of the book that was read that day and "get in the head" of the character, telling about the events of the day and how they feel about what has happened. Although the students are reading a wide variety of books, Ms. Bersarian notices that there are several of the students who are simply summarizing the events in the stories without taking the point of view of one of the characters. She decides that a lesson on perspective taking is needed.

Because the students are all familiar with *Charlotte's Web,* Ms. Bersarian decides to use that book as an example in the perspective-taking lesson. She looks through the simulation journal and identifies the students who are not writing from the perspective of one of the characters and she calls the group together.

Ms. Bersarian begins by reading aloud the first chapter of *Charlotte's Web* to the students. She then asks the students to name the characters introduced in the chapter. As the students name the characters, Ms. Bersarian lists the character names across the top of the chalkboard. She then asks the students to tell what they know about the characters. See Figure 42.2 for the list of characteristics they created.

After the attributes of the characters are listed, Ms. Bersarian acts as the local television news reporter and asks each student to take the role of one of the five characters introduced in the chap-

Fern	**Mr. Arable**	**Mrs. Arable**	**Avery**	**Wilbur**
8 years old	farmer	farmer's wife	10 years old	runt
passionate	practical	practical	heavily armed	white
outspoken	loves Fern	cooks breakfast	jealous of Fern	pink ears
fights for	willing to	helpful	sleeps late	good appetite
right	give Fern	supports husband's	wants a pig too	
	a chance	decisions		

Figure 42.2 Attributes of the Characters in Chapter One of *Charlotte's Web*

ter. Ms. Bersarian asks each character questions about the morning events on the Arable farm and the students pretend to be the character and answer the questions from the point of view of the character they are playing. The student playing Avery acts as though he were disgusted with his sister and the student playing Fern acts very excited that she saved the life of Wilbur, the runt pig. The student playing Wilbur, with the help of a pig puppet, tells the news reporter how grateful he is that Fern saved his life (Herrell & Fowler, 1997).

Ms. Bersarian has prepared five simulation journals, each one identified with the name of one of the five characters in the first chapter of *Charlotte's Web*. In Fern's journal, Ms. Bersarian and the students decide what Fern would write that day about her adventure. Ms. Bersarian and the students negotiate the sentences and she chooses one student to be the group scribe. Their entry says,

Dear Diary,
Today I saved a life. My dad was going to kill a runt pig just because he was too small. I grabbed his ax and held on tight. I said, "Would you have killed me if I had been small at birth?" I cried a lot and now I have charge of a tiny pig. Boy, is Avery mad! He wants a pig too. Dad says he only gives out pigs to early risers. Maybe Avery won't be so lazy after this. I'm really excited! I named the little pig Wilbur because it's such a pretty name.
Fern

After the group wrote the entry for Fern they did journal entries for each of the other four characters introduced in the chapter. Ms. Bersarian concluded the lesson by reminding the students that they are all writing simulation journals for the books they are reading in reading workshop.

"Today, I want you to do exactly what we have done with the characters from *Charlotte's Web*. Read your chapters and then tell the events in the chapter from your character's point of view. Pretend to be the character and explain how you feel and what happened to you," says Ms. Bersarian. "If you have trouble getting started, raise your hand. Or come back and look at the journal entries we made about the *Charlotte's Web* characters today."

As the students complete their simulation journals that day, Ms. Bersarian reviews them with the students. She finds that all but two of the students now understand what to do and with a little support those two students are able to take their character's perspective in the journal entries. Ms. Bersarian plans to monitor those two students' entries carefully for a few days to support their successful perspective taking. If the students are still experiencing difficulty, Ms. Bersarian will form a new skills group for the two struggling students and teach another lesson on perspective taking for those two students.

● ●

Mr. Tyler is reading his eleventh-grade essays, and he notices that a number of the students are still having difficulty with the proper use of the homophones *there, their,* and *they're*. As he reads the essays he makes a list of the students who are still confusing these words. A little later he notices several students who are confused about when to use an apostrophe in *it's*. Several of these same students are also using apostrophes inappropriately with nouns, sometimes creating possessives when they really need plurals. After Mr. Tyler completes the reading of the essays he has three skills group lists and decides that he will use some of the class time each day for the next week to work on these specific skills.

Mr. Tyler has identified the need for skills grouping in his classes. He has an additional problem because his classes only meet for 50 minutes and he must find time to teach skills groups while not wasting the time of the students in his classes who do not need this instruction. Although he is surprised that the students he has identified as misusing simple grammar and vocabulary in their essays are not all in his basic writing class, he realizes that he cannot ignore these types of errors in students nearing high school graduation.

Mr. Tyler designs a group assignment lesson that will enable him to teach the skills he has identified and still maintain the momentum for the rest of his class. Then he divides each class into cooperative groups. He calls students into a skills group to work with him on the skills he has identified. The rest of the class works in cooperative groups to identify a writing goal and design a presentation for the class using literature to demonstrate the ways in which different authors accomplish this goal. Mr. Tyler begins the class by conducting a brainstorming session in which the class identifies some of the writing goals they have. The list includes writing good dialogue, building tension in the plot development, using a rich vocabulary to make the writing interesting, developing interesting characters, understanding the use of metaphor and simile, determining approaches to creating and developing a problem and solution. After the list is generated, Mr. Tyler divides the students into cooperative groups, placing one student from his skills group into each of the cooperative groups. The cooperative groups each identify a goal they want to research and begin to look at the literature they have been reading for good examples.

Mr. Tyler calls his skills group together and introduces the problem he has discovered in reading their essays, "I will be working with this small group for a short time each day for awhile to help you to overcome a problem that I discovered in reading your essays," he begins. Mr. Tyler gives an explanation of the differences among the homophones *there, their,* and *they're* and how important it is that the words be used correctly. He sends the students back to their cooperative groups to begin to look for the examples needed for the group presentations on the way the professional writers approach the goals identified by the class. The skills group has one added task. They are to find sentences in the literature that demonstrate the correct usage of the homophones they are studying and copy at least one sentence that employs each of the homophones. For homework that night the skills group is assigned a paragraph to be written about an imaginary group of people. The skills group is to find a way to use all three forms of the homophone in their paragraph.

Mr. Tyler finds that the system he has set up works well. He identifies needs for skills groups and then provides time for cooperative group work, which can continue while he conducts quick skills instruction. He follows up with short assignments in which he monitors for understanding of the skills. He uses one additional technique to help the students in monitoring their own progress. He duplicates copies of the skill or vocabulary rules for the students to attach to the inside cover of their writing folders. Before they turn in any assignments they must work collaboratively with another student on editing, proofreading their writing for the types of errors that give them difficulty. Mr. Tyler finds that making the students aware of the errors they are committing helps them to self-monitor and self-correct. They are refining their use of the English language (Swain, 1993).

••

CONCLUSION

Skills grouping is a way to provide focused instruction for small groups of students with shared needs. Because skills groups are created to address a specific need, they are not long-standing groups. Instruction is given, skills are practiced and monitored, and the groups change. If some students require further instruction, that instruction is provided, but only for those who need it. This form of grouping is effective because students are receiving lessons tailored to their needs and the other students in the class are given assignments that allow them to practice their skills at appropriate levels without being bored by instruction they do not need.

References

Gibbons, P. (1993). *Learning to learn in a second language.* Portsmouth, NH: Heinemann.

Herrell, A., & Fowler, J. (1997). *Camcorder in the classroom: Using the video camera to enrich curriculum.* Upper Saddle River, NJ: Merrill/Prentice Hall.

Krashen, S. (1985). *The input hypothesis: Issues and implications.* New York: Longman.

Swain, M. (1993). The Output Hypothesis: Just speaking and writing aren't enough. *The Canadian Modern Language Review, 50,* 158–164.

White, E. B. (1952). *Charlotte's web.* New York: Harper and Row.

SORTING ACTIVITIES

43

SUPPORTS

- ● Comprehensible input
- ✔ Increased verbal interaction
- ✔ Contextualized language
- ✔ Reduced anxiety
- ● Active involvement of the learner

Sorting activities (Bear, Invernizzi, Templeton, & Johnston, 1996) are activities that require the students to sort objects, words, phrases, and sentences according to set parameters. Sorting activities are appropriate for use with English language learners because they provide a way for students to manipulate objects and written symbols to show their understanding of concepts, while acquiring the vocabulary and structures needed for verbal interaction.

Sorting activities can be used in a wide range of curricular areas and are appropriate from kindergarten through twelfth grade with careful planning and adaptations. See Figure 43.1 for suggestions in the use of sorting activities.

STEP BY STEP

The steps in implementing sorting activities are:

1. Identify a skill that can be practiced or demonstrated using sorting. See Figure 43.1 for suggestions. Prepare the materials to be sorted, including containers or pocket charts in which to place the sorts.
2. Explain the activity, model what the students will do, and provide some guided practice before asking the students to sort independently. Decide whether you want the students to sort individually, in pairs, or small groups. If practice of the concept is the purpose of the sort, individual sorts are effective. If you want the sort to include practice in using English vocabulary and communication, paired or small-group sorts are more effective.
3. Establish a routine for the students to use when they complete their sort. Some teachers encourage the students to take a Polaroid picture of the sort and turn the picture in, others require a written response that explains the sort, and others simply have a peer check the sort.

Grade Level	Curricular Area	Description of Sorting Activity
Kindergarten	Phonemic awareness	Using small objects or pictures, students sort by matching sounds.
	Phonics	Using small objects or pictures, students sort by initial sound/letter representation.
	Math	Using small objects or math manipulatives, students size, shape, or number.
	Science	Using animal pictures, children sort by attributes such as fur, feathers, and scales.
	Social studies	Using pictures depicting weather conditions, students sort by season.
Primary	Phonics	Using small objects, pictures, or words, students sort by ending sound, vowel sounds.
	Math	Using number sentences, students sort by sum or difference.
	Writing	Using short sentences written on sentence strips, students sort by type of sentence (declarative, question, exclamation).
	English	Using word cards, students sort by parts of speech (nouns, verbs, adjectives, etc.)
	Science	Using leaves, students sort by leaf shape. Using animal pictures, students sort by classification (mammal, reptile, amphibian, bird).
Upper Elementary	Reading	Using sentence strips with sentences written on them, students sequence them to form a topic sentence and supporting details.
	Math	Using cards with word problems written on them, students sort them into stacks representing the four operations (addition, subtraction, multiplication, and division).
		Using cards with word problems written on them, students sort them into stacks estimating their correct solutions (1–5, 6–10, 11–15, 16–20, etc.)
	Vocabulary	Using word cards, students sort words into categories such as synonyms, antonyms, etc.
Secondary	Science	Students sort rock samples into classifications. Students match description cards with scientific samples, slides, experiments.
	Literature	Students sort plot summaries into genre classifications. Students match main character description with literature titles.
	Learning strategies	Students sequence cards with learning strategy step descriptions.
	Life skills	Students sequence cards with job application procedure descriptions. Students sort descriptions of job application and interview behaviors into piles marked *Positive Behavior* and *Negative Behavior.*
	Social studies	Students sequence the steps in the legislative process. Students match attributes of nations to the names of the nations.

Figure 43.1 Suggestions for Using Sorting Activities

APPLICATIONS AND EXAMPLES

The students in Mr. Avedesian's kindergarten class are learning how to sort objects by listening to the beginning sounds of the words. Each student has an empty milk carton with the top cut off. On the table in the sorting center is a tray full of small objects such as balls, pencils, erasers, bracelets, hearts, apples, baby bottles, crayons, and markers. The students are looking for objects that begin with the same sound as their names. Mr. Avedesian reminds them to say their names and then say the name of the object to see if the sound matches.

Michael says, "Michael, ball," then shakes his head and returns the ball to the table and picks up the marker.

"Michael, marker," he says and smiles as he places the marker into his milk carton.

After the students have found the items that begin with the same sound as their names, they bring their milk cartons to Mr. Avedesian and show him the items they have found. Mr. Avedesian asks them to say the names of the items and then they can return the items to the table. Mr. Avedesian keeps a list of the students who are successful with this initial sort and pairs them the next day to search for items for their partners' names. He plans to match Michael and Simon for the second day. Michael will be looking for items that begin like Simon's name and Simon will be looking for things that match Michael's name.

Gradually through the year, Mr. Avedesian will move through the initial consonants and begin to have the students sort for items that match the letters of the alphabet.

The twelfth graders in Ms. Tan's pre-employment class are getting ready for practice job interviews. She has designed a series of picture and description sorts to help them make good decisions as they practice interviewing and begin to apply for jobs. The first sort involves pictures of people in various forms of dress. The students sort the pictures into piles according to the job interviews for which the dress is appropriate.

This first sort is a picture to picture sort. The students simply match the pictures of the people to pictures of places of employment. After the students complete the sort they fill out a form, which lists the places of employment, and the students enter the number of a picture of a person next to the place of employment. After all the students have completed the sort, the class discusses the responses and why certain dress is appropriate for certain jobs.

The second sort involves reading a series of employment advertisements and matching pictures of people with their education and experience listed on the back with the jobs for which they are most qualified. Again, the students fill out a brief form which matches the letters that identify the job ads and the numbers that identify the applicants. The class discusses the meanings of the ads and the qualifications that would be needed for each.

The third sort involves placing a series of job application forms into piles marked *Definite NO, File, Interview,* and *Top Candidate.* The students place the names of the applicants on a list with the same indicators at the top. For the list marked *Definite NO* they are asked to state why they placed the application on this list. They are asked the same question for the names on the *Top Candidate* list. The class discussed the sort after everyone has completed the "paper screen."

"You mean you would get placed on the *Definite NO* list just because of a few misspelled words on the application?" asks Jerome with indignation in his voice.

"For this particular job, spelling is a major requirement," replies Karen. "You are painting signs and decorating windows for sales. Besides, why would you hire someone who isn't careful enough to double check his spelling on something as important as a job application?"

"Exactly," confirms Ms. Tan. "Remember, you are probably not the only applicant for the job. The employers are looking for the best candidates. They don't want to waste time interviewing people who are probably not qualified to do a good job."

CONCLUSION

Sorting activities provide hands-on experiences with the manipulation of pictures, letters, words, and longer texts. Sorting activities provide practice in making decisions and differentiating among concepts but also illustrate a technique for studying and organizing materials. Although sorting activities have a wide range of applications, they are highly effective for use with English language learners because they provide the students with an opportunity to demonstrate their understanding with reduced reliance on language skills. Asking the students to justify their sorts creates an opportunity for verbal interaction based on visual cues, which is supportive of emergent English speakers.

References

Bear, D. R., Invernizzi, M., Templeton, S., & Johnston, F. (1996). *Words their way: Word study for phonics, vocabulary, and spelling instruction*. Upper Saddle River, NJ: Merrill/Prentice Hall.

STORY REENACTMENT

44

SUPPORTS

✔ Comprehensible input
● Increased verbal interaction
● Contextualized language
✔ Reduced anxiety
● Active involvement of the learner

S tory Reenactment is a strategy that encourages students to act out stories after they have heard them read or have read them themselves. This strategy involves creating props for the students to use in reenacting stories so that they can use the book language they have heard or read, and better comprehend the text by acting it out in sequence.

Props for story reenactment may consist of costumes for the students to wear or prop boxes containing props made of clay, flannel, or laminated photos. Part of the effectiveness of this strategy is the planning and active involvement of the students in discussing the stories and creating the needed props.

STEP BY STEP

The steps in story reenactment are:

1. Read a story to the students or have them read the story independently.
2. Have the students retell the story in sequence and list the props that will be needed in order to be able to accurately reenact the story.
3. Provide materials for the students to use in creating the props for the prop box. The materials might be clay, dough for baked dough-art, felt, or drawing materials. Encourage the students to sign up for the props they will make. See Figure 44.1 for instructions for making dough-art props.
4. After the props are made, painted and sealed, decorate a shoebox in which to store the props. The box can be labeled with a photograph of the cover of the book so the students can easily identify the story props.
5. Encourage the students to use the prop boxes to retell and reenact the stories, working in pairs or small groups.
6. Listen to the story retellings and encourage the students who are using the "book language" and vocabulary. This is a good opportunity to document language usage and take anecdotal records.

4 cups flour (NOT self-rising)   I cup salt
I ½ cups water
Mix ingredients together. Mixture will be stiff.
Knead for I0 minutes.

Make shapes desired, separate by thickness (poke holes in thick pieces).
Bake at 325–350 degrees (½ hour per ¼-inch thickness)
Cool.

Paint to resemble figures in the storybook.
Use acrylic paints or tempera mixed with Elmer's glue (half and half).

Other suggestions for prop boxes: Paper doll figures, flannel board figures, magnetic tape on the back of pictures, overhead transparency pictures, actual dress-up clothes, and larger props.

Figure 44.1 Baked Dough Recipe

APPLICATIONS AND EXAMPLES

Ms. Brown's kindergarten students are making dough-art props for the Gingerbread Man story. They are rolling out the dough and using cookie cutters to make the props. After the props are baked and cooled, the students paint them using a mixture of tempera paint and white glue. Once the props are dry they enjoy retelling the story, loudly proclaiming, "Run and run as fast as you can. You can't catch me. I'm the Gingerbread Man!"

Once the props for the Gingerbread Man are made, the students ask Ms. Brown, "Can we make props for The Little Red Hen now?" Ms. Brown decides to have an ongoing center where the students can make story retelling props. They are enjoying the props and she sees a lot of language practice going on as they use the props to retell the stories they have read.

Story reenactment is a strategy that seems to be made for English language learners. It provides a script for them to follow as they retell favorite storybooks. The props or costumes give them support in remembering the sequence of events. They gain confidence in their oral English abilities with each new retelling.

Mr. Zarras's sixth grade English language learners are making props for the story, *Where the Wild Things Are* (Sendak, 1963). The students read and reread the story many times so that they can tell it by heart. After the props are complete, the students will retell the story, with props, to their first-grade book buddies. The day finally comes when all the props are complete. The sixth graders enter the first grade classroom with broad smiles on their faces. The first graders sit enthralled as they listen to their sixth-grade friends reenact one of their favorite stories with the small clay props they have created. As soon as the sixth graders finish their production, Janey, one of the quietest of the first graders, shyly raises her hand. "Can I do it?" she asks. Soon all the first graders are clamoring for a turn to retell the story using the props. The lesson is a great success.

The first graders are in awe when the sixth graders announce that they will leave the prop box in the first-grade class for the first graders to use. The book and the prop box are presented solemnly to the first-grade class as a gift from their book buddies. The sixth graders are very proud of their ability to present the story so well and of their handmade gifts. Mr. Zarras is even prouder of his wonderful idea. It has boosted the self-confidence of his English language learners immensely.

CONCLUSION

Story reenactment can be used at any grade level. High school students enjoy the reenactment of literature they have read by using minimal costumes and props and by acting out the parts. Students can create overhead transparency props or computer graphics that they can use to reenact stories in the form of a slide show as an alternative to actual role playing.

Story reenactment provides a unique opportunity for the teacher to observe and evaluate the students' comprehension of the stories reenacted and the students' use of unique vocabulary and sentence structures. No matter which mode of prop is used in story reenactment, the students benefit by increased interaction with story plot, language, and structure.

References

Sendak, M. (1963). *Where the wild things are*. New York: Harper/Collins.

SYNTAX SURGERY

45

SUPPORTS

- ● Comprehensible input
- ✔ Reduced anxiety
- ✔ Active involvement of the learner

yntax surgery (Herrell, 1998) is a strategy that allows students to see the relationship of elements within a sentence that may be confusing to understand. Because English syntax often differs from the word order found in students' home languages, English language learners sometimes encounter difficulty in comprehending sentences they read or confuse word order when speaking or writing in English (Baltra, 1998).

Syntax surgery involves writing a sentence on a sentence strip and then cutting the sentence apart to rearrange it into more understandable pieces. Because the students actually witness the pieces of the sentence being moved, they are more likely to understand and remember the English syntax rules when called upon to use them in the future. Syntax surgery is also helpful in refining the students' understanding of the elements of writing and speaking that make their English difficult for others to understand; therefore, the use of this strategy helps them to be more confident in their use of English. Swain (1993) calls this refining of the spoken and written product vital to the development of fluency in her description of output theory.

STEP BY STEP

The steps in implementing syntax surgery are:

1. Identify a sentence that is causing difficulty. It may be a sentence that the student has spoken where the home language word order is in conflict with the English word order, or it may be a complex sentence encountered in reading that is causing confusion.
2. Write the sentence on a sentence strip and reread the sentence aloud with the student or students involved in the speaking or reading activity. For example, if the sentence that was written by the student says, "She was wearing a sweater green." Take a pair of scissors and cut the sentence apart in the place or places of difficulty. "She was wearing a sweater green," would be cut before the words *sweater* and *green*.
3. Rearrange the words in a pocket chart or on the chalk rail in the correct English sequence. Place "She was wearing a green sweater," on the chart and say, "This is the way we say it in English," reading the sentence with the correct English word order. Reaffirm the students' knowledge of the home language by rebuilding the sentence in the original order and say, "This would be the right order of the words in Spanish" (or other language), "but we say it this way in English," and put the words back into the correct order for English. Have the student read the corrected sentence along with you and then explain the difference in the word order as simply as you can.

4. Write a few more sentences with the same word pattern on sentence strips and have the students read them along with you for additional practice.

5. Be careful not to use this lesson in a way that interrupts communication with the student. If the message the student was conveying was clear, respond to it modeling the correct English syntax. Write the student's sentence down and return at a later time to use the syntax surgery strategy to support the refinement of the student's English. Be observant of other students who might benefit from the explanation and use the opportunity to give instruction to several students at a time.

APPLICATIONS AND EXAMPLES

Ms. Newsome's fifth graders are reading a series of books by Beverly Cleary when one of her English language learners comes to her with a puzzled look on his face. "Ms. Newsome, this sentence doesn't make any sense."

"Let me see, Jorges," says Ms. Newsome. She reads the sentence aloud, "'She pushed her bed out from the wall so that something reaching out from under the curtains or slithering around the wall might not find her.' I see what you mean," Ms. Newsome says.

"Let's see if we can figure it out," Ms. Newsome says. "Let's write the sentence on a sentence strip." As she writes the sentence on a sentence strip she reads it aloud with Jorges.

"OK, the first part of the sentence says, 'She pushed her bed out from the wall,'" says Ms. Newsome. "Do you understand what 'out from the wall' means?"

Jorges nods, "It means she moved the bed away from the wall."

"Exactly!" exclaims Ms. Newsome and she cuts that part of the sentence away from the rest of it.

"The next part says 'so that,' which means that the next part is going to tell us WHY she moved the bed," says Ms. Newsome as she cuts off the words *so that*.

"Here's where it gets tricky," explains Ms. Newsome. "'Something reaching out from under the curtains or slithering around the wall,' now did the story say anything about something behind the curtains or on the wall?"

Jorges shook his head, "No. That's why I'm confused."

"The key is the next word, *might*," says Ms. Newsome. "She's thinking there *might* be something behind the curtains or there *might* be something slithering around the wall. She's scared of things that *might* be in her room."

"Oh," says Jorges. "Now I get it." He takes the scissors and cuts *might* and then *not find her* away from the rest of the sentence. He arranges the sentence again to show the relationships among the clauses. "This makes sense," Jorges says as he looks at the new arrangement.

"The words *something* and *might* are important. They give you clues that this is all in her imagination," says Ms. Newsome as she underlines the two words. "You're really good at this, Jorges," Ms. Newsome smiles. See Figure 45.1 to see how Jorges arranged the sentence.

Mr. Reynolds teaches tenth-grade English in a high school with a large number of Hispanic students. Mr. Reynolds finds that his students enjoy literature but need a lot of support in understanding some of the more formal language in the classic tales they read.

While in the midst of a study of Arthurian legends, Mr. Reynolds shows a video of *King Arthur and His World* and then shares a beautifully illustrated children's story book, *Young Lancelot,* by Robert D. San Souci (1996) to give the students a feel for the history, culture, and language of the times. The students then read *The Lady of the Lake and Excalibur* by Sir Thomas Malory, translated by Keith Baines (1996), which is a part of their literary anthology. The students are reading the tale, taking individual parts and trying their best to read with expression so the story will be as exciting as Mr. Reynolds's reading of *Young Lancelot.* The language is difficult, however, and they often have to stop and discuss the meaning. Mr. Reynolds has used syntax surgery with his students on

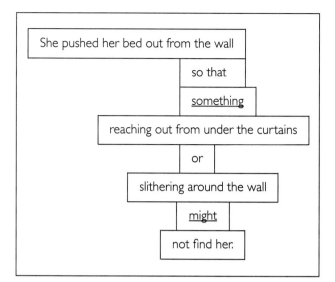

Figure 45.1 Jorges's Arrangement of the Sentence

several occasions and decides to do it in a shortened version during the reading to move the process along so the meaning of the passage doesn't get lost in the analysis. As the students read aloud, Mr. Reynolds writes sections of a sentence on the chalkboard whenever the reading appears to be choppy or without expression. As Mr. Reynolds writes the phrases or sentences on the board he separates the elements of the sentences that cause difficulty. For example, as a student reads:

> Riding once more through the forest, Sir Lancelot came upon a black brachet, eagerly pursuing a trail. Sir Lancelot followed and soon noticed traces of blood. The brachet kept glancing over its shoulder as if to insure that Sir Lancelot was still there, and finally came to an ancient castle which had been built on a green marsh. The brachet led the way across a shaky bridge and into the hall. A dead knight lay on the floor. The brachet went up to him and started licking his wounds, and then a lady appeared, haggard with grief and wringing her hands. (p. 131)

As the reader is reading this section Mr. Reynolds is writing brief notes on the board. See Figure 45.2 for Mr. Reynolds's notes to the readers.

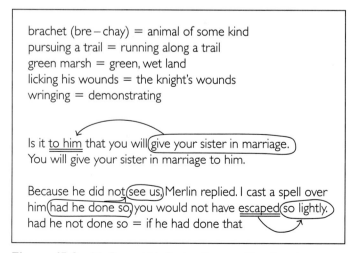

Figure 45.2 Mr. Reynolds's Syntax Surgery Shorthand

The student watches Mr. Reynolds and rereads the problem sentence using the clues Mr. Reynolds writes. The reading of the Malory tale goes smoothly using this strategy and the students don't lose the meaning in the process.

CONCLUSION

Syntax surgery is a strategy for making English syntax visible to the students. By using written diagrams as Mr. Reynolds does or cutting sentences apart as Ms. Newsome does, the students can both see and hear the differences in the word order in English or separate the thoughts within a complex sentence. By using several avenues to reinforce the English syntax, the students' understanding and memory are supported.

References

Baines, K. (1996). *Malory's Le Morte d'Arthur*. New York: Penguin Books.

Baltra, A. (1998). Hispanic ESL students reading in English: The language problem. Unpublished manuscript. Fresno, CA: California State University, Fresno.

Herrell, A. (1998). Strategies for supporting English language learners as readers. Manuscript submitted for publication.

San Souci, R. D. (1996). *Young Lancelot*. New York: Doubleday.

Swain, M. (1993). The output hypothesis: Just speaking and writing aren't enough. *The Canadian Modern Language Review, 50,* 158–164.

TOTAL PHYSICAL RESPONSE

···
SUPPORTS

- Comprehensible input
- Contextualized language
- Reduced anxiety
- Active involvement of the learner
···

Total physical response (Asher, 1982) is an approach to second language acquisition based on first language acquisition research. In first language acquisition children listen and acquire receptive language before they attempt to speak, they develop understanding through moving their bodies, and they are not forced to speak until they are ready. In total physical response, the teacher gradually introduces commands, acting them out as she says them. The students initially respond by performing the actions as the teacher demonstrates them. Gradually the teacher's demonstrations are removed and the students respond to the verbal commands only.

STEP BY STEP

The steps in teaching a total physical response lesson are:

1. Choose vocabulary that will be used in the classroom such as verbal directions, colors, and parts of the body, and list the words the students will need to know. Think of simple commands that can be given using the target vocabulary and that require a movement response such as "stand up," "sit down," "touch your head," or "show me the red block."

2. Introduce two or three commands at first, giving the command while demonstrating physically. For example, "Stand up," is accompanied by standing up. Motion for the students to do it with you. Introduce the next command and demonstrate. After you have introduced three commands, randomly alternate them, still demonstrating and encouraging the students' responses.

3. After the students have practiced the commands as you demonstrate each time, and they appear to know what to do without waiting for your demonstration, drop the demonstration and encourage them to respond to the verbal commands.

4. Add new commands, no more than three at a time. Always start with demonstrations as you introduce new commands, practice until the students appear to know what to do, and then drop the demonstrations.

5. Find new ways for the students to demonstrate their understanding of the vocabulary being practiced—such as pointing to pictures, drawing pictures, taking turns demonstrating commands—just to add practice and variety while the students are gaining confidence.

6. Play a game with a student volunteer giving the commands once the students gain confidence. Gradually encourage new student volunteers to give the commands as they become comfortable speaking the words. Never force students to speak the commands. Wait until they are confident enough to volunteer.

APPLICATIONS AND EXAMPLES

Mr. Tong's kindergartners are learning the names of body parts. Because he has a number of English language learners in the class, Mr. Tong decides to use total physical response to support their understanding of the English names for the parts of the body. He begins the lesson by saying, "Point to your head," as he demonstrates. He motions for the students to join him in touching their heads, nods, and smiles as they follow his lead. He then introduces, "Touch your chin," as he demonstrates. He alternates the two commands for a few minutes and then adds, "Touch your nose."

Mr. Tong repeats these three commands several times before he drops the demonstrations and gives just the verbal commands. He watches the students very carefully as he drops the demonstrations to make sure that the students are still able to follow along. He continues this game for a few days, until the students respond to commands to touch or point to their heads, chins, noses, ears, eyes, shoulders, feet, toes, knees, hands, arms, and elbows.

Mr. Tong changes games once he observes the students responding to verbal commands to identify each of the parts of the body. The second game he plays with the students involves their drawing body parts on a big chart. Mr. Tong begins by drawing a circle. He accompanies the drawing of the circle with the statement, "I am drawing a head."

He then asks for volunteers to draw each of the rest of the body parts on the chart. He follows the drawing of the body with requests for students to come up and point to body parts of the drawing.

Mr. Tong notices that several of the students are using the names of the body parts in their oral communications in the classroom, so he plans a game that will involve students giving directions in English. Mr. Tong begins the game by demonstrating. He pairs the students and tells them to touch heads, and he demonstrates with his partner. Then he tells them to touch hands, demonstrating with his partner. He asks for a volunteer to give the directions and one child eagerly raises his hand. Mr. Tong gives up his partner to pair him with the volunteer child's partner and helps the volunteer to demonstrate the commands as the student gives the directions and the others follow them. This game is played for a few minutes a day for about a week to give additional volunteers a chance to be the leader. Even the native English speakers enjoy playing.

Ms. Lopez teaches seventh-grade science and she is very concerned about safety with her students. Because she wants to make sure that everyone understands the safety procedures, she decides to teach them through a total physical response lesson. She introduces the terms pitcher, beaker, Bunsen burner, and the directions "tip the beaker" and "pour carefully" at the beginning of the lesson with the burners turned off. She demonstrates exactly how to tip the beakers to make sure the liquid doesn't splash as she says, "Tip the beaker slowly toward the pitcher and pour carefully."

After she is sure that the students understand the terms and directions with the accompanying demonstration, she repeats the directions without demonstrating as she walks around the room. Ms. Lopez observes the students as they practice transferring liquid from the pitcher to the beaker and placing the beaker into the holders, and she feels much more confident about their understanding of the safety precautions. The next day she plans to introduce the lighting of the burners and the procedures to be followed in case of an emergency. She will review today's lesson before she introduces a new one, however.

- Movement directions (stand up, sit down, line up, walk, run, kneel, skip, hop, etc.)
- Students' names
- Color words
- Number words
- Shapes
- Body parts
- Prepositional phrases
- Directions (up, down, left, right, high, low, etc.)
- Classroom procedures
- Content vocabulary/picture sorts

Figure 46.1   Applications for Total Physical Response

CONCLUSION

Although total physical responses are generally used with young children or English language learners with very little English knowledge, they can be used to introduce new procedures and vocabulary at almost any level. Figure 46.1 shows many ways in which this strategy is effective.

Total physical response is an active learning approach for supporting comprehension in a low-anxiety atmosphere (Krashen & Terrell, 1983). For this reason it is very popular with English language learners and teachers alike. Total physical response is also highly effective in teaching vocabulary associated with content-area knowledge. Teachers can introduce vocabulary and have students respond by drawing, pointing, putting pictures in order, or any other physical response that encourages active involvement and verifies understanding.

References

Asher, J. (1982). *Learning another language through actions: The complete teachers' guidebook.* Los Gatos, CA: Sky Oaks.

Krashen, S., & Terrell, T. (1983). *The natural approach: Language acquisition in the classroom.* Oxford: Pergamon Press.

VISUAL SCAFFOLDING

47

Visual scaffolding is an approach in which the language that is being used in instruction is made more understandable by the simultaneous display of drawings or photographs that allow students to hear English words and connect them to the visual images being displayed. In order to use this strategy, the teacher builds a file of visuals such as photographs or drawings and organizes them so that they can be easily accessed for teaching. See Figure 47.1 for suggestions of resources for visuals.

STEP BY STEP

The steps in planning and implementing visual scaffolding are:

1. Identify the vocabulary in the lesson to be taught that can be scaffolded with visual images, such as drawings or photographs.
2. Find (or take) photos or line drawings that can be used to visually support the understanding of the vocabulary needed in order for the students to understand the lesson.
3. Reproduce the visuals on transparency film and organize them in a way so that they can be easily used during teaching. Sequential order works well for a specific lesson, but you may want to organize your growing picture file alphabetically so that the pictures can be used easily for future lessons. Since pictures to be projected on an overhead projector need not be large, they can be stored in a shoe box on the overhead projector cart.
4. Encourage the students to use the transparency picture file in their presentations or as a way of asking and answering questions.
5. Continue to build your file on an ongoing basis.

APPLICATIONS AND EXAMPLES

Visual scaffolding can be used effectively at all grade levels and across curricular areas. In Mr. Chavez's second-grade class he is teaching a social studies unit on community. Because his students all walk to school and many of their parents use the city buses for transportation, many of the students have never been more than a few blocks away from the school. Mr. Chavez tries to plan the community unit to build the students' sense of pride in their community. Mr. Chavez takes photographs of local community helpers and institutions such as the local post office, postal work-

- Teacher-, student-, parent-taken photos
- Illustrations in old textbooks
- Line drawings from old black-line masters or workbooks
- Line drawings from children's coloring books
- Illustrations from big books
- Children's artwork

(All of which can be converted to color transparencies)

- Vacation videos
- Commercial videos
- Class-made videos

To make color transparencies from photos or illustrations:
Take the original to a commercial copying center. They will enlarge the picture and convert it to a transparency in one operation.

Storing transparencies:
A three-ring notebook with pockets can be used to organize transparencies so they are easily located.
    Small transparencies of individual pictures can be stored alphabetically in a shoebox and kept adjacent to the overhead projector.

Figure 47.1 Visual Scaffolding Resources

ers, the neighborhood grocery store, the local grocer, the crossing guard at the corner, a local fire-fighter, and police officer. These are all places and people with whom his students are familiar. Mr. Chavez has the photographs he has taken copied onto transparency film at the local copy shop.

As he leads a discussion of community helpers, where they work and what they do, Mr. Chavez uses the photos to connect the discussion to local places and people so that the vocabulary being used is identified with people and places the students know. The original photographs are then displayed in the room with written labels so that the students can begin to learn the written forms of the words.

Mr. Chavez and his students then take a field trip into the central part of town where the students are introduced to a supermarket. Mr. Chavez is busy taking pictures with a Polaroid camera and the students join in the discussion back in their classroom as they compare the pictures of the supermarket with the ones of their little neighborhood grocery.

"So many food!" exclaims Mercedes as she looks at the photo of the supermarket produce aisle piled high with fruit and vegetables. "Mr. Santos have only some," she says as she points to the picture of Mr. Santos's small store.

Mercedes' observations are just the beginning of the conversations Mr. Chavez hears among his students over the next few days. He has placed the photos in the writing center and the students are writing about the sights they have seen on their bus trip to the supermarket. The photographs have provided support in the students' understanding of their community. They have also provided a source for verbal stimulation and comparison that lasts for many days.

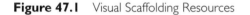

In Ms. Hammond's high school history class, her students are studying ancient Egypt. Ms. Hammond has transferred her vacation pictures of Egypt onto transparency film and the students are enthralled as she describes her feeling of being extremely small as she stood in front of the pyramids. The students are particularly interested in how the pyramids were built and they listen intently as Ms. Hammond displays transparencies she has made from David McCauley's book *Pyramid* (1976). The students begin a glossary of words they are learning as they study ancient Egypt.

They illustrate their glossary using sketches they make of the pictures she displays to support their discussion. As a follow-up to their discussion of the pyramids, the students form groups to research various segments of daily life in ancient Egypt. They add to their glossaries, work together to give oral presentations, and prepare transparencies of their own to demonstrate the facts they are learning about their area of research. As the students present their reports, Ms. Hammond finds they have followed her example. All of the groups have made line drawings of costumes, artifacts, and reproductions of Egyptian art to support their presentations.

CONCLUSION

Although visual scaffolding requires some planning, there is an abundance of resources for visuals. Photos can be copied from books and magazines and transferred to transparency film to build the picture file for use in scaffolding vocabulary and concept understanding. Photos taken on vacation can often be used in classroom teaching and may even make part of your trip tax deductible. Parents can often contribute photographs that you can copy for your growing file. Send out a request for photos of hard-to-find items to give the parents an opportunity to lend support.

Line drawings, photographs, maps, and realia are not the only visuals that can be used in scaffolding. Video is another visual support that is useful. It is often possible to film brief video clips in advance of a lesson so that students get a moving scaffold as a topic is discussed. Again, vacation video is a rich source of support.

Reference

McCauley, D. (1976). *Pyramid*. Reading, MA: Addison-Wesley.

VOCABULARY ROLE PLAY

SUPPORTS

- ● Comprehensible input
- ✔ Increased verbal interaction
- ● Contextualized language
- ✔ Reduced anxiety
- ● Active involvement of the learner

Vocabulary role play (Herrell, 1998) is a strategy used to encourage learners to make connections between their past experiences, the content currently being studied, and vocabulary that is new or being used in an unfamiliar way. Students are introduced to new vocabulary and given an opportunity to discuss and use the vocabulary in context through role playing. Often several groups of students are given the same vocabulary and asked to write and perform a skit in which the words are used and demonstrated. Since the groups are likely to write and perform skits in which the vocabulary words are used in different contexts, the skits serve to show multiple uses of the same words. In this way, English language learners are given an opportunity to see the vocabulary words used in context, as well as demonstrating several different contexts in which the words may be used appropriately.

▶ STEP BY STEP

The steps in implementing vocabulary role play are:

1. Determine the vocabulary words that will be used in a lesson or reading. Make cards with the words written on them.
2. Show the cards to the class, one by one, and ask the students to talk about ways in which they have seen the words used. Use this opportunity to introduce the context in which the words will be used in the lesson.
3. Divide the class into small groups of three to five students and give each group a set of four or five words. Make sure that each group has at least one member who is a strong reader. Instruct each group to write a skit in which all their words are used.
4. Give the groups time to work on their scripts and practice performing their skits. Encourage the groups to make and use simple props.
5. Give each group a chance to perform the skit that they have written. Discuss how the words were used after each skit is performed.
6. Compare and contrast the uses of the words by the groups, emphasizing the differing contexts used in the skits and the similarities and differences in the ways in which the words were used.

APPLICATIONS AND EXAMPLES

Ms. Lee has brought her calico cat, Muffin, to school to visit the children in her first-grade class. Many of the children express fear at the possibility of handling Muffin, but Ms. Lee wants them to become more comfortable with her. She chooses a very special book about a calico cat to share with her class. As she sits in the big rocking chair in the corner of the classroom with Muffin sleeping in her lap, Ms. Lee shows the cover of the book she holds, which has no picture on it.

"The title of this book is *The Third-Story Cat* (Baker, 1987). There is no picture on the cover to help us guess what it is about. What do you think it might be? What is a third-story cat?" asks Ms. Lee.

"Maybe there were two other stories about the cat," suggests Jacob.

"That's an idea," agrees Ms. Lee.

"Have you ever heard the expression *third-story* before?" she asks.

"I think my uncle lives on the third-story," answers Tony tentatively. "You have to go up a lot of stairs to his apartment."

"That's right, Tony. Third-story means the same thing as third floor," Ms. Lee opens the book to the title page where the students can see a lovely watercolor painting of an apartment building with three floors. In the apartment on the third floor you can see a calico cat sleeping on the window sill.

"Look up here in the window. Do you see a cat that looks just like Muffin?" asks Ms. Lee.

"O-o-o-h," sigh the students. "It does look like Muffin."

Ms. Lee then uses the illustration of the apartment building to show the meaning of the word *third-story*. She sweeps her hand across the first floor of the apartment building in the picture and says, "The people who live on this floor can walk out their doors and be on the sidewalk. This is the first floor or first-story." She points to the doors that open onto the sidewalk and to the sidewalk itself as she says the words.

"The people who live on the second floor, or second-story, have to go up some stairs to their apartments," Ms. Lee points to the doorway and moves her hand up to the second floor as she explains.

"The people who live on the third-story have to go up even more stairs," Ms. Lee explains as she points to the third floor.

"There are a lot of big words in this story," says Ms. Lee. "The author of this book, Leslie Baker, uses a lot of wonderful words to tell us about all the exciting things this cat does one day. Let's read the story and find out what adventures the cats have."

Ms. Lee reads the story aloud to the students, using the beautiful illustrations to help them understand the new vocabulary that is introduced in the story. She stops to demonstrate the meaning of the word *startled* as the cat is surprised by a butterfly flying up out of the geranium box. She has one of the children demonstrate the word *crept* as the cat is balancing along the ledge on the three-story building. As the story is read the children are exposed to a number of new words describing the ways in which cats move: *paraded, prowled, twitched, leaped.* Some other words require some physical practice like *winked* and *stroked.*

After the story is read, Ms. Lee goes through the new words again and has the children make a large circle. They walk around the room and act out the movements the cats made in the story. They wink, and creep, and twitch, and parade until they are all very silly. They show the difference between being startled and being frightened, between winking and blinking, between parading and prowling, and between patting and stroking. When they sit back down in the circle, Ms. Lee shows them cards with the new words printed on them and as she holds each card up a child volunteers to act it out.

Ms. Lee leaves the new vocabulary word cards in a part of the room near the pocket chart and shows the children how they can use the cards to fill in the blanks in the pocket chart story. They are invited to make new sentences with the cards during center time and they even have a new pointer with a calico cat on the end of it to use as they read the sentences they are making. The pocket chart sentences are shown in Figure 48.1

Vocabulary Words	Pocket Chart Sentences
crept	Alice _____ along the ledge.
startled	The butterfly _____ Alice.
leaped	Alice _____ to the roof.
winked	The tiger cat _____ at Alice.
paraded	The cats _____ by the grandmothers.
prowled	They _____ under the bench.
stroked	They hoped to get_____ .
twitched	Alice _____ her tail to say good-bye.

Figure 48.1   Pocket Chart Center

Note: Once the sentences from the story are built, the words can be rearranged to make new sentences. The children can chose to write and illustrate their sentences after they are built.

Ms. Lee smiles as she watches the children busily building sentences with the new vocabulary words. One of the children is carrying Muffin around the room with her as she acts out the new words she has learned from *The Third-Story Cat.*

• •

Mr. Valdez's fourth graders are studying Florida history. They are reading about the barefoot mailmen who brought the mail down the beaches to the first settlements and the ways in which the various people came to Florida to establish permanent residences. Some of the vocabulary is unfamiliar to the students and Mr. Valdez wants to make sure that the words are understood by all his students. Going through the Florida history book, Mr. Valdez selects the words, *barefoot, cypress, brackish, humid, Everglades, tidepools,* and writes the words on sentence strips. After he reads the section from the Florida history book aloud to his class, Mr. Valdez asks the students to talk about the ways in which they have heard the words used before. Jonah starts the discussion by saying, "I like to go barefoot in the summertime. My mother is always telling me to put my shoes on."

"I know what is means to go barefoot," adds Katie. "I just don't understand why the mailmen were barefoot."

Mr. Valdez takes the time to explain that since there were very few roads in the early days, the easiest route down the state was walking along the beach and so the mailmen often got their feet wet. To protect their shoes, they walked barefoot until they came to places where they needed to wear shoes. They would then stop and put their shoes back on.

Carla talked about brackish water and how her dad is often worried about the salt water at their beach house invading the drinking water. "That's what he calls brackish water," she explains. "It's when the salt water invades the fresh water."

"Yes," Mr. Valdez agrees. "But in some places in the state it's a natural thing for water to be brackish." Some of the rivers empty into the ocean and there is an area in which the salt water and fresh water mix. That's also brackish water."

The discussion continues until each of the words has been discussed. Mr. Valdez then divides the students into groups of three and asks them to write a short skit in which they use as many of the new vocabulary words as they can. One member of the group is assigned as the note-taker and the skits are written. The students are given 15 to 20 minutes to make simple props and each group is given a chance to act out its skit. Some of the groups have one of the members read the script while the other two do the acting. One group chooses to do a charade and asks the class to guess which word they are portraying. Another group has a complete dialogue with each of the speakers emphasizing a few of the new vocabulary words. One of the groups even performs a rap routine using the new words. By the time all six groups perform, all the new words have been demonstrated multiple times in many different contexts. Mr. Valdez feels confident that the new vocabulary is thoroughly understood by everyone.

CONCLUSION

Vocabulary role play provides the link between learning a new word and using the word in context, or multiple contexts. Role play enables the student to create experiences with which to link the new vocabulary. The study of words, their multiple meanings, and origins can also be effective with the use of vocabulary role play. Students can add brief videos to illustrate word meaning, create animated computer dictionaries, publish vocabulary books, and illustrate word posters—all of which increase their interactions with and understanding of English vocabulary and multiple meanings.

References

Baker, L. (1987). *The third-story cat.* Boston: Little, Brown and Co.

Herrell, A. (1998). *Exemplary practices in teaching English language learners.* Fresno, CA: California State University, Fresno.

WORD WALLS

49

W ord walls (Tompkins, 1997) are alphabetical lists of words created in the classroom for the purpose of word study and vocabulary development. They can be as simple as a list of words written on a large sheet of butcher paper. In classrooms where students are learning English as a second language it is helpful to create bilingual (or multilingual) word walls with the words written in several languages and illustrated. These word walls then serve as a reference for students as they write or interact verbally. Some teachers prefer to create a number of different word walls in the classroom, one containing high frequency words, which the students use for reference in writing, and others related to words being studied in connection to a literature or science focus unit. When the class moves on to another literature focus the words collected for the previous study can be placed on a word ring and kept for the students' reference. Placing a picture of the cover of the book to which the words are related helps the students to locate words by simply recalling the context in which the words were studied. See Figure 49.1 for suggestions on types of word walls and ways to display them.

STEP BY STEP

The steps in implementing a word wall are:

1. Decide on the format you wish to use (see Figure 49.1) and begin by brainstorming a list of words with the students. In order to arrange the words in alphabetical order for easy access write the words on individual cards and tape them on a wall or place them in a pocket chart. For a multilingual classroom add translations and illustrations to the words to support the students' use of the words in writing and speaking. Involve the students in selecting words to be added to the word wall. With young children you might want to begin your word wall by placing the students' names on the wall alphabetically and then adding words they encounter in the books they are hearing read aloud.

2. Refer to the word wall whenever a word is discussed. Help the students to see the possibilities for the use of the word wall. If a student asks for the spelling of a word that is posted, draw the students' attention to it. If it is a word that is not on the word wall, add it (along with translations and an illustration when appropriate).

3. Use the words for activities such as word sorts, definition games, practicing syllabication, and phoneme segmentation. As word studies in literature, science, and social studies are completed the words should be transferred to word cards and placed on a metal ring by

High frequency words	Alphabetical lists on large sheets of butcher paper.
	Laminated sheets of construction paper onto which individual word cards are attached.
	Large bulletin boards onto which individual words are added in alphabetical order.
	Clotheslines strung across the room onto which large cards with a single alphabet letter are attached. Word cards are then stapled to the alphabet letter to form the word list for each letter.
Literature word walls	Interesting, difficult, and unusual words from the story being studied are placed in a pocket chart and arranged alphabetically.
	The words may be arranged on a sheet of butcher paper in the shape of something related to the story like a covered wagon or hot-air balloon.
	The words may be collected in a container that relates to the story such as a witch's cauldron or miniature windmill.
Content-area word walls	Interesting words are written on cards and displayed on a pocket chart.
	Words are collected by entering them in the computer and printing out a large poster that is updated periodically. If the computer has a display screen attached, the list can be projected on a blank wall or projection screen.

Figure 49.1 Types of Word Walls and Suggestions for Displaying Them

punching a hole in the corner of each card. The ring can then be stored on a nail or hook in the classroom placed at a level so that the students can easily access it.

APPLICATIONS AND EXAMPLES

The lizards are crawling all over the terrarium in Ms. Romero's first-grade classroom. The students are watching intently as they crawl on the rocks and hop from plant to plant. As they observe, the students are writing their observations on sheets of paper attached to clipboards and trying to spell words like *lizard* and *amphibian*. Ms. Romero has started a science word wall by placing key words in a pocket chart located near the terrarium. Because a number of her students speak Spanish at home, she has the Spanish words alphabetized on the same chart. The English words are written in green, the Spanish words in blue. All the words are illustrated, some with small magazine pictures the students have found and cut out, others by drawings made by the students. Everyday Ms. Romero and the students reread the words from the wall and use them for some type of activity so that the students will gradually come to recognize them all.

Ms. Romero has another word wall in her classroom. This word wall is arranged on the doors of the closets and organized by using 9-by-12 sheets of laminated construction paper in a checkerboard pattern of primary colors. The first words added to this word wall are the students' names, then over the first few months of school the color and number words are added. Gradually more and more high frequency words are added. Because the high frequency word wall was filling quickly, Ms. Romero decided to keep her science and literature word wall separate and build them on word cards in the pocket chart. She's glad she made that decision because she now has 20 different word rings holding the words the class has studied in various subjects. Her students seem to know just where to go to locate a word when they need to use it for something they are writing.

Jonathan comes up to Ms. Romero with his observation log in hand. "I have a new word for the science word wall, Ms. Romero," he says. "The green lizard just *torpedoed* off the top of the plant into the pond. How do you write *torpedoed*?"

"I think you can spell that one, Jonathan," says Ms. Romero. "It just sounds hard. Let's sound it out."

Ms. Romero picks up a card and she and Jonathan sound out the word as she writes it.

"It wasn't hard at all," grins Jonathan. "I spelled it!"

"Now the hard part," says Ms. Romero. "Where does it go in alphabetical order?"

"That's not hard, Ms. Romero. It goes right after *terrarium,*" says Jonathan.

"I see I can't fool you," replies Ms. Romero. "Can you draw a picture for your new word? And don't forget to ask Alberto if he knows the Spanish word for *torpedoed.*"

"If he doesn't know it, his father will," smiles Jonathan as he trots off to talk to Alberto.

Later that day, Ms. Romero uses the words on the science word wall for a word sorting activity. The students choose a group of words from the wall and tell how the words are related. Jonathan chooses *jumped, hopped, climbed,* and *torpedoed* and explains that he has chosen these four words because they are all things he has seen the lizards do.

Alberto chooses the words *verde, amarillo, anaranjado,* and *pardo* because they are all words that tell about the colors of the lizards.

Teresa chooses *tiny, bumpy, spotted,* and *striped* because they all tell about the way the lizards look.

Once everyone has a chance to select words and tell how they go together, Ms. Romero and the students recite the alphabet and the words are replaced on the pocket chart in alphabetical order. See Figure 49.2 to see how Ms. Romero's word walls are displayed.

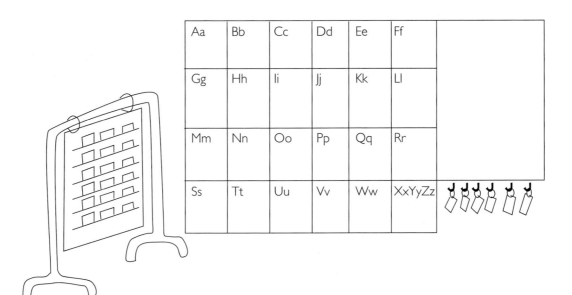

Figure 49.2 Ms. Romero's Word Walls

Valentina is standing in front of the word wall in her seventh-grade classroom wearing a puzzled look on her face. "What is the problem?" asks Mr. Stalvo.

"I can't find exactly the word I need for the story I am writing. I thought maybe I could locate one on the word wall," replies Valentina.

"That's a good strategy, Valentina," says Mr. Stalvo with a smile. "What other possibilities do you have?"

"I could use the thesaurus," grins Valentina, "but I can usually find a word on the word wall."

"You're right, Valentina. Our new literature focus book has a lot of interesting words in it."

Mr. Stalvo's seventh graders are reading . . . *and now Miguel* by Joseph Krumgold (1953). They are combining the literature study with a study of geography and finding a number of fascinating words. The word wall in front of which Valentina is standing is almost full. Soon they will have to take it down. See Figure 49.3 for the list of words on the word wall.

Since Valentina seemed reluctant to consult the class thesaurus, Mr. Stalvo decides to use the word wall to help the students create their own personal thesaurus. Later that day he gives directions for the students to bring a new three-ring folder to class the next day. "You don't need a huge one," he says. "A half-inch notebook and fifty pages of notebook paper will be enough."

The next day Mr. Stalvo and the students begin their classroom thesaurus project by labeling their notebooks and brainstorming all the ways they can say *walk* when they are writing. The students come up with *saunter, creep, tiptoe, parade, shuffle, prowl,* and *stomp.* After they brainstorm the list they go back and write a short descriptive phrase explaining the words. When they are finished they have a list that looks like this:

saunter—to walk at a slow, casual pace
creep—to walk at a snail's pace
tiptoe—to walk on the tips of your toes
parade—to walk proudly with head held high as if marching in a parade
shuffle—to walk slowly dragging your feet
prowl—to walk slowly and carefully as if trying not to be heard
stomp—to walk as if angry, banging your feet on the ground and making a loud noise

Once the class completes this exercise, Mr. Stalvo gives them their next assignment. "Over the next few weeks we are going to write our own thesaurus, beginning with the words we have collected from our literature focus book. Once we get some basic words entered we will be updating our vocabulary books regularly all year. I can't wait to see how many new words you can learn this year. I expect you to be using these books for many years to come. They should be very helpful in making your writing more exciting, too."

The first things the class does is to match up the words on their literature word wall, putting words together that mean the same, or approximately the same, thing. Mr. Stalvo arranges the class into cooperative groups, making sure that each group has at least one fluent Spanish speaker in it. They then divide up the words from the word wall and begin to create their new vocabulary notebooks—or thesaurus. The Spanish speakers are assigned the task of explaining the nuances in meaning for the Spanish words and making sure that the translations for the English words are accurate.

"Mr. Stalvo, I'm sure glad my dad insisted we speak Spanish at home!" exclaimed Tomas. "I couldn't do this assignment if I hadn't kept up in Spanish."

"Your father is a wise man," smiles Mr. Stalvo.

CONCLUSION

Word walls can be very supportive to students in their study of words and the expanding of their vocabularies. However, it is very important that the students be made aware of the ways in which the word walls can be used. Students will use the word walls when the teacher models the ways in which they can be used as resources.

absolutely	**adobe**	**alfalfa**
apron	arrange	arroyo
balance	bare	beneath
bundle	burlap	burracho
burro	cactus	canvas
canyon	champion	comforter
corral	coyote	crawl
cyclone	elbow	engineer
ewe	fetch	flock
fractions	grain	graze
government	heave	huddled
imagine	lamb	liniment
lonesome	mesa	mesquite
mistake	mutton	necessary
orphans	partidero	patron
particular	pasture	peeping
perfect	permission	permit
pickaxes	promised	pueblo
reason	remarkable	remembered
remind	scratch	shearers
shepherd	shivering	shovels
skidding	sopaipillas	squeaks
stamped	stovewood	straggling
stretched	traitor	trout
underneath	vamanos	veranda
windshield	whisper	wrestling

Figure 49.3   Word Wall for . . . and now Miguel

Teachers encourage the use of the word walls by referring to them frequently, calling attention to the words, playing guessing games by giving clues related to the words on the wall, adding new and interesting words on a regular basis, and relating content-area words to special word walls reserved for this use. The students should play an active role in the building of the word walls, suggesting words to be added, writing words themselves, even creating their own "special word walls" with small cards taped to the sides of their desks.

References

Krumgold, J. (1953). . . . and now Miguel. New York: Harper Collins.
Tompkins, G. E. (1997). Literacy for the 21st century: A balanced approach. Upper Saddle River, NJ: Merrill/Prentice Hall.

WRITING WORKSHOP

SUPPORTS

- ● Comprehensible input
- ● Increased verbal interaction
- ✔ Contextualized language
- ✔ Reduced anxiety
- ● Active involvement of the learner

Writing workshop (Graves, 1983) is an approach to teaching writing in which the students choose their own writing topics and move through prewriting, drafting, revising, editing, and publishing their work as though they were professional authors (Tompkins, 1994). Writing workshop is especially supportive to English language learners because students are encouraged to discuss their ideas, work with a partner or group in revising and editing, and interact verbally with others (Diaz-Rico & Weed, 1995). The classroom environment in which students work together to give each other support as they work through the stages in the writing process provides the support necessary to lower anxiety and motivate students to write. The opportunity to write on self-chosen topics validates each student's experiences. The stages in process writing are shown in Figure 50.1 with suggestions for supporting English language learners.

STEP BY STEP

The steps in implementing writing workshop are:

1. Introduce the writing process stage by stage, modeling each stage with your own writing. Talk about the need for prewriting to get ideas flowing and model a prewriting strategy such as webbing, listing, drawing, or brainstorming. Do your own prewriting using an overhead projector or chart so that the students can see the process and then give them an opportunity to prewrite. Follow this same pattern through each of the subsequent stages in writing, using your own developing piece as an example.
2. Provide writing materials and time to write each day. As students complete first drafts schedule writing groups to give them feedback and suggestions. Set the classroom up to encourage interaction among the students as they write, revise, edit, and publish. Provide resources such as dictionaries, thesaurus, and content-area reading for reports.
3. As you see the need, teach mini-lessons on skills and additional strategies for each of the stages. These lessons can be whole-group, small-group, or individual. Encourage the students to work at their own pace, writing and publishing on topics that relate to other curricular areas or to their own experiences.
4. As students complete the writing, find ways to celebrate their accomplishments and include their published works in the class library. Always give students an opportunity to share their

Writing Process Stage and Definition	Adaptations for English Language Learners
Prewriting. Strategies for getting and organizing ideas	Allow first language usage if needed. Model more than one strategy using visuals and actual writing idea being developed. Include realia. Encourage first language partner or small-group work.
Drafting. Getting some ideas down on paper.	Model putting a draft down on paper using an overhead or chart. Think aloud as you write. Write on every other line to allow for revisions. Model crossing out ideas, writing between lines, making changes as ideas begin to flow. Encourage collaboration and discussion of ideas among students. Allow writing in first language.
Revising. Focusing on the content of the piece, asking questions if parts are not clear, giving suggestions to the writer. This stage can be repeated as needed.	Model a writing group using your writing. Encourage the students to give you feedback and ask questions about the piece of writing you are doing. Work with a small group. Encourage translation to English if the piece is written in another language. Authors can use student translators for both the reading of the piece and feedback and suggestions given. Authors decide which revisions to make based upon the group suggestions.
Editing. Correcting mechanics.	Model the editing process using your own writing. Teach proofreading symbols so that students can work together to correct all spelling, punctuation, capitalization, and other mechanical errors. Encourage partner work. Provide resources such as dictionaries, thesaurus, and English grammar textbooks. After student editing, teacher can serve as final editor.
Publishing. Putting the writing into a final form such as mounting for the bulletin board, binding into a book, creating a shape book, pop-up book, or other novelty form.	Model the publishing of your writing. Introduce the publishing possibilities by modeling each of them. Encourage the students to choose their publishing mode and work with a partner. Take photos of the authors for an "About the Author" page in the book.
Celebration. Sharing the finished work with classmates or others.	Student whose book is published sits in the *Author's Chair* and read the newly published book or writing aloud. Principals, other teachers, and parents can be invited.

Figure 50.1   Writing Process Stages Adapted for English Language Learners

published works and include their photos and an "About the Author" page in the published books.

APPLICATIONS AND EXAMPLES

The fourth graders in Mr. Heil's classroom are using their writing workshop time to write plays for the dragon puppets they have created in art. Since the students are reading fantasy books in reading class, they have decided to write plays about dragons and damsels in distress. To prepare the students to write plays, Mr. Heil has brought in several scripts so the students can see the format they will use. The class brainstorms the elements of fantasy they remember from the stories they are reading and list several possibilities for plays. Mr. Heil organizes the students into groups so that each group has at least one strong writer and the English language learners have a language buddy who can translate for them if needed.

The groups start to work by looking at the puppets they have made and brainstorming a list of characters in their play. Each of the students is assigned an additional puppet to make and the script writing begins.

The students work in groups for several days, producing a rough draft, revising, and editing. Once their script is complete, they bring in the puppets they have made at home and begin to practice their puppet plays. Mr. Heil provides a puppet stage and the groups decide they must have backdrops to make the productions more realistic. At the end of the week, almost all of the groups are ready to perform.

Mr. Heil's class is using writing workshop to create a collaborative project. They are providing support for the English language learners by working as a group to support the creation of a play. Once the script is complete all of the group members participate in the performance. Because the script provides a strong scaffold for the oral presentation, all the students are confident reading their parts.

Ms. Martin teaches a senior humanities class in a large high school. She finds the final grading period in the senior year to be difficult since the students are eager to graduate and move on. Ms. Martin decides to try a new project for her senior group. Using a writing workshop format, she suggests that the students look back over the past four years and create a scenario based upon a current event, stage play, or film that will encourage the other seniors to recall something memorable about their high school experience. They begin by brainstorming a list of possibilities and then a list of characters who might be included in the scenarios.

The final lists provide some hilarious suggestions and the students choose topics on which to write. Some of the students choose to write alone, others in pairs and small groups. Since the high school is named Hoover High, the students decide to produce a publication entitled, "Hoover History Hash." Their stories change the history of the last four years in slightly wacky ways. One story has the principal as the hero of a local happening in which one of the students drove his car into the river. Mr. Posten, the principal, is hailed as the hero of the story and the events changed just enough to make the story laughable.

Once the stories are written, Mr. Posten is so impressed with their originality that he chooses the best five to read over the intercom during the last week of school. The stories are so popular that the student publication is sold out.

CONCLUSION

Writing workshop is a strategy that has many possibilities. Because writing workshop is intended to simulate the procedures that real authors follow as they prewrite, write, revise, edit, and publish, students have multiple opportunities for context-based verbal interactions as they research, confer, give, and receive feedback on their own and their colleagues' writing. Because the students choose their own topics for writing, students' ideas and experiences are validated. Writing in students' home languages is valued and collaboration in order to create bilingual (or multilingual) books can contribute to the growing library of such books in the classroom. See chapter 5, Bilingual Books and Labels, for more information on this topic.

In order for writing workshop to be effective, students must be given writing time daily. A structure must be set up in the classroom to support all the stages in the writing process and the students must be given instruction in ways to support one another in reading drafts, giving feedback, and editing collaboratively. When the workshop is encouraged and student interaction supported, there is nothing that provides a more collaborative classroom environment than writing workshop.

References

Diaz-Rico, L., & Weed, K. (1995). *The crosscultural, language, and academic handbook.* Boston: Allyn and Bacon.

Graves, D. (1983). *Writing: Teachers and children at work.* Portsmouth, NH: Heinemann.

Tompkins, G. E. (1994). *Teaching writing: Balancing process and product* (2nd ed.). Upper Saddle River, NJ: Merrill/Prentice Hall.

APPENDIX A

....

▶ AN INFORMAL MULTIPLE INTELLIGENCES SURVEY

Mark the face that shows how you feel about each statement.

I. Linguistic Intelligence

Reading books makes me feel

Listening to the radio makes me feel

Nonsense rhymes, tongue twisters, or puns make me feel

Playing word games like Scrabble, Anagrams, or Password makes me feel

Using big words in speaking or writing makes me feel

In school, English, social studies, and history make me feel

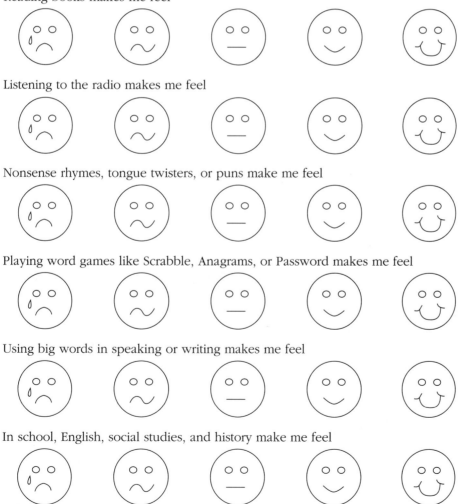

When people talk about books they've read or things they've heard, I feel

When I have to share something I have written, I feel

II. Logical-Mathematical Intelligence

When I'm asked to compute numbers in my head, I feel

In school, math and/or science makes me feel

Playing number games or solving brainteasers makes me feel

Finding ideas for science fair projects makes me feel

Having to "show all my work" on my math paper makes me feel

Finding errors in someone else's math or logic makes me feel

Measuring, categorizing, analyzing, or calculating makes me feel

Watching science and nature shows on television makes me feel

III. Spatial Intelligence

When I am asked to "close my eyes and visualize," I feel

When I'm asked to draw in pencil and not allowed to use color, I feel

When I read a book without pictures, I feel

When I read a book with actual photographs as illustrations, I feel

When I do jigsaw puzzles, mazes, and other visual puzzles, I feel

When I have to find my way in an unfamiliar building or neighborhood, I feel

When I have to do math without writing it down or drawing pictures, I feel

When asked to draw something from "a bird's-eye view," I feel

IV. Bodily-Kinesthetic Intelligence

When I play sports or other physical activities, I feel

When I have to sit still for long periods of time, I feel*

When I work with my hands at concrete activities such as sewing, weaving, carving, carpentry, or model building, I feel

When I spend time outdoors, I feel

When I have to talk without using my hands or body language, I feel*

When I have to look at something without touching it, I feel*

When riding on a roller coaster ride, I feel

When asked to try a new physical movement, I feel

V. Musical Intelligence

When asked to sing "Happy Birthday," I feel

When someone is singing off-key, I feel*

When listening to music on radio, records, cassettes, or compact disks, I feel

If I had to take music lessons, I would feel

If I had to listen to music without tapping my fingers or feet, I would feel*

When someone asks me to sing a tune, I feel

If I had to study without listening to the radio, I would feel*

If there were no more music programs in school, I would feel*

VI. Interpersonal Intelligence

When someone comes to me for advice, I feel

When we have to play team sports at school, I feel

When I have to work out a problem without talking to anyone about it, I feel

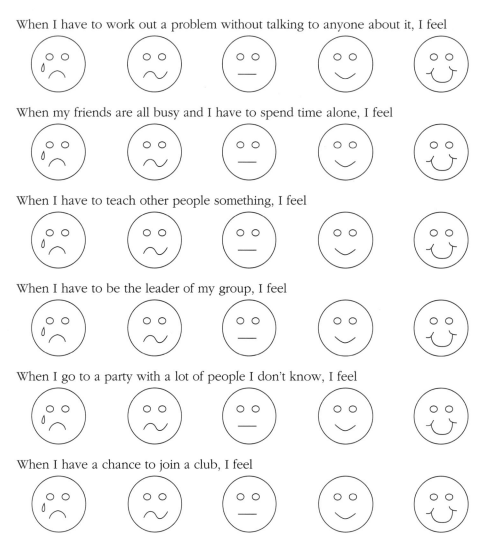

When my friends are all busy and I have to spend time alone, I feel

When I have to teach other people something, I feel

When I have to be the leader of my group, I feel

When I go to a party with a lot of people I don't know, I feel

When I have a chance to join a club, I feel

VII. Intrapersonal Intelligence

When I spend time alone reflecting, or thinking about important things, I feel

When I don't get picked for something, I feel

When I spend time with a hobby or interest that I have to do by myself, I feel

When I think about important goals for my life, I feel

When I think about my own strengths and weaknesses, I feel

If I had to spend time alone (safe) in a mountain cabin, I would feel

When my friends want to do something I don't want to do, I feel

If I had my own business, instead of working for someone else, I would feel

Adapted from *7 Kinds of Smart* by Thomas Armstrong, (1993). New York: Putnam.

Scoring Instructions

All people possess all seven intelligences in some combination, and this exercise gives you an idea of the relative strengths of your personal intelligences. For most of the items, add the total of your points for each question in each section using the scale of 0–1–2–3–4 (from left to right, crying to big grin) for the face you marked. For the items marked with an asterisk, simply reverse the scoring from left to right, 4–3–2–1–0. Add the total points scored in each section. The sections in which you score the most points indicate your strongest areas of intelligence. The lower scores indicate your weaker areas of intelligence. The stronger areas of intelligence are those in which you will learn and demonstrate understanding most easily.